Nearly Free Tuition

Nearly Free Tuition

Let the IRS Pay for Your Child's Education

Alexander A. Bove, Jr.

Viking

VIKING
Viking Penguin Inc., 40 West 23rd Street,
New York, N.Y. 10010, U.S.A.
Penguin Books Ltd, Harmondsworth,
Middlesex, England
Penguin Books Australia Ltd, Ringwood,
Victoria, Australia
Penguin Books Canada Limited, 2801 John Street,
Markham, Ontario, Canada L3R 1B4
Penguin Books (N.Z.) Ltd, 182–190 Wairau Road,
Auckland 10, New Zealand

First published in 1985 by Viking Penguin Inc.
Published simultaneously in Canada

LIBRARY OF CONGRESS CATALOGING IN PUBLICATION DATA
Bove, Alexander A., 1938–
    Nearly free tuition.
    1. Income tax—United States—Deductions—Expenses.
2. Gifts—Taxation—Law and legislation—United States.
3. Trusts and trustees—Taxation—United States.
4. Tax planning—United States.   5. College costs—United
States.   I. Title.
KF6395.E3B68   1985   343.7305′23   84-40070
ISBN 0-670-31354-8   347.303523

This publication is designed to provide accurate information in regard to the
subject matter covered as of the date of publication. Since tax laws and
government regulations change periodically, it is sold with the understanding that
the publisher is not engaged in rendering legal, accounting, or other professional
service. If legal advice or other expert assistance is required, the services of a
competent professional person should be sought.

Printed in the United States of America
by The Book Press, Brattleboro, Vermont
Set in Times Roman
Designed by Ann Gold

Preface
"All the World
Should Be Taxed ..."

"And it came to pass in those days, that there went out a decree from Caesar Augustus that all the world should be taxed ..." says the New Testament.

And so it was, and so it is, and so it probably always will be. But that doesn't mean we can't do anything about it. In the days of Caesar the tax laws were so simple that there was little one could do to avoid or reduce taxes legally. Today our tax laws are infinitely more complicated, and it is the very complexity itself which creates the options to allow us to arrange our affairs to pay the least possible tax. Most people narrowly associate this planning with income taxes, but there is no reason why educational costs can't be included—and that's what this book is about.

Although educational expenses *per se* are not tax-deductible, they can be made so. With a knowledge of the tax laws and with the help of your (professional) friends, you can take advantage of legal and effective ways of actually reducing educational costs through tax savings. In most instances, your key to savings is to develop and then implement the right plan or plans to suit your family's circumstances and educational needs.

In that sense, you should think of this book as an idea book and *not* as a do-it-yourself book. Saving many thousands of tax dollars by clever use and application of complicated tax laws is not exactly like fixing a leak or building a picnic table. It is serious business and should only be done in consultation with your professional advisors. The problem is that they are probably not sitting up all night thinking of ways you can make your children's education tax-deductible, or even tax favored. More often than not, the ideas must be presented to them. And that is exactly what you can do with the help of this book.

I will take you step by step through those known, as well as some hitherto unknown, maneuvers for tax-favored educational plans and offer you and your advisors all you need to know to develop and implement the ideas. And to satisfy the skeptical advisor, each chapter is appended with appropriate technical references and case citations supporting the major ideas in that chapter. For instance, Chapter 5 discusses the attractive arrangement of a gift (to a child), then a borrowing back of the funds by the parent, so that the parent may regain the use of her or his money and at the same time begin paying tax-deductible interest to the child for educational use. Some advisors may be skeptical about this too-good-to-be-true deal, but two cases I have cited hold that this tactic is perfectly permissible under the law; viz., *Cook v. U.S.* and *Potter v. Commissioner of Internal Revenue*.

In addition to instructions and references on the use of the numerous ideas, the book does something else that no other book has done: it tells you of the special planning that is needed for the *child* who has been accumulating educational funds, as well as estate planning considerations for both the child and the parents. For example, many parents create custodial accounts for children naming themselves (the parent) as custodian without realizing that this will cause the amounts in those accounts to be included in the parent's taxable estate should the parent die. Chapter 10 explains how this can be avoided.

Finally, and most important, you will learn how to put the tax laws to work in your favor, and feel comfortable about it. A saying inscribed on a six-thousand-year-old Sumerian clay tablet reads: "You can have a Lord, you can have a King, but the man to fear is the tax collector." Today, six thousand years later, little has changed. Most people still fear the tax collector, largely because they don't understand the tax laws and the extent of what they can legally do. As far as tax planning for educational costs is concerned, this book will help dispel your fear of the tax collector and educate your children in the bargain.

Acknowledgments

The unique experience of writing a book compels every author to pay his respects to those persons whose presence, assistance, and/or support have combined to enable the author to complete his ominous task successfully. Accordingly, it is appropriate that I offer due acknowledgment to the following important persons, each of whom played or plays a very special role in my literary life: my good friend and literary mentor, Stuart Vidockler; my other literary mentor and good friend Rupert Ingram; my partner Fred Kuhn, for his excellent and knowledgeable critique of my manuscript; and my partner, teacher, and keeper, Stanley Charmoy.

In addition, special thanks and acknowledgments are due my associate Patricia Spinney, tax lawyer, for her diligent and thorough research talents and helpful comments in completing this work.

To my parents,
Mary M. Bove and
Alexander A. Bove, Sr.

Contents

Nearly Free Tuition

1

. . . .

Some Basic Tips— How the Rockefellers Did It

Everyone likes tax deductions. To get them, we are willing to spend a great deal of time, mental energy, and even money searching for the arrangement which allows us to legally pay as little in taxes as possible. And rightly so. But one of the most overlooked areas for potential tax savings is one that affects just about every family with children: educational costs.

Each year as these families pay for college or private school expenses with after-tax dollars, they are losing thousands of dollars in potential tax deductions which can never be recovered. It need not be that way.

. . . .

What This Book Can Do for You

If you have a child in (or who may enter) private school or college, and you are the primary source of funds to pay for that education, this book can tell you how to make all or part of those costs tax-deductible, or at least how to make them subject to a lower tax than you are presently paying, depending, of course, upon your individual circumstances.

This book will *not*, however, make you an expert on taxes or tax planning. Let's make it quite clear right up front that, with the possible (and qualified) exception of gifts, *this is not a do-it-yourself book*. It is a book that allows you to *educate yourself so that*

1

you can save money. The huge amounts of money and time you will invest in a child's education are far too important to risk on some casual homemade scheme to save taxes through the use of a few "tear-out" forms, and I can assure you that the tax laws are much too savvy to allow that.

To get the best and most effective use of the many ideas in this book, then, you must have the help and advice of someone familiar with the tax laws, usually your attorney and/or accountant. This is not to imply that every attorney and accountant has the required tax expertise, but in most instances they will be more familiar with the risks and requirements than you and have greater access to an outside specialist if one is required. Chapter 11 tells you how to get the best advice and ways to find a specialist.

But the fact that your attorney or accountant does have some expertise in tax law does not necessarily mean that he or she has a monopoly on all the ideas that may be used to save taxes. This is where you and this book come in. By familiarizing yourself with the plans and fundamentals presented here, you can work *with* your advisor to determine the best tax plan to fund your family's educational expenses based on your particular circumstances and objectives, which no one can know better than you. To assist your advisor, at the end of each chapter there are technical references to sections of the Internal Revenue Code and Treasury regulations, as well as cases and revenue rulings for all the major points covered in that chapter.

. . . .

The "Key" to Your Tax Deductions

Your key to making educational costs tax-deductible is to educate yourself in the various ways these objectives may be accomplished. Such maneuvers may involve gifts or trusts, loans or leases, purchases or sales, or perhaps combinations of one or more of these. The following chart will give you an idea of the many different arrangements possible depending upon the nature of the family and the family's assets:

If your family has:	Then for a tax-favored educational plan you should consider:	You will find this thoroughly covered in:
Savings	Gifts	Chapter 4
	Custodial gifts	Chapter 5
	Gift & borrowback	Chapter 5
	Clifford trust & borrow-back	Chapter 6
A home, but no sub-stantial savings or other investments	Clifford trust & borrow-back	Chapter 6
Income-producing securities	Minor's trust	Chapter 5
	Clifford trust	Chapter 6
	Gifts	Chapter 4
	Custodial Gifts	Chapter 5
Low-cost securities with a high current value	Gifts	Chapter 4
	Custodial gifts	Chapter 5
	Minor's trust	Chapter 5
Income-producing real estate	Clifford trust	Chapter 6
	Employment of child	Chapter 8
A family business	Employment of child	Chapter 8
	Clifford trust	Chapter 6
	Family partnership	Chapter 8
	"Subchapter S" corpo-ration	Chapter 8
	Gift & leaseback	Chapter 8
	Educational benefit trust	Chapter 8
A professional practice	Employment of child	Chapter 8
	Gift & leaseback	Chapter 8
	Educational benefit trust	Chapter 8
Tax shelters that will produce income	Clifford trust	Chapters 6 & 9
	Independent trust	Chapters 6 & 9
Access to loans or gifts from family members or other "friendly" sources	Clifford trust & borrowback	Chapter 6

All of the accepted as well as some of the more aggressive (but still legal) ways of saving on taxes are discussed in detail in this book, with notes of caution where the risk may be a little greater than usual. As with all risks, great or small, they must be weighed against the potential reward. In the case of rising educational costs, the reward can be great, and as time goes by, it will undoubtedly become even greater.

In 1963, for example, the *average* cost of a four-year undergraduate college education including tuition, books, and dormitory expenses, was about $7,000. In 1973, it was $13,000; today, it is over $36,000! And this is the *average* cost; many schools are double that!

Where is the "average" family going to get $36,000 in cash, *after* taxes? While it's true that there are still some financial aid programs available from the federal and state governments and even from many colleges, it is also true that the bulk of the funds from these programs generally go to families earning less than $30,000 per year. As family earnings climb higher and higher above this figure, the financial aid becomes less and less. Even where there is financial aid, more often than not it covers only a *fraction* of the total educational costs and is usually contingent upon the parents' agreement to "make up the difference." To make matters worse, amounts contributed by the parents for a child's education are *not* tax-deductible, despite some legislative efforts in this direction. Those laws that may be enacted propose a deduction (or tuition tax credit) that is so insignificant in comparison to the cost of the education, it might as well be nonexistent.

If parents could structure their payments for a child's education in a way that would effectively render these payments tax-deductible, then the college costs paid by the parent could be reduced by as much as 50 percent! Looking at it another way, failure to do this can as much as *double* the cost of the education, depending upon the tax bracket of the parents.

Present tax laws provide that a married couple filing jointly will be in the 50 percent tax bracket if their taxable income for 1984 exceeds $109,400. A single person qualifying as head of household* need only have $81,800 of taxable income to be in the 50 percent bracket, and a single person not head of household, only $55,300 of taxable income. For any of these people, this means

---

*A person qualifies as head of household if she maintains a principal residence for herself *and* one or more qualifying dependents.

that paying $5,000 of nondeductible college expenses *actually costs $10,000 of earnings*! The other $5,000 is lost forever to Uncle Sam for taxes. However, if that payment could be structured as a tax deduction, the parent could save as much as $5,000.

· ·

How the Rockefellers Did It—A Simple But Effective Plan

The case of the Rockefellers is a good example of how to use a "simple" method to make college costs deductible. Irving and Sadie Rockefeller had to come up with about $6,000 each year to cover their daughter's college expenses. Being in the 50 percent tax bracket, Irving had to earn $12,000 to pay the $6,000 of college expenses (after taxes). Quickly tiring of this, he went to his bank and took out a short-term loan of $40,000. He then made a gift of the $40,000 to his daughter, which he subsequently borrowed back from her at a rate of 15 percent interest (or $6,000 per year). With the borrowed funds from his daughter, he paid off his bank loan, and is now paying $6,000 per year *deductible interest* to his daughter, which she in turn is using to pay for college.

In effect, Irving has saved $6,000 cash per year simply by making a gift *which he will recover in tax savings in about six and a half years*. The arrangement is quite legal and, from a tax standpoint, low risk, if done properly. Of course, Irving still owes his daughter $40,000, and this must be dealt with at some point. How the story could end is discussed in Chapter 5.

· ·

Planning Ahead to Save Tax Dollars

Taxpayers who finally decide to plan for tax-favored educational costs can generally be divided into two groups: those who plan ahead and the rest of us. If you fall into the first group and you are planning now for the education of children who will be going to college five, ten, or fifteen years from now, congratulations! (You probably also have perfect teeth and always file your tax returns on time.)

If you fall into the second group and your child is about to enter college (or is already there), it is a bit more difficult to save money, but *not* impossible. Of course, the more time you (or the child) have to accumulate funds in a lower tax bracket, the more money will be saved, and the better off you and the child will be. For shorter-term planning, the crucial factor is often how much money is available with which to effect the savings. For example, a substantial gift and borrowback can generate large tax savings in the very first year, as can the various forms of shifting income from a successful family business. The amount of the savings will simply depend on the amount of cash available. The famous Crown case, although a bit extreme, is a perfect example of this. In that case, Mr. Crown and his partners made interest-free loans of about $18 million (!) to several *trusts* for the benefit of their children. If invested at only 10 percent, these funds would produce income of $1.8 million annually for the children, before taxes. At these levels, the question of tax savings—even *I* must admit—becomes somewhat moot, but it does illustrate the point that the tax savings are often directly proportional to the amount of money or property generally available to the family. (See Chapter 7 for a thorough discussion of interest-free loans.)

Do not let these numbers discourage you, however, because in most families *any* tax savings can be helpful. After all, if with simple planning you could save, say, $500 per year, wouldn't it make sense to do it, provided it cost less than $500 to arrange to do so?

Furthermore, you will find that in many, if not most instances, the suggestions made in this book can also save some *state* income taxes, as well as federal income taxes, in those states that have an income tax. Of course, in a state where there is no income tax, there will be no difference.

Finally, you must realize (if you don't now, you will before you finish this book) that the tax laws are extremely complex, and to add to this, each of the various types of taxes—income, estate, and gift taxes—may have a bearing on a transaction that is intended primarily to deal with only one type of tax—the income tax. For example, although our major concern in this book is saving *income* taxes to pay for college, many of the ideas and plans discussed have certain *estate* tax implications, and most involve some aspect of *gift* taxes, both of which will be covered. Nevertheless, some of the coverage is basic simply to introduce you to the ideas, and you must constantly be aware of the importance of getting expert advice, even though (after reading this book) you may be the one to give your "expert" the ideas that you want to use to fund the education of your children.

One way for you to come up with some ideas is to see how other families with similar situations might handle their particular college expense problems. In the next chapter, there are a number of hypothetical family case studies which will help you focus on the problems and ways they can be solved. Each case study refers to the related chapter in this book to give you (or your advisor) more details about the idea involved. Try not to rely on any one case, however, since there may be ideas in others that can be equally helpful to you. Once you have a "feel" for the various ways taxes can be saved on educational costs, you'll be on your way to developing your own plan for tax-favored educational costs.

REFERENCES FOR CHAPTER 1

1. (Interest-free loan) *Lester Crown v. Commissioner,* 67 TC 1060 (1977), *aff'd,* 585 F. 2d 234 (7th Cir. 1978) (Illinois), but overruled by the S. Ct. in 1984. See Chapter 7 for a thorough discussion of interest-free loans.
2. (Gift and borrowback) *Cook v. United States,* 78-1 USTC Par. 9114 (W.D. La 1977) (Louisiana).

NOTE:
IRC = Internal Revenue Code.
Regs. = U.S. Treasury Regulations.
RR = Revenue Ruling (by Internal Revenue Service).
Letter Ruling = Ruling for a Taxpayer by the Internal Revenue Service (not published in IRS Bulletin).
TC = U.S. Tax Court Decision (TCM = U.S. Tax Court Memorandum Decision, not the full court).
F. = Federal (U.S. Circuit Court of Appeals) Decision, (F.2d = Federal, 2nd series).

Cir. = Circuit (area of the U.S. served by that court).
aff'd = affirmed lower court decision.
rev'd = reversed lower court decision.
S. Ct. = U.S. Supreme Court Decision.
USTC = U.S. Tax Cases, Commerce Clearing House.

2

. . . .

How to Find Yourself
in This Book—
Some Case Studies

. . . .

How to Use the Case Studies

The following stories of several families who were faced with educational costs under a variety of circumstances and conditions illustrate, in every case, that there was a better way to plan for and pay for these costs than the particular family had originally thought. Your own circumstances and conditions may differ somewhat, so you should not look for an exact match to your family situation, but rather find similarities that seem to jibe. It may be that a combination of ideas will be best for you, or perhaps a modification of some. The important thing in reading these case studies is to keep an open mind about rearranging your property or finances and to realize the importance of attention to *detail and follow-through*. When dealing with the tax laws, the slightest sloppiness can at times be fatal to a transaction.

For example, if you plan carefully and correctly to make your educational cost tax-deductible, but then casually sign an agreement with the school stating that you will be legally responsible for the tuition payments, you will *lose* the benefit of your tax deduction, no matter how meticulous you were with the rest of your plan. (This trap, and how to avoid it, is discussed thoroughly in Chapter 3.)

Finally, the case studies are not all-inclusive. They are intended as an aid to focusing on the types of ideas that may be useful in your situation and to orient your thinking to the field of tax planning for educational purposes. You should be aware that there are still more ideas embodied in the various chapters which could well apply to some of the case studies, as well as to your particular situation, and perhaps, after reading the material, you and/or your expert can come up with even a few more.

. . . .

A Married Couple (both working; some assets, little cash)

John and Abigail Adams have two children, ages 9 and 11. Their combined earnings are about $55,000, but it is just recently that the Adamses began earning "decent" money so they haven't been able to save very much. Like most parents, they are concerned about their children's educational costs, but they haven't really thought about where the money will come from. The Adamses' assets consist mainly of their home and a rental property that Abigail inherited from her mother. Aside from this they have little else.

The rental property is a three-family home with no mortgage that generates a net monthly income of about $700. The Adamses hope that this will help pay for their children's education, but they are not sure of the best way for it to do so. At present, they are simply saving as much as they can from this plus their other income and trying to "set aside" about $6,000 per year for education. The Adamses are in the 40 percent tax bracket, meaning that it will require $10,000 of income to "set aside" $6,000—the remaining $4,000 is lost forever to taxes.

Instead of simply "saving" their money, John and Abigail should consider creating a ten-year (Clifford) trust for their children. This type of trust will last for ten years and at the end of that time the property in the trust will be returned to the Adamses. During the ten-year period, all the *income* from the property can be taxed to the children, at a much lower tax rate. For example, if the rents generate a profit of $8,400 per year, the Adamses will pay a tax of about $3,400, leaving them with about $5,000. On the same income the children will pay a total tax of only $800 (a savings of $2,600 every year), leaving them with about $7,600. Using this method, the Adamses will "set aside" much more than their objective of $6,000 per year and will have saved themselves money in the bargain. And the same approach would work as well with other types of investments, such as stocks or bonds, which produce an income that is desirable to "shift" to the child.

(Ten-year trusts and all the special rules involved are discussed in detail in Chapter 6.)

. . . .

A Married Couple
(both working; some cash)

Frank and Elizabeth Franklin are earning about $85,000 per year. They have a home with a mortgage and Frank has about $60,000 in money-market-type accounts, generating about a 10 percent return. Their 17-year-old son, Benjamin, will be attending college in about a year and they have done very little planning for this, since what they have finally been able to accumulate is earmarked for their retirement. For this reason, they have never felt they could "afford" to make cash gifts to Benjamin. If they must, they will dip into their savings to pay for his college, but of course they would rather not.

They estimate that Benjamin will need about $7,500 annually for school, of which he can earn about $2,000 from his writing and sales of bifocals. The balance will have to be paid by them. After talking to their advisor, they realize they are in the 44 percent tax bracket and this means they will have to earn nearly $10,000 each year in order to have $5,600 left to give to Benjamin for school. The balance of $4,400 is lost to taxes forever.

The Franklins should consider placing the $60,000 savings in trust for the benefit of Benjamin. The terms of this trust (I call it the Shortcut Clifford trust, see page 121) would coincide with Benjamin's anticipated educational plans, say four years, and at the end of that period, the principal (in this case $60,000) would be paid to *Elizabeth* rather than Frank (tax laws prohibit it from coming back to Frank in less than ten years).

In the meantime, the trustee of the trust can invest the $60,000 for Benjamin's benefit, and all the income will be taxed to Benjamin if paid out (or to the trust, if not paid out). If the trust continues to earn 10 percent as the Franklins have done, Benjamin will receive $6,000 per year and pay a tax of about $680. This will leave him with just about what he needs for school, at a tax savings of nearly $2,000 each year for the family.

Four years later, when Benjamin finishes school, the trust will terminate and Elizabeth will receive the $60,000. Over that period, the family will have supplemented Benjamin's educational costs to the tune of about $22,000 *without using any of their principal*, while *saving* about $8,000 in taxes in the bargain!

(The Shortcut Clifford trust as well as other types of trusts are discussed in detail in Chapter 6.)

. . . .

A Married Couple (one working; plenty of bills, no cash)

Abraham and Mary Lincoln have no savings, no investments, and little prospect of either. All they have is their home, which they bought many years ago for $45,000, now worth about $160,000. The mortgage is nearly paid. They have three children, ages 17, 14, and 12. The 17-year-old will be entering college within a year, and, of course, the others will follow in due course. Although Abe earns about $65,000 a year, his current living and family expenses are such that he simply cannot save any money, so he and his wife are quite concerned about how they will pay for their children's education, especially their son's, which is imminent.

They have tentatively decided that they will try to squeeze what they can out of earnings and perhaps borrow the rest. In other words, every dime they pay will come from before-tax dollars, so that an annual college expense of $7,000 will cost the Lincolns about $12,500, and the difference of $5,500 each year will be lost forever to taxes. There is a way they can save nearly the entire amount.

The Lincolns should consider creating a ten-year trust for their children, and "funding" it with, say, $52,000 cash. They will then *borrow back* the cash from the trust at 15 percent interest, and, if done properly, the interest they pay will be fully tax-deductible to them, while it may be used by the trust to pay for the children's education.

One hitch, you say—where are they going to get $52,000? Easy—from the bank.

Here's how it can work. The Lincolns apply to the bank for a $52,000 loan, using their home as collateral. The bank consents (and it will, because there is adequate equity in their home), and loans them $52,000 as a "short-term" second mortgage. They contribute the $52,000 to the ten-year trust and some time later (thirty–sixty days), they borrow the $52,000 from the trust at a fair rate of interest, say 15 percent, pledging their home as collateral for the loan. They use the $52,000 to repay the bank, which releases the collateral (the home), and now the trust has adequate collateral (the home) for the loan.

For the next several years (as long as the loan is outstanding), the Lincolns must pay the interest to the trust, which should be fully tax-deductible to them. As the ten years come to a close, the Lincolns should pay off their note to the trust. If they still do not have the liquid funds, they may borrow once again from the bank and pay off the loan from the trust, which in turn terminates (because the ten years are up). On termination, the trustee returns the principal (the $52,000) to the Lincolns. They then may repay the second bank loan and everyone (except perhaps the IRS) is happy.

(There are several important and very delicate steps involved in this particular transaction; all are discussed in detail under ten-year trusts in Chapter 6.)

. . . .

A Married Couple
(one working; some savings)

George and Martha Washington are in their late forties and have two children about to enter college. The children have accumulated some funds to help with their education, but not enough to pay for it entirely. It appears that the Washingtons will have to come up with about $6,500 each year to cover the balance of tuition costs. George runs a small nation and earns about $70,000 per year but seems to have little extra cash. He could afford to pay the $6,500, but in his tax bracket it will consume about $10,800 of his earnings. The balance of over $4,000 each year will be lost forever to taxes. Their assets consist of a home plus about $60,000 in savings which they would like to use to buy a vacation home, although they recognize their "responsibility" to educate their children and thus they have not yet purchased the second home.

Since the Washingtons want to purchase the vacation home for the whole family, there may be a way for the children to participate in the purchase while the Washingtons get a tax deduction for the tuition costs.

Say that the Washingtons make a tax-free gift of $20,000 to each child. Later, the children loan the $40,000 back to their parents at a rate of 17 percent. The parents use the $40,000 to purchase their vacation home and give the children a mortgage on the home (although the mortgage, in this case, is not a necessary step).

The interest payments on the loans will total $6,800 per year ($40,000 × 17%), fully tax-deductible to the Washingtons, and enough to cover the tuition payments for the children.

One potential problem with this loan arrangement is that at some point the loan must be paid back. In some cases, this could be relatively "painless." For example, when the children are through school, their mortgage on the vacation home could be converted to an equity interest in the home. That is, they would exchange their $40,000 note for a percentage ownership of the home. Since we are dealing with parents and children, it would probably end up this way in any event.

There are some other tax considerations here, but nothing too serious. Since the parents are exchanging $40,000 of debt for a share of the home, they will be treated as having sold that share for $40,000, and so, depending on the cost of the property and the value at the time of the exchange, they may have a taxable gain. However, it would be taxed at the lower capital gains rates and would be negligible compared to the thousands of dollars they saved in taxes by "deducting" the tuition payments over the previous several years.

(Gifts and borrowback are discussed in detail in Chapter 5.)

. . . .

A Married Couple
(who has sold property)

When Tom Jefferson completed his job with the government, he and his wife decided to sell some property they would not be needing. They sold one piece for $60,000, taking $10,000 cash and a note for the balance. The $50,000 note called for annual interest payments of only 15 percent, and the full $50,000 principal due in ten years (a "balloon" payment).

As it turned out, Tom continued to do well financially and did not need the $7,500 yearly interest payments on the note, but despite his love for his country he did not enjoy paying 40 percent of it back to the government in taxes. Further, their son would be going to college in a few years and he felt he should begin to prepare for this. What to do?

Mr. and Mrs. Jefferson should create a ten-year trust for their son's education, and transfer the $50,000 note to this trust. If properly done, all the interest payments can be used for the child's education and will be taxed to the child; none of it will be taxed to the Jeffersons. And, at the end of the ten years, the $50,000 will be returned to them without further tax consequences (except for their original gain on the sale).

(Ten-year trusts and all the special rules involved are discussed in detail in Chapter 6.)

. . . .

A Single Parent
(working; some savings)

Joanne Kramer is divorced. She has a daughter, age 13, who attends private school at a cost of about $2,500 per year, presently paid for in full by Joanne, since her "ex" is a deadbeat who was last seen working as a surfing instructor at Lake Tahoe. Joanne lives in an apartment in New York City and her primary asset is a bank certificate for $20,000. She pays for her daughter's schooling out of her $38,000 earnings. She realizes that even though she is not in a "high" tax bracket, the educational expense is costing her more than it might if she were able to take advantage of some "gimmick." She's right.

Joanne is in the 40 percent tax bracket. Paying $2,500 for tuition with after-tax dollars *costs* her about $4,200; the balance of about $1,700 each year is lost forever to taxes. If Joanne were to create a ten-year trust for her daughter, she could contribute the $20,000 to the trust and later borrow back her $20,000 at, say, 14 percent interest. If properly done, the interest of $2,800 per year would be fully tax-deductible to Joanne. Her daughter would pay a tax of about $210, and there would still be more than enough to pay her private school tuition. In the meantime, Joanne would have recovered the use of her $20,000 and could reinvest it as she pleased (except in tax-exempt bonds).

(The ten-year trust—how they work and what you must know—is discussed in detail in Chapter 6.)

. . . .

A Widow with Young Children

Maryanne's husband died about two years ago, leaving her with their three children, ages 8, 9, and 11. Fortunately, there was life insurance totaling about $250,000, but the income generated by this together with the $7,000 she earns from part-time employment is only just enough to get by. Although $250,000 "sounds" like a lot of money, that's all there is, and she does not want to use the principal, if at all possible. She is worried about how she can educate her children without jeopardizing her own security.

Maryanne can set up a trust for the children's education which will not only generate adequate funds but will protect her principal, and in fact return it to her after the educational funds are accumulated. If Maryanne contributes $75,000 to a ten-year trust, naming the children as beneficiaries, and if the trust invests the $75,000 at 10 percent, in ten years it will accumulate about $100,000 (allowing a reasonable amount for the payment of income taxes over that period) *over and above* Maryanne's original $75,000. The trust funds should adequately cover their educational costs. Further, there will be no additional income tax on those funds when they are distributed to the children from the trust, nor will there be a tax when Maryanne recovers her $75,000 at the end of the ten-year period.

(Ten-year trusts—how they work and what you must know— are discussed in detail in Chapter 6.)

. . . .

A Business Owner

Gerard has a small but successful window-shade business. After paying his employees and other expenses, he nets about $75,000 per year. He usually draws about $60,000 and leaves the rest "in the business," although he pays income taxes on the whole amount. He has two children, 17 and 18, and he hopes that they will work in the business after they finish college. In the meantime, he has to concern himself with just that—their college education.

Gerard is in the 44 percent tax bracket and he estimates that to cover the projected college expenses for the two children, which will be about $18,000 per year, he will have to earn about $32,000 before taxes. The difference of $14,000 each year will be lost forever to taxes; if there were a way to make these costs deductible to Gerard, or at least not taxable to him, he would save up to $14,000 per year!

Gerard can easily change his business from a sole proprietorship to a partnership—a *family* partnership. If done properly, the family partnership arrangement will cause each "partner" to be taxed on his share of the partnership income. So, if a partner has a 30 percent interest and the partnership income is $20,000, he can receive, and be taxed on, $6,000 of income.

If Gerard can give each of his children an interest sufficient to give them about $10,000 each per year, they will have enough left over after taxes to cover their tuition expenses, and the tax effect to Gerard is a savings of $12,000 each year. If, for some reason, the children do not enter the business or it is not desirable to retain them as partners, Gerard could "buy back" their shares at some future date. In the meantime, he has saved a small fortune in taxes.

(Family partnerships are discussed in detail in Chapter 8.)

. . . .

Another Business Owner

Harrington has a small medical supply company. It is a successful incorporated business with about twelve employees, and generates enough income to place Harrington in the 50 percent tax bracket. Harrington has three children, ages 18, 10, and 9, and would like to do some planning to help reduce present and future educational costs. His 18-year-old son is about to enter college and the costs are projected to be about $8,000 per year. No plans have been established yet for the other two children. Considering taxes, Harrington will have to earn $16,000 to have $8,000 left to pay for his son's education each year.

If instead Harrington hired the oldest child, he could pay him, as wages, the $8,500 per year necessary to cover his college expenses after taxes. Assuming the wages were fair considering the work his son did, they would be fully deductible to Harrington. They would also be income to his son, who would pay a tax of about $700 on that income. If necessary, the difference between the salary and education costs could be made up by additional salary, gifts, or loans. This simple maneuver will save Harrington over $7,000 each year in taxes!

As for the two younger children, because of their ages it would probably be difficult to employ them and justify much of a salary, but Harrington could shift income to them by transferring a portion of his shares in the company to a trust for their benefit, then electing to have his corporation treated as a partnership for tax purposes (called a "subchapter S" election). During the period of the trust, a portion of the corporate profits would be taxed to the trust at a much lower tax rate, and the funds could accumulate for their education. At the end of the trust period, Harrington could arrange to get his shares back and, if advisable, terminate the subchapter S arrangement. Assuming Harrington remains in the 50 percent bracket, he could save in taxes as much as 50 percent of all amounts that are paid to the trust.

(Hiring children and making a subchapter S election are discussed in Chapter 8.)

. . . .

A Doctor

Doctor Cosgrove has a busy and lucrative medical practice which she operates out of a small professional building she purchased several years ago. Because of the relatively low cost for the building and the fact that she has been there for a number of years, she is presently realizing only nominal tax benefits through depreciation and expenses.

Doctor Cosgrove has children—four of them—who range in age from 9 to 14 and will soon be needing funds for education. What to do? She could create a trust for her children, transfer the building to the trust, then lease it back from the trust for her medical practice. This arrangement should be accompanied by a written lease, and the trust should have an independent trustee, but if all the necessary requirements are met, Doctor Cosgrove will enjoy a *larger* tax deduction than she is presently getting for the property, and all the rental payments will be made to the trust, tax-deductible, to accumulate for the children's education.

The type of trust could be either one where the real estate would ultimately be owned by the children, or one where the real estate would be returned to Doctor Cosgrove after ten years. In either case, Doctor Cosgrove will be entitled to deduct the rental payments made to the trust even though the funds are to be used for her children's education.

(Trust and leaseback arrangements are discussed in Chapter 8.)

. . . .

A Dentist

Doctor Krane has a busy "group" dental practice, which has grown from one to six dentists over the past twelve years. Just about all the dental equipment used in the practice has been fully depreciated (run out of tax benefits) so Doctor Krane has more taxable income than was previously the case. In addition, he is faced with the educational costs of his three children, at roughly $6,000 per year each, and realizes painfully that the $18,000 annual educational expenses will, in his tax bracket, cost him about $36,000. What to do?

Doctor Krane should create a trust for the benefit of his children, make a gift of the dental equipment to the trust, then lease back the equipment for use in his dental practice. If a fair yearly rate for the equipment were $3,000 for each of the six dental offices in his practice, he could pay the trust $18,000 of *tax-deductible* lease payments. These funds could be used toward the children's education, at a savings of about $18,000 per year for the doctor. In short, he would be generating an $18,000 tax deduction where there was *none* before, and better still, the $18,000 is paid to the children for college expenses.

(Gift and leaseback of equipment or similar property is discussed in detail in Chapter 8.)

. . . .

Going Further

These case studies should give you an idea of the myriad possibilities for structuring a particular family's situation to achieve deductibility of educational costs. The solutions offered in the examples are presented in a very simple way to show direct results. Although the actual results can be equally direct, the laws behind the simple concepts are not always as straightforward. What follows is a more detailed coverage of all the ideas and tax concepts contained in the case studies presented so that you and your advisors can determine whether a given plan fits into your situation and, if so, exactly how to carry it out.

IMPORTANT REMINDER: Regardless of the plan you use, if any of the child's income, *whether from a trust or any other source,* is used to satisfy a parental obligation, *the income so used will be taxed to the parent,* despite the care taken with the rest of the plan. To avoid falling into this trap, be sure to review the discussion of this point in Chapter 3 (pages 26–33).

REFERENCES FOR CHAPTER 2

(No References—See individual chapters cited with each case study.)

3

. . . .

Shifting Income
to Save Money—
An Overview

The basis for accomplishing "deductibility" of educational expenses is either a tax-free or a tax-deductible shifting of taxable income to the child, to be taxed in the child's lower tax bracket. There are numerous ways to "shift" income, some relatively simple, some more complicated. In this book we will cover all the accepted and tested ways, as well as some of the more "creative" ones. Where there is a risk, we will tell you what it is, and you and your advisors can take it from there.

Shifting income is by no means new to the tax-planning field. In fact, because of the tremendous incentive in the form of virtually guaranteed tax savings (if properly done), it has been the topic of numerous court cases embodying ingenious methods of transferring taxable income from one party to another. Although the concept is agreeably simple, the underlying tax laws involved are disagreeably not so simple.

The starting point in your understanding of what you can or cannot do in this regard is the basic principle of how income is taxed, as embodied in the income tax code. Simply stated, the law provides that income will be taxed to the person who *earns* it. Breaking this down a little further, we can say that taxable income is for the most part attributable to the *services* or *property* of a particular person or entity. That is, if I paint your house for $750, I have earned $750 of income as a result of my *services*. But if I own stocks that pay annual dividends of $500, than I have $500 of income attributable to my *property* (the stocks).

Under the tax laws, I cannot "shift" the $750 of services income, because once I have "earned" it, it will be taxed to me when I receive it. But what if I don't receive it? What if I say to you, "I have legally transferred my right to receive your payment of $750 to my son, and therefore, you are to pay him directly." Will my son be taxed on the $750? Or what if I write my broker, stating, "I have legally assigned my $500 of dividends to my son; please pay him directly." Will he then be taxed on the $500?

The tax laws (and hundreds of court cases) clearly say, "No." This, they say, is an "assignment of income" and I will be taxed on the $750 earnings or the $500 dividends even though they are paid to someone else, since *I* (or *my* property) "earned" them and, therefore, only *I* had the right to receive them. In this same line of reasoning, you are also unable to assign *future* income from services. In other words, I cannot arrange that "one-third of all legal fees I earn for the next four years" shall be payable to my daughter. Since *I* will be doing the earning, *I* will likewise be responsible for the taxes, regardless of any legal assignment I might try to make.

This does not mean that there is no other way to accomplish the same end. This book describes the many ways you can do so. Reading through the following chapters, you will see that arrangements can be made to lead to a similar result, without running afoul of the tax laws.

Shifting income which is attributable to *property* can be a little clearer, although nonetheless tricky. If the underlying property interest itself is shifted, then the earnings on that interest will also be shifted. For example, if a hundred shares of stock are gifted to a child, then all the dividends earned on that stock from the date of the gift will be taxed to the child. Variations on this "simple" concept, however, can lead to traps and tax costs.

The Horst case, a landmark in this area, is a good illustration of this. In that case, Mr. Horst had purchased some "bearer" bonds (bonds that are not registered in the name of any particular owner and are therefore payable "to the bearer" or person in possession of them). Such bonds, in order to enable the payment of interest, have "coupons" attached to them. To collect an interest payment, the bearer simply clips off the coupon and presents it to a bank, and the bank makes the interest payment to the person who turned in the coupon.

Mr. Horst clipped all the coupons from his bonds and made a gift of the *coupons* to his son, who collected the interest and reported it for income tax purposes. The IRS contended that the interest was taxable to Horst, not his son, since it was the *bonds* that generated the interest and it was *Horst* who owned the bonds. Horst argued that since the coupons were separate and negotiable in their own right, and since he had given up all control over them, he should not be taxed.

The case went all the way to the United States Supreme Court, which held that Horst's actions were clearly an assignment of income, that the gift was one of *income* and not of the income-producing *property*, that the underlying property that produced the income was still owned by Horst, and that therefore Horst (and not his son) should be taxed on the interest.

These examples illustrate a very important tax principle in the shifting of income, metaphorized as the "fruit and the tree" doctrine by Justice Holmes in the 1930 case of *Lucas v. Earl*, which should help you better understand the concept of shifting taxable income. Simply stated, the IRS and the courts will *not* recognize, for tax purposes, an "arrangement by which the fruits are attributed to a different tree from that on which they grew." Horst, in other words, gave his son the "fruit" (the interest) but kept the "tree" (the bonds). To shift the tax burden, the Supreme Court says, you must transfer the "tree" as well.

In the Horst case, transfer of the "tree" could have been simply and conclusively done by an outright gift of the bonds to his son. Not every family situation (nor every option for the shifting of income) is the same, however, and some "trees" are much more difficult to uproot. Horst obviously didn't mind giving away the interest, but for some reason, he wanted to keep the bonds. Actually, if this happened today, he could have arranged to have his son taxed on the interest without giving up complete ownership of the bonds through the use of a ten-year trust (see Chapter 6).

Whether you use simple or complicated maneuvers or combinations of both, the basic principle of shifting income to save money will remain the same, and that is to cause the income in question to be legally taxed to someone in a lower tax bracket than yourself. The effective savings each year will be equal to the difference in actual taxes paid on the income before and after the "shift," and can be as high as *50 percent* of the income involved.

. . . .

Tax-Deductible vs. Tax-Free Shift

From the parents' income tax standpoint, shifting income can either be a nontaxable transaction or a tax-deductible transaction. The nontaxable transaction would include, for example, the making of a tax-free gift. A tax-free gift is one that does not result in a gift tax. (In some cases, the making of a gift can produce a gift tax on the transfer; see Chapter 4.) By nontaxable, I mean there are no immediate income tax consequences, either in taxes paid or in taxes deducted on the transaction itself. The *making* of a gift is not deductible on your income tax return nor is the *receipt* of the gift taxable to the recipient. You should realize, however, that although the gift may be a nontaxable transaction, it is made with after-tax dollars—that is, money on which an income tax has probably already been paid.

With a nontaxable transaction such as this, the tax savings come about when the *income* from the gift is taxed to the child or the child's trust. For example, if Dad gives Daughter $10,000 and she invests it at 11 percent, there is no tax benefit to Dad on making the gift, but Daughter is now taxed on the $1,100 income earned from the gift. If Dad is in the 50 percent tax bracket, he would be saving $550 per year on that $1,100 income which, prior to the gift, would have been taxed to him.

An important aspect of a nontaxable transaction is that it is made with *after-tax* dollars. If you are in a 50 percent income tax bracket, you must earn $50,000 in order to have $25,000 left over to use in a nontaxable transaction. If you have a choice, a tax-deductible transaction is almost always better.

A tax-deductible shifting of income would come about when the income-shifting maneuver is structured so as to permit an income tax *deduction* to the parent for payments made to the child.

A simple illustration of this would be the case where the parent borrows money from the child and makes interest payments on the loan. If properly structured, the interest payments are tax-deductible to the parent and taxable income to the child. The fact that the child uses the funds for college education should not affect the deductibility of the payments.

Another simple example is where the parent employs the child in a business. Amounts paid to the child for services will be deductible to the parent or to the business, and taxable income to the child.

The IRS itself has ruled that such payments will be fully deductible if they are fair and reasonable under the circumstances (see Chapter 8). The "fair and reasonable" test is an objective one and may be determined by simple common sense. For example, if the going wage for window washers in your city is $5 per hour, it would not be considered fair and reasonable to pay your child $10 or $12 per hour to wash your office windows.

. . . .

Important Mistakes to Avoid After Shifting Income

Once the income has been legally shifted to the child or student, you are home free, right? *Maybe not!* There are two *important* details you must watch out for *after* the shifting of income to be sure there are no adverse tax results to you.

Trap #1—Support Obligations

The first and most important of the two details has to do with "support obligations" you have to your child. There are certain responsibilities every parent has to a child, which include the legal obligation to provide food, clothing, maintenance, shelter, and any of the other necessities of life. Since you have the legal obligation to provide this support, if it is paid for from the income you have previously shifted, then the amount of income applied for that purpose will be taxed to you.

For example, say that you have successfully shifted income of

$1,000 per year to your child. In a particular year, the child has dental work done which costs $350 and this is paid out of the child's $1,000 income. If this happens, *you,* the parent, will pay an income tax on the $350 and the child will be taxed on the remaining $650, because $350 of the child's income was used to satisfy your obligation to provide and pay for the dental work.

Exactly what constitutes a support obligation has, like many other tax issues, been the subject of a great deal of litigation. As a general rule, however, it would certainly include all of the reasonable "necessities" mentioned above, viewed in the light of the particular family's lifestyle. Further, it is important to note that your support obligations cease when the child becomes an adult. Once the child becomes an adult, the income may be used for just about any purpose relating to the child without being taxed to you, as long as use of the child's income does not satisfy some other legal obligation of yours.

In many states, a child becomes an adult at age 18, in others at 20 or 21. You should check the law of your particular state to see which age applies.* This is extremely important in the context of paying for college education with tax-favored dollars, since the age at which a child usually enters college is 18. If your state's age of majority is not 18, but 20 or 21, the question may arise as to whether college or other educational expenses are a support obligation of yours, as the child is still a minor. If they are a support obligation, then the income used to provide the education could be taxed to you, and the tax savings from shifting the income would be lost, to that extent. Some states are very clear as to whether support obligations include or exclude secondary and private education, but the IRS does not specifically limit the criteria to "state law" for tax purposes. That is, state law may exclude college education as a parental support obligation, but the IRS may nevertheless attempt to include it on account of the particular family's circumstances, viz., the family's ability to provide more. But, in some cases, the IRS may have state law on its side.

In a 1941 Minnesota case, for example, a circuit court agreed

*See Appendix A for the laws of each state.

with the IRS that private school and college expenses were a support obligation of the parents under Minnesota law, and the parents were taxed on the child's trust income used to pay those expenses. On the other hand, in a 1972 Montana case, a circuit court held that trust income similarly spent was *not* taxable to the (high income) parents, even though Montana law provided that the parent should provide support and education "suitable" to the parents' circumstances. A further illustration of the possible variation of the law from state to state and of the extreme position some courts can take is provided by a 1984 New Jersey case.

In that case, Fred and Marjorie Braun established two Clifford-type trusts for the benefit of their two children, and the trustees used the trust income to pay private school and college tuition costs for the Brauns' children. The IRS contended, among other things, that the payment of such expenses satisfied a legal support obligation of the Brauns, and therefore should be taxed to them as income.

In an extraordinary decision which was against the general authority on the point, the court held that the income so used *was* taxable to the Brauns on the basis that "they were both able and willing to do so, a college education was imminently reasonable in the light of the background, values and goals of the parents as well as the children, and the parents brought forth no arguments which would militate against the recognition of this obligation on the part of these particular parents." In other words the court said, if they could clearly afford it and it was clearly a part of their "background, values and goals," the Brauns had a legal obligation to provide for private school *and* college costs for their children.

This decision is *not* the majority holding, but it does show how courts can arrive at surprising decisions. Although this extreme decision should *not* discourage planning for educational costs, for those parents in New Jersey it should at least warrant the careful investigation of their particular circumstances as well as a professional opinion on the effect of such payments by a trust or other source. And despite this decision, I'm sure that Clifford trusts will continue to be a popular vehicle to reduce educational costs in New Jersey.

In contrast with the New Jersey decision, some states go to lengths to make it quite clear that a child's income (or income from a trust for the child) *may* be used to provide educational costs *without* affecting the parents' obligation of support. The result would be that the parents would not be taxed on the income used to pay for college or private school, even though the parents themselves may have created the educational trusts, as long as they were not personally liable for payment as discussed in Trap #2 below. Rhode Island, for example, has a law that states:

> To the extent that any such minor child has property or an estate of his or her own, or that there is income or principal of any trust used for his or her benefit, which may be used to provide such child with an education in a college, university or private school, such (parents) shall not be obligated either jointly or separately to provide such an education. The foregoing sentence shall not be deemed to create by implication any obligation to provide such an education where none would otherwise exist.

When the legislators wrote this law, it almost seems they had a book like this in mind. But not all states have such a law. In states that do not, it is a question that may turn on the facts of each individual case.

In short, the law is not crystal clear, and you will be much better off if the educational expenses are paid (from the child's income) *after* the child reaches the age of majority. If it must be paid before that time, such as for private school tuition, see if state law includes such payments as part of your support obligations. As a general rule, it appears that *private* school costs for a minor are *not* considered a parental obligation, but in any event, be additionally careful not to fall into the second trap.

Trap #2—Other Legal Obligations

The second trap many people unsuspectingly fall into occurs when the parent has *contracted* to pay the child's educational expenses and then uses the shifted income to pay the bills. This tax problem is similar to the one discussed above, except that instead of a *support* obligation, we have a *contractual* (legal) obligation of the parent being paid with the child's income. When this happens, the income is *taxed to the parent*, because it is being used to satisfy a legal obligation (i.e., a debt) of the parent. If this happens, the tax will apply even if the child is an adult, since the question is not one of minority and support, but rather one of using the child's income for payment of an *actual debt* of the parent.

To circumvent this problem, you should not legally commit yourself to pay for the educational expenses that are to be paid from the child's income. If there is a trust involved, the *trustee* of the trust can agree to pay the bills (on behalf of the trust and not as an individual), or if the child is old enough and the school will accept the child's promise, the *child* can agree to pay. If financial "backing" is necessary and as a last resort, parents can *guarantee* the loan or contract, but in no event should the parents be primarily liable if they intend to use the child's income to pay the educational expenses.

For example, the Evergreen school wants a commitment that your child's tuition will be paid even if the child doesn't finish the year. They won't settle for the child's signature alone. If you have an educational trust or a custodial arrangement, you should have the *trustee* or the custodian guarantee payment of tuition. If for some reason this can't be done (i.e., where there is no trust or no custodian), you can be a guarantor of the child's debt. That is, if for any reason the child does not pay the total tuition, the school may look to the guarantor (i.e., to the trustee, to the custodian, or to you, as the case may be) for payment. Since the guarantors are liable only if the primary obligor (the child) does not pay, the debt will not be treated as your obligation, so if tuition in such a case is paid by an educational trust on behalf of the child, you will have avoided this trap and the tuition payments will not be taxed to you.

Trap #3—Divorce Agreements

Clients who are in the process of divorce frequently ask me if I can devise a way to utilize some of my tax-saving ideas for education in connection with their divorce agreement. This is because most divorce agreements will require one of the parents (usually the husband) to provide funds for the child's education with *after-tax* dollars. Unfortunately, from the perspective of the many tax maneuvers discussed in this book, the chances of accomplishing this are somewhere between slim and none, and in fact, if you try to use one of those ideas, you will probably find yourself caught in the jaws of both of the tax traps described above. Here's why.

When a divorce takes place, it is the result of a court decree, and that decree normally orders the parties to carry out the terms of the divorce agreement and/or the court's decision. A court decree (or even a separation agreement ordering the parties to do something) creates a *legal obligation* for the parties, even though none may have existed before the decree, and if that obligation is satisfied through some other source (such as an educational trust), it will result in adverse tax consequences, as discussed above.

For example, say that Jekyl and Heidi get a divorce, and the court decree states that Jekyl must provide a college education for his eighteen-year-old daughter. Under the laws of their state, a person is an adult at eighteen and therefore, were it not for the court decree, Jekyl would *not* be legally obliged to pay for her college education. The decree *creates* a legal obligation for him to do so, where none previously existed. And, if after the court decree Jekyl were to establish and fund a Clifford trust to provide for his daughter's education, all of the trust income so used would be taxed to Jekyl, because the trust would be satisfying *his* legal obligation to pay those costs as ordered by the divorce decree.

If the children are minors, the parents already have the obligation of support, but as discussed earlier in this chapter, it may not be clear in the particular state involved whether the parental obligation of support includes such things as private school costs or early college admission. Usually, the court dispels any confusion on this point by making it the clear obligation of one or both parents under the court decree, thereby restricting, if not eliminating, any opportunity for tax planning. If the obligation of private school or college is *not* mentioned in the decree, however, one or more of the ideas in this book may be effectively used (and this is something to keep in mind).

Despite the above, there may be at least one opportunity to realize some tax savings on educational costs in the face of a divorce, but it will require cooperation from both spouses. Briefly, it is done by having the spouse in the *lower* tax bracket agree to the obligation of educating the child, while the spouse in the *higher* tax bracket increases alimony payments accordingly.

For example, in the case of Jekyl and Heidi, say that before alimony payments Jekyl has a taxable income of $100,000 per year and agrees to pay for their daughter's education (at a cost of $8,000 per year), plus make alimony payments to Heidi of $32,000 per year. Under this arrangement, Jekyl would pay a tax of about $22,200, and Heidi a tax of about $6,000, for a combined tax of $28,200.

If, instead, Heidi agrees to become obligated to pay their daughter's educational costs and Jekyl agrees to pay Heidi $11,600 in *additional* alimony each year, for, say, six years, the tax results would be quite different. (The reason Jekyl would agree to pay $11,600 more instead of $8,000 is to help cover Heidi's additional income tax on the higher alimony payments.) Under this arrangement, Jekyl would pay a tax of about $17,000, and Heidi a tax of about $9,600, for a combined tax of about $26,600, *and a savings of about $1,600 each year!*

The greater the difference in tax brackets between the spouses, the better this plan will work, but, unfortunately, there may be some drawbacks, as noted below. Before you consider rearranging payments and obligations, you must have your tax advisor review the "numbers" as well as the tax laws governing alimony payments and confirm that there will be a worthwhile savings. Furthermore, it will, as noted above, require the cooperation of *both* spouses, which is not always obtainable.

If you already have a divorce decree and are required to meet these obligations at a high tax cost, it still may not be too late. If both spouses will agree, and if the proposed change in payments is approved by your tax advisor, your attorney may be able to modify the court decree to realize the educational objective and the tax savings.

There are two potential drawbacks to the idea of rearranging alimony payments and shifting the burden of educational costs to the lower bracket spouse. The first is the tax law itself. Alimony payments under divorce or separation agreements executed after December 31, 1984 must meet certain requirements in order to be deductible to the paying spouse. One requirement is that payments over $10,000 per year must be made for at least six consecutive years. This in itself may not pose a problem since actual alimony plus the educational "addition" would probably exceed $10,000. There is an additional provision, however, that says that, if *during* the six-year period payments fluctuate by more than $10,000 per year, the excess (over $10,000) will not be deductible to the paying spouse. In other words, in our example, if Jekyl's payments drop off by $11,600 in the sixth year (after his daughter's education is completed), a portion of that amount ($1,600) could be disallowed as a deduction. If the payments don't drop until after the sixth year, there should be no problem.

A second potential drawback is the possible vulnerability to an IRS attack that this whole arrangement is just to avoid taxes and an attempt to make the obligation to educate the child a deductible item. They could try to disregard the court decree and disallow at least a portion of the "alimony" deduction on this basis. It is not at all clear that the IRS would be successful in such an attack, especially if this is what the original decree provides (i.e., if it is not a modification of an old decree), and if your advisors agree, the tax savings could make the calculated risk quite worthwhile. In Jekyl's case, for example, they will save about $10,000 over the six-year period—about a year's free tuition!

. . . .

Social Security Numbers
and Other Tax ID Numbers

A Child's Social Security Number
and the Tax Consequences

Because each of the plans in this book directly or indirectly involves the child as a separate "taxpayer" (paying as little as possible, we hope), it is important that the child have his or her own Social Security number for tax identification purposes. If your child does not have one, you should apply for one as soon as possible by calling your local Social Security office. They will send you an application, which you must complete on behalf of the child and then send to the central Social Security office in Maryland. It usually takes about four–six weeks to obtain a number.

Having a separate Social Security number for the child is very important not only for filing his or her income tax return but also because banks and certain other payers of interest and dividends are required to *withhold* 20 percent from those payments if no number is given. Further, the IRS is authorized to impose other penalties for failure to supply a tax ID number.

Remember, the Social Security number is purely for purposes of identification of the particular taxpayer. *It does not, by itself, operate to shift income or create a new taxpayer.* Many people are under the mistaken impression that placing a child's number on a joint bank account or "trustee" bank account (i.e., parent as trustee for child) will cause all the interest on that account to be taxed to the child. *This is not so.* In those cases, the income on that account will be taxed to the parent as the owner of the account and as the person who has *control* over the account. The fact that you or someone you know may have been doing this for years (and having the child pay the tax) means only one thing—that you or they haven't yet been audited on this point by the IRS. If you want to shift income to your child, this book will tell you the right way to do it, without fear of an audit.

Trust and Custodial ID Numbers

If part of your plan to shift income for educational purposes involves the use of a trust, such as a minor's trust, or a ten-year trust (discussed in Chapter 6), the trust itself will also have a separate tax identification number. This number, however, is not given by the Social Security Administration but by the IRS, and like the Social Security number, it is purely for purposes of identification of the taxpayer involved—in this case, the trust. When the trust files its own tax return, as it will for purposes of this book, it will use its own ID number on the return. Your accountant or attorney will usually apply for this number when the trust is created. In any event, you will still need a separate Social Security number for the child (regardless of his or her age).

If you make gifts to a custodian for the child under the Uniform Gifts to Minors Act (see Chapter 5), the custodian does *not* need a separate tax ID number. He or she will simply use the child's Social Security number for any investments or accounts held as custodian under the Gifts to Minors Act. So, for example, if you make a gift to a custodian for the child and then borrow back the funds, the custodian will receive all the interest payments on the loan and report them under the *child's* number on the *child's* tax return. The custodian himself has no personal tax liability and need not file a separate return as custodian.

SUMMARY

Separate taxpayers need separate tax identification numbers. In the case of a child, this means a Social Security number, so anyone interested in shifting income to a child for educational (or any other) purposes should apply for a Social Security number for the child as early as possible. Separate trusts will also have separate tax ID numbers, but custodians under the Gifts to Minors Act need not. The number itself has *no legal effect* and is for no other purpose than tax identification, so it is important to understand that shifting income involves much more than shifting ID numbers.

. . . .

The Double Dependency Exemption

One additional advantage of shifting income to a child, especially where the funds are to be used for college, is that a "double" exemption is available. That is, the $1,000 per dependent exemption allowed under the federal income tax laws will be available not only to the parent for the child but also to the child for himself. For example, if a minor has only $1,000 of income in a given year, the child will pay no tax because he may apply his own $1,000 exemption to offset the income. At the same time, the parents may claim the child as a dependent on their income tax return, getting an additional $1,000 deduction for the same year.

Briefly, a child will be a dependent, regardless of the amount he earns, until reaching the age of 19, or any age if he is a full-time student, as long as the parent provides more than half the child's support. A child is considered a student if he is a full-time student at an educational institution or an institutional on-farm training program during a period of at least five calendar months (not necessarily consecutive) during the year. Night school does not qualify. An "educational institution" is one with a regular faculty, a regular student body, and an established curriculum.

There could be cases, however, where the child/student is not a child of the taxpayer and where the extra exemption is lost, for example, where the student is the "dependent" of a relative other than his or her parents. In that case, once the student earns more than $1,000 for the year, the child may of course claim himself, but the extra dependency exemption to the relative is lost for that year.

In the typical case, though, the student will be the child of the taxpayers and as long as the other dependency requirements are met, the double exemption will be available.

IMPORTANT REMINDER: Regardless of the plan you use, if any of the child's income, *whether from a trust or any other source*, is used to satisfy a parental obligation, *the income so used will be taxed to the parent*, despite the care taken with the rest of the plan. To avoid falling into this trap, be sure to review the discussion of this point in Chapter 3 (pages 26–33).

REFERENCES FOR CHAPTER 3

Shifting Income and Saving Money
1. *Helvering v. Horst*, 311 U.S. 112, 61 S. Ct. 144 (1940) (Assignment of income).
2. *Lucas v. Earl*, 281 U.S. 111 (1930) (Assignment of income).

Important Mistakes to Avoid After Shifting Income
1. *Mairs v. Reynolds*, 120 F.2d 857 (8th Cir. 1941) (Minnesota) (Private school costs).
2. *Brooke v. U.S.*, 468 F.2d 1155 (9th Cir. 1972) *aff'd*, 300 F.Supp. 465 (DCC Mont) (Montana) (Private school costs).
3. *Morrill, Jr. v. U.S.*, 228 F.Supp. 734 (DC Me. 1964) (Maine) (Private school costs).

4. *Braun v. Comm.* TCM 1984-285 (College and private school costs taxable to parents).
5. Rhode Island General Law, Section 33-15-1 (Using child's funds for education).
6. IRC, Sections 108 and 677(b) (Payment of your debt with the child's funds).
7. *Sperling v. Comm.* 84-1 USTC 9176 (1984) (Divorce, where parent pays tuition).

Social Security and Other Tax ID Numbers
1. IRC, Section 674 (Parents Taxes on Trustee Bank Accounts).
2. IRC, Section 6109 (Tax Identification Numbers).
3. Reg. Section 35A. 9999-1 (20% Withholding If No ID Number).

The Double Dependency Exemption
1. IRC, Section 152 (Dependent defined).
2. IRC, Section 151(e) (Additional exemption for dependents).

NOTE:
IRC = Internal Revenue Code.
Regs. = U.S. Treasury Regulations.
RR = Revenue Ruling (by Internal Revenue Service).
Letter Ruling = Ruling for a Taxpayer by the Internal Revenue Service (not published in IRS Bulletin).
TC = U.S. Tax Court Decision (TCM = U.S. Tax Court Memorandum Decision, not the full court).
F. = Federal (U.S. Circuit Court of Appeals) Decision, (F.2d = Federal, 2nd series).
Cir. = Circuit (area of the U.S. served by that court).
aff'd = affirmed lower court decision.
rev'd = reversed lower court decision.
S. Ct. = U.S. Supreme Court Decision.
USTC = U.S. Tax Cases, Commerce Clearing House.

4

· · · · · · · · · · · · · · · · · ·

Gifts and
Gift Taxes

Many of the ways to shift income for educational purposes involve the use of gifts in one form or another, so when making a gift, one must be aware of the potential gift tax traps. It comes as a surprise to many people that there is a separate and distinct tax on the "privilege" of making a gift. In fact, the gift tax laws are more than fifty years old and were enacted to impose a tax on the *transfer* of property by gift. In many instances, however, if the gift takes advantage of certain allowances stipulated under the gift tax laws, there will be no tax on the transfer.

If gifts are involved in your particular plan to save taxes on educational costs, it is important to understand the basics of gifts and gift taxes, so as to minimize, if not eliminate, any gift tax exposure that may be present in the plan. Throughout, you should try to keep in mind the distinction between gift taxes and income taxes, and remember that gifts are generally made with *after-tax* dollars, so that if you are in the 50 percent income tax bracket, you must earn $20,000 in order to make a nondeductible gift of the $10,000 you have left.

· ·

How the Gift Tax Works

The federal gift tax is not a tax on the actual property one individual gives to another, nor is it a tax on the receipt of the property by the donee (the person receiving the gift). It is a *separate tax on the transfer*, when the transfer is made for less than the fair value of the property given. In most cases, the donor of the gift receives nothing in return and the amount of the gift is clear—the full fair value of the property given. In some cases, however, the recipient may pay or exchange something in return for the gift, and the value of the gift will be the difference between the two.

Your gift may be one of money, stocks, bonds, or real estate; a life insurance policy; or even a copyright interest in a book. It can be anything that is capable of ownership and transfer. When a taxable gift is made, the gift tax is imposed on the *donor* (the person making the gift), although if the donor can't be found or has no money to pay the tax, the IRS has the means to reach the gifted property in the hands of the donee to collect any gift tax due. But as a practical matter, most gifts will not involve the actual payment of a gift tax, as you will see.

The amount of the gift tax is based on the *fair value* of the property given *on the date of the gift*. It does not matter that the donor himself paid considerably less or considerably more for the gifted property. For example, say that Dad purchased some stocks many years ago for $1,000 and today they are worth $15,000. He decides to give them to Daughter so that she can sell them (in her income tax bracket) and use the proceeds for her educational expenses. When Dad gives the stocks to Daughter, he would be making a gift to Daughter of $15,000, the fair value of the stocks *on the date of the gift* and would be subject to a gift tax. (Daughter's income tax treatment is discussed in detail in Chapter 5, but, simply stated, the gain would be passed on to her.) The general rule, then, is that for gift tax purposes, the value of the gift is the *fair value* of the gifted property *when the gift is made*.

. . . .

A "Sale" for One Dollar

Remember, a gift only occurs if the transfer is, in fact, a gift. That is, a bona fide *sale* is not a gift, nor is a *loan* of money, since in both cases each party gave up something but in turn received something of equal value—what the IRS refers to as "full and adequate consideration." To the extent there is *less* than full and adequate consideration for the property transferred, then it will be considered a gift. Because of a lack of understanding of the "full and adequate consideration" concept, many people *mistakenly* think that creating a "sale" for one dollar is a sale and not a gift.

Merely calling something "a sale" does *not* take it out of the gift category. A purported "sale" of something for one dollar will clearly be a *gift* unless the property sold is really worth only one dollar. Similarly, transfers for "love and affection" are not considered bona fide sales. A bona fide sale for tax purposes is one at a price and under terms which "a willing buyer would accept and a willing seller would pay, neither being under any compulsion to buy or to sell, and both having reasonable knowledge of all relevant facts." The farther you stray from this, the greater the gift tax exposure, and in some cases, it is very difficult to determine the "fair value" of property involved.

Taxpayers frequently attempt to get around the "sale" question by charging *something* for the property (i.e., more than one dollar), but not quite enough, thinking that the "donor," being the owner of the property, can charge whatever he likes, and that therefore a sale at any price will be "legal." It might well be perfectly "legal," but it will just as well be taxable (at least in part) as a gift. For example, when Mother sells her $50,000 vacation home to Son for a price of $30,000, a gift of $20,000 has been made as clearly as if she had collected his $30,000 and given him back $50,000, except in this case, she gave him a home worth $50,000. In fact, this is called a "bargain sale" and in some cases could produce a capital gain as well as a taxable gift to Mother!

For example, say that Mother originally paid $20,000 for the property (now worth $50,000) and "sold" it to Son for $30,000. The IRS would argue that because Mother received more than her cost back, she had a taxable gain, and at the same time, because she sold it to Son for less than its fair value, she made a taxable gift. The gain and gift are computed as follows:

Since she paid $20,000 and received $30,000 on the "sale," Mother will have a capital gain of $10,000.

Since the property had a fair value of $50,000 (she could have sold it for that amount) but was transferred to Son for only $30,000, the difference of $20,000 is a gift to Son.

. . . .

Timing of Your Gifts

The time a gift takes effect can often be important for tax purposes, since once the gift does take effect, the donee is taxed on all the income earned on the gifted property from that point. As a general rule, the gift is complete when the transfer is effective and delivery has been made to the donee. Delivery can be an actual delivery or it can be "constructive" i.e., a transfer of the *right* to something rather than the something itself. Delivery of a bank book to the donee is constructive delivery of the funds in the bank; delivery of the keys (and title) to a car is constructive delivery of the car; delivery of endorsed stock certificates to the donee is constructive delivery of the right to obtain new stock certificates, and delivery of property to the trustee of donee's trust can be constructive delivery to the donee.

When you give bonds or stock certificates, timing can be especially important, since they usually generate continuous income. The IRS insists that unless there is a physical delivery of endorsed certificates to the donee or his agent, the gift is *not* complete until the stocks are registered in the name of the donee on the books of the corporation. To be on the safe side, you should be sure the endorsed certificates are delivered to the donee (or trustee) or to the donee's brokerage account within the desired time.

. . . .

The Gift Tax and "Tax-Free" Gifts

When the gift tax applies, it ranges from 32 percent to 50 percent of the amount given (the value of the gift at the time it was made), and, as previously noted, it is the *donor's* responsibility to pay the tax, if one is due. As a general rule, *all gifts are taxable* for federal gift tax purposes, but as a practical rule, most gifts do not require the actual payment of a gift tax. One reason for this is the "tax-free" gift exception.

Certain gifts to individuals that do not exceed a specified amount are not subject to a gift tax and for this reason are called "tax-free" gifts. The term tax-free does NOT mean that the gift gives the donor an income tax deduction (see Gift Taxes vs. Income Taxes, page 46); it simply means the gift is *free of gift taxes*.

To qualify for this tax-free status the gift must be one of a "present interest" to the donee. This is a legal term designed to distinguish gifts that can be used and enjoyed *presently* from gifts given under a "future interest," another legal term meaning that the donee must wait to enjoy the money or property. The requirement that the gift qualify as a present interest is vital to the annual gift tax-free exclusion. IRS regulations define a *present interest* as one where the donee has "an unrestricted right to the immediate use, possession or enjoyment of or the income from property, such as a life estate or a term certain."

An outright gift to a donee clearly qualifies as a "present interest" since once the donee owns the property, he can do with it as he pleases. Further, an outright gift to a guardian or to a custodian for a minor (see Chapter 5) also qualifies for the present interest exclusion, since the minor or other child, through the custodian or guardian, can immediately begin to enjoy the property, and in any event, the child has "possession" through the guardian or custodian. Gifts in trust, although a little trickier, can also qualify for the present interest exclusion as discussed later.

Now for the numbers. Prior to 1982, the maximum gift a donor could make to each donee under the annual exclusion was $3,000. Beginning with gifts made in 1982, the annual per-donee exclusion has been increased to *$10,000*. The exclusion is measured annually and on a "per-donee" basis for each donor. There is no limit to the number of $10,000 gifts a donor can make each year, but he or she may not give more than $10,000 to any one donee without incurring a gift tax, with the following two exceptions: gifts for medical expenses of a dependent may be made in excess of the $10,000 per-donee limitation without incurring a gift tax; and gifts to a child for tuition payments may also exceed the

$10,000 limitation. But do NOT let this latter exception mislead you into thinking that this is any kind of a meaningful tax savings for educational purposes. The real tax savings will come when you shift the income to the child and let the child pay his own tuition and other nondeductible costs.

Getting back to the $10,000 annual exclusion, it means that Stuart, who has five children, can give each child up to $10,000 during the year (a total of $50,000) without incurring a gift tax. And if his wife, Linda, either wants to make her own gifts or consents to having Stuart "use" her exclusions, then an additional $50,000 may be given to their children in the same year, for a total of $100,000 in "tax-free" gifts. Since it is only measured on an annual basis, they may continue this year in and year out until they run out of money, which would probably be soon at that rate! It is easy to see that if you have a spouse and enough donees (they do not have to be children) to whom you want to give gifts, you can give away a great deal of money (or any other property) without worrying about a gift tax at all.

Finally, remember that the infamous "lifetime exemption" was repealed in 1976. Although previously you were allowed a lifetime exemption for gift taxes on gifts of up to $30,000 (over the old $3,000 exclusion), this is no longer the case.

. . . .

Gift Tax Returns—When to File

Like the gift tax itself, the gift tax return comes as a surprise to many people. We all realize that an income tax return must be filed whenever we have a certain amount of income in a particular year. Similarly, a *gift tax return* must be filed *by the donor* whenever a certain amount of gifts are made during the year.

Any gifts by a donor which exceed the annual exclusion (or exceptions) discussed above require the filing of a gift tax return, as do any gifts of "future interests" (where the donee does not have immediate possession or enjoyment of the property or its income), regardless of the amount of the gift.

For example, if Carolyn makes a gift of $12,000 to her nephew Alex, she has made a $2,000 taxable gift ($12,000 − $10,000 exclusion) and must file a gift tax return. If Carolyn's husband allows her to use his exclusion as part of that gift, tnere will be no tax, but a gift tax return must nevertheless be filed to show her husband's consent to use his exclusion. If they each made separate gifts to Alex of $10,000 or less, no gift tax return would be required.

The gift tax return is due by April 15th of the year following the year in which the gifts were made. Therefore, if there is a gift of $25,000 in January of 1985, a gift tax return must be filed by April 15, 1986.

. . . .

Gift Tax Credits

You will be pleased to know that unless you make huge gifts in excess of the annual exclusion, there will probably be no gift tax to actually pay. This is because everyone is entitled to what is called a "unified credit" to apply toward any gift tax that may be due. It works this way. In the example above, Carolyn made a $2,000 taxable gift (the $12,000 gift less the $10,000 exclusion) and if she had no husband to consent to use of his exclusion (only spouses can consent) then she would owe a gift tax of $360 on the $2,000 gift. However, unless she had made large gifts in the past and already used up her unified credit, she would not have to actually pay the $360 tax. She could merely apply $360 of her unified credit, and the tax would be considered "paid."

The credit allowed to every U.S. citizen and resident alien is $121,800 for 1985, and it gradually increases to $192,800 in 1987 and thereafter. The table below shows the various credits and the corresponding dollar value of gifts that would use up the credit:

Year	Tax Credit	Value of an Equivalent Gift
1982	$ 62,800	$225,000
1983	79,300	275,000
1984	96,300	325,000
1985	121,800	400,000
1986	155,800	500,000
1987 and after	192,800	600,000

In other words, a gift tax credit of $79,300 is the "equivalent" of an outright gift of $275,000, or conversely, a taxable gift of $275,000 would produce a gift tax of $79,300.

As you "gain" more credit each year, it may be used or simply carried forward. It would not matter, for example, that in 1983 you used up your credit of $79,300, because in 1984 you would pick up another $17,000 of credits due to the gradual increase.

If in a given year you exceed your allowable credit, you will then have to come up with the tax due. For this reason, if you intend on making large gifts, you should *be sure to time them so you get proper use of the credit*, since if you exceed your 1985 credit in 1985, you will have to pay the difference in tax, even though your credit may be increased in 1986.

Further, if it is advisable to make gifts, you should always try to get maximum mileage out of the $10,000 annual exclusion since it will not use any of your unified credit. For instance, if you wish to make a $20,000 gift, you may make a $10,000 gift in December and another in January of the following year (thereby using two years' exclusions) without being subject to any tax and without using any of your credit. If the full gift must be made earlier, you may give the first $10,000, "loan" the other $10,000, then forgive the debt early the next year. The IRS could say that you made a gift of the "use" of the $10,000 for the few months, but even if this did happen, the exposure would be quite nominal and much less of your unified credit would be used in that manner (for a more detailed discussion of loans, see Chapter 7).

. . . .

State Gift Taxes

Our discussion is limited to the federal gift tax laws. However, many states have adopted a gift tax (see Appendix D) and if yours has, the laws should be checked to avoid incurring a state gift tax even though a federal gift tax may not be due.

. . . .

Gift Taxes vs. Income Taxes

A great deal of confusion seems to have developed around the relationship between gift taxes and income taxes. There is none.
While it is true that gifts can shift the income tax liability on the
gifted property, the gift tax is a separate and distinct tax from the
income tax. Perhaps the greatest confusion lies in the misappre-
hension that gifts or gift taxes are deductible from your income
taxes. They are not. When we speak of tax-free gifts, we mean
gifts that are free of *gift* taxes, and except for gifts to charities,
gifts in themselves do not create an income tax deduction and are
made from after-tax income.

The good news, however, is that gifts *are not considered as income to the donee*. In short, for gifts within the annual exclusion,
there are no immediate tax consequences, neither gift nor income,
to either the donor or the donee. For example, Mother gives
$9,000 to Son in 1983. Mother does not "report" the giving of
the gift on her income tax return and neither does Son on his, but
Mother at some point probably paid a tax on the $9,000 she ac-
cumulated to make the gift. The advantage is that all the *income*
earned on the $9,000 *after the gift* is taxed to Son and not to
Mother. This is the objective in shifting income.

Another aspect of gifts that affects the donee's income taxes is
the treatment of subsequent sales of the gifted property. When a
donee sells property that she received as a gift, how does she determine whether there is a gain or loss? As a general rule, the donee takes the same basis (the cost for tax purposes) as the donor
had in the property at the time of the gift. If the donor paid additional gift taxes (over his credit), then a part of this may be added
to the donee's basis, but use of the donor's *credit* (without actually paying a gift tax) does *not* increase anyone's basis in the
gifted property. In addition to taking the donor's cost basis, the
donee also "adds on" the donor's holding period in the property.
For example, if a donor purchases some securities in January of
1984 and in December of 1984 makes a gift of them to donee,
then donee is treated as if he held the stocks since January of

1984. Or say that Grandma makes a gift to Grandson of her Cape Cod summer home, which she purchased fifty years ago. Grandson can sell it the next day, but as far as the tax laws are concerned, it's as if he held it for fifty years.

The substituted basis and holding period rules can produce a favorable and easy income-shifting opportunity. For example, say that Dad has securities he purchased on November 30, 1984, for $2,000, which in November of 1985 are worth $10,000. He then makes a gift of the stocks to Daughter, who sells them only a few days later, on December 2, 1985. Daughter will have a *long-term* capital gain of $8,000, the tax on which ought to be substantially less than Dad would have paid.

NOTE: There is a special (and somewhat complicated) rule when gifted property is sold by the donee at a "loss." In effect, the special rule provides that a donor is *not* allowed to "shift" a tax loss to the donee merely by making a gift of the property.

The following table should help illustrate the different treatment of gift and income taxes, gains and losses, in different situations:

If you make an outright gift:

and your cost for the gift was:	and the value of the gift on the date of the gift is:	there will be a gift tax of:	if the donee immediately sells it at the gift tax value there will be:
$ 1,000	$ 8,000	none*	a $ 7,000 gain
$10,000	$12,000	$360**	a $ 2,000 gain
$15,000	$ 7,000	none*	no gain/no loss***
$ 1,000	$25,000	$4,900**	a $24,000 gain

*No gift tax because the value of the gift when made is under the $10,000 tax-free exclusion.

**If you are able to apply your gift tax credit, no actual tax will be paid. If you actually pay a gift tax, the donee's gain will be reduced by the amount of the gift tax attributable to the gain.

***In this situation, there will be no gain unless the sale price exceeds $15,000 and no loss unless the sale price is less than $7,000. Anything in between produces no gain/no loss to the donee.

. . . .

Gifts in Trust

Because of the very extensive use of trusts in the various possible maneuvers associated with shifting income to children for educational purposes, it is very important to understand the possible gift tax implications of transfers to trusts for that purpose. This is not a discussion on trusts (that follows in Chapter 6), but rather on the gift tax considerations where transfers are made to trusts. When property is transferred to a trust, particularly a trust designed for educational purposes, a gift has probably been made.

The confusion and complications come about, however, because the gift is not made directly to the donee, but instead to a *third party* (the trustee) to hold for the donee. This is what a gift in trust is about, and the logical questions arise: If the donee does not yet *have* the gifted property, is the gift "complete" for tax purposes? And who is actually the donee in that case?

In principle, a gift in trust does not differ from an outright gift in that once the donor has given up ownership and control over the gifted property, the gift is complete. Whether a donor who makes a gift in trust has in fact given up the necessary ownership and control is not always clear, since the trust arrangement in a sense intercedes between the donor and the donee, and, therefore, it is the *terms* of this trust arrangement that will determine whether a gift has been made.

For instance, when a gift is made to a trust, the *donee* of the gift in trust is the beneficiary (or beneficiaries) of the trust and *not* the trustee. If the terms of the trust allow the beneficiary to presently use and enjoy or to withdraw the funds, then the gift (to the beneficiary) is one of a *present* interest and the $10,000 annual exclusion will apply to the gift even though made in trust. For example, say that John transfers $10,000 to a trustee, *in trust* for his son, Jonathan. The trustee is instructed to hold and manage the $10,000 in trust, except that Jonathan may request the funds from the trustee at any time. Since Jonathan, the beneficiary, has a right to withdraw the $10,000, this is considered a gift of a *present interest* and the gift will qualify for the $10,000 present interest exclusion. (This is so, regardless of Jonathan's age.)

If, on the other hand, the terms of the trust provide that the trustee is required to "accumulate" income (so it will not be paid out at least annually to the beneficiary), or that the beneficiary has no right to withdraw funds, or any other provisions that prevent the beneficiary from present use and enjoyment of the funds, then the gift will be one of a "future interest" and the $10,000 exclusion will not apply. (There is an exception to this under a minor's trust, discussed in Chapter 6.)

If the "gift" to the trust is *incomplete*, then no gift is made and the gift tax rules will not apply, but more important, you will *not have succeeded in shifting the income* to the beneficiary. For purposes of our discussions relative to shifting income, it is very important to have a completed gift, since we want the income on the gifted property to be taxed to someone in a lower tax bracket.

Incomplete gifts will result if you, the donor, reserve too many rights or powers over the trust or over the gifted property, allowing the IRS to argue that by exercising one or more of these powers, you could *change* the disposition of the gifted property and therefore you did not give up sufficient ownership and control over the property to have a completed gift.

For example, the right to amend, revoke, or terminate the trust will render the gift incomplete, since you could change the entire disposition of the property merely by changing the terms of the trust, or merely by terminating the trust. This is the main reason that so-called *trustee bank accounts* are virtually useless as a means of shifting income, particularly where the donor is also the trustee on the account. As trustee, he has the right to simply withdraw the funds and terminate the trust. Further, with such an arrangement the "beneficiary" may receive nothing during the donor's lifetime, depending on the whim of the donor. Under these conditions, how could anyone argue there was a completed gift? And since there was no completed gift, all the interest earned on that account will be taxed to the donor/trustee, as many people sadly discover when audited by the IRS.

Another situation that will render the gift incomplete occurs when the donor reserves the right to decide at some future date to change the shares of the beneficiaries or to add new beneficiaries to the trust. Although there are exceptions, suffice it to say that the more powers you reserve under the trust, the thinner the ice you're on for purposes of successfully shifting the income to save taxes. Further, as you will later see, you are generally better off to have an independent trustee to help convince the IRS that you have, in fact, parted with ownership and control of your property, as well as to comply with some of the specific tax laws relating to dealings with trusts.

Some unfortunate results can come about if you trip up with an incomplete gift. While a completed gift successfully shifts the income to the donee, an incomplete gift does not, and, as noted above, the income, therefore, is taxed to you, the donor, as it would have been prior to the gift. This is so even though the income is *paid over* to the beneficiary. And when the income *is* paid to the beneficiary, you then would have a completed gift *of the income* at that time, while the underlying property is still treated as belonging to the donor.

For example, say that Joseph owns $100,000 in bonds paying interest at 12 percent. He wants to give these to his son Christopher and so creates a trust for this purpose and transfers the bonds to the trust. However, he reserves the right in the future to by-pass Christopher and substitute one of his other sons. In the meantime, the trust provides that all the annual income will be paid to Christopher.

Because of the right reserved by Joseph to change beneficiaries, the gift is incomplete. But because of the terms of the trust, the $12,000 income will still be paid out to Christopher until Joseph exercises his right to change that. Since the gift is incomplete, the $12,000 income will be *taxed to Joseph, even though he does not receive it*. Further, each year the $12,000 is paid out to Christopher, it is considered a *gift* from Joseph to Christopher, and subject to a gift tax (or use of the gift tax credit). It should be easy to see how important it is to have a properly structured trust and a completed gift.

Another complication to watch for where gifts in trust are concerned is with gifts of appreciated property to a trust. There is a special income tax rule that says if you transfer appreciated property to a trust by gift, and if the trust sells or exchanges that property at a gain within two years of the transfer, then the trust will pay basically the same tax on the gain (existing at the time of the transfer) that you, the donor, would have paid. For instance, Stanley bought some stocks for $8,000 that are now worth $28,000, and he made a gift of these stocks to his children's educational trust. If the trust sells the stocks at a gain (of up to $20,000) within two years of the date Stanley made the transfer, then the trust will pay at least the same tax that Stanley would have paid had he sold the stocks himself. This is an easy trap to overlook and it can cause substantial tax savings to be lost. However, it applies only to transfers of appreciated property to a trust, and only when that property is not held for more than two years before it is sold. The rule does not apply to an outright gift to a child or even to a custodial gift (as discussed in Chapter 5). This does not mean that a trust should not be used simply because appreciated property is involved. Unless there is a requirement or need that the transferred property be sold within the two-year period after transfer, a trust may still be considered.

NOTE: This chapter has presented only a general overview of gifts and gift taxes as they relate to the topics covered in this book. It is offered to help you understand the important gift tax considerations involved in carrying out some of the ideas for shifting income for educational purposes suggested in this book. No final action should be taken on any of these ideas without the benefit of expert advice.

IMPORTANT REMINDER: Regardless of the plan you use, if any of the child's income, *whether from a trust or any other source*, is used to satisfy a parental obligation, *the income so used will be taxed to the parent*, despite the care taken with the rest of the plan. To avoid falling into this trap, be sure to review the discussion of this point in Chapter 3 (pages 26–33).

REFERENCES FOR CHAPTER 4

How the Gift Tax Works
1. IRC, Section 2501 (Imposition of tax).
2. IRC, Reg. Section 25.2511-2 (Dominion and control).
3. IRC 2512 (Valuation of gifts).

Timing of Your Gifts
IRC, Reg. Section 25.2511-2.

The Gift Tax and "Tax-Free" Gifts
1. IRC, Section 2502 (Gift-tax rates).
2. IRC, Section 2523 (Gifts to spouse).
3. IRC, Section 2522 (Gifts to charities).
4. IRC, Section 2503(b) (Tax-free gifts).
5. IRC, Section 25.2503-3 (Gifts of future interests).
6. IRC, Section 2503(e) (Gifts of educational and medical expenses).
7. IRC, Section 2513 (Gift-splitting by husband and wife).

Gift Tax Return—When to File
IRC, Section 6019.

Gift Tax Credits
IRC, Section 2505.

Gift Taxes vs. Income Taxes
1. IRC, Section 1015 (Cost basis of gifted property).
2. IRC, Section 1223(2) (Holding period of gifted property).
3. IRC, Section 102 (Gifts are not income to donee).

Gifts in Trust
1. IRC, Sections 2010 and 2505 (Estate and gift tax credits).
2. IRC, Section 2501 (The gift tax).
3. IRC, Section 2012 (Gift tax credit).
4. IRC, Section 644 (Appreciated property—two-year role).

NOTE:
IRC = Internal Revenue Code.
Regs. = U.S. Treasury Regulations.
RR = Revenue Ruling (by Internal Revenue Service).
Letter Ruling = Ruling for a Taxpayer by the Internal Revenue Service
(not published in IRS Bulletin).
TC = U.S. Tax Court Decision (TCM = U.S. Tax Court Memorandum
Decision, not the full court).
F. = Federal (U.S. Circuit Court of Appeals) Decision, (F. 2nd = Federal, 2nd series).
Cir. = Circuit (area of the U.S. served by that court).
aff'd = affirmed lower court decision.
rev'd = reversed lower court decision.
S. Ct. = U.S. Supreme Court Decision.
USTC = U.S. Tax Cases, Commerce Clearing House.

5

. . . .

Gifts to Minors and
Other Children

Once you understand the basics of gifts and gift taxes, you can begin to investigate the numerous ways to use gifts as a means of shifting income. One of the problems frequently encountered, however, is that the donee may not be capable (from a legal, if not a physical standpoint) of accepting the gift. Minors, for example, cannot legally "own" securities or real estate in their own name. If a situation does arise where securities or real estate are accidentally placed in the name of a minor, you will find that virtually nothing can be done with the property until certain (expensive and involved) court action (usually a legal guardianship) is taken. This and other chapters will cover the various ways that minors can "own" property without the risk or necessity of such court action.

. . . .

The Uniform Gifts to Minors Act

One of the advantages of a person's "owning" property is the opportunity to put it to profitable use and perhaps sell or exchange it for other property. With only special exceptions, minors are unable to do this since anyone dealing with a minor does so "at his peril." In other words, a minor either does not have the legal capacity to enter a contract or at least (depending on state law) has the right to simply cancel it at his whim, even *after* the fact. Many cases exist, for example, where a minor has purchased an automobile, wrecked it, then returned the wrecked car to obtain his money back *in full*. Similar cases exist with securities, which were returned by the minors after the securities dropped drastically in value, and the brokers were forced to return full payment, since the minor had the right to "avoid" the contract of sale.

As a result, for many years the only way a minor could "own" property was through a guardian or through a trust. "Guardian" did not mean simply a parent, but rather a court-appointed guardian, since a parent is the natural guardian of the minor's *person* but not of his *property*. Fees and responsibilities attached to the court-appointed guardianship route made this choice quite unattractive in most cases, especially where only comparatively small gifts of money or securities were involved. And although trusts have been and still are quite useful, they are at the same time somewhat complicated and generally are more strongly indicated where larger gifts are involved, or where the desired maneuver is a bit too sophisticated for a simple gift (such as a gift and lease-back arrangement as discussed in Chapter 8), or where the tax laws effectively require it (such as a ten-year trust, as discussed in Chapter 6). There was no easy way, in other words, to make a small gift to a minor without making a big production out of it. Enter the Uniform Gifts to Minors Act.

I don't know who thought of it first, but gradually all states, as well as the District of Columbia, the Panama Canal Zone, and the U.S. Virgin Islands now have a Uniform Gifts to Minors Act (referred to hereafter as the UGMA). The UGMA was designed to provide a simple, inexpensive, and *uniform* way of making relatively small gifts to minors without the necessity of court involvement or expensive legal documents. Unfortunately, many people forget that the UGMA had "small" gifts in mind and they often accumulate huge amounts of money and securities under the UGMA without realizing the attendant risks, which are discussed in the sections that follow. Although the UGMA varies slightly from state to state (see Appendix C), the differences are slight and the basics discussed here will generally apply in any state.

The Custodian—The Person in Charge

Basically, the UGMA requires that the gift to the minor be made to a "custodian" on behalf of the minor. The custodian may be any competent adult or it may be a trust company, appointed in writing by the donor. Of course, it may be a parent or other adult member of the minor's family, including the donor, but where the donor is also the custodian, there will be estate tax problems, as discussed later.

If the original custodian ceases to serve as custodian, then a successor custodian may be appointed, in writing, by the resigning custodian. If the original custodian dies or for some other reason is unable to appoint a successor, then a successor will be appointed by a local court. The successor custodian will normally be an adult member of the minor's family, a guardian of the minor, or a trust company. If the minor is age 14 or over, he may nominate his own custodian, subject to approval of the court. Certain states' UGMAs allow for automatic succession of custodians, but this is not the general rule (see Appendix C for reference to the laws of your state).

Investments and Fees

Once the property is transferred to the custodian, he is responsible for "managing" the gifted property during the period of minority, and this includes collecting and holding the income, dividends, or whatever other proceeds are received, and possibly selling the property (if he feels it desirable) and reinvesting the proceeds. He is not required to simply hold the gifted property for the entire period, but he certainly may if he feels it is prudent to do so. And "prudent" is the key word. As a standard for his investment activities, the custodian is bound by the so-called "prudent man rule," which, simply stated, requires that he be conservative and careful, keeping within accepted investment principles.

The custodian may receive compensation for his services, but if he receives none (most individual custodians do not take a fee), he will be liable only for losses resulting from intentional wrongdoing, gross negligence, or failing to exercise "prudence" in managing the funds.

Types of Property—What Is Allowed

The types of property that may be given under the UGMA are somewhat limited, and this is largely owing to the original purposes of the act, which was to facilitate "small" gifts, say, a couple of thousand dollars. As a general rule, the custodian may accept only gifts of money, securities, life insurance policies, or annuity contracts. The most common, of course, are money and securities, such as shares of stocks and mutual funds. Except in certain states, real estate may *not* be given under the UGMA, nor may tangible personal property, such as gold, antiques, coins, or other collections, or works of art. Appendix C details the allowable investments in your state.

How to Make the Transfer

To effectively transfer eligible property to a custodian under the UGMA, it is *critical* that the donor make the proper title designation; otherwise the gift will *not* fall under the UGMA, and the legal and tax benefits of the UGMA could be *lost*. The appropriate designation for any transfer to a custodian is: "(Name of Custodian), Custodian for (Name of Minor) under the (Name of State) Uniform Gifts to Minors Act." Often, you will see it abbreviated like this: "Grover Lambeck, custodian for Clover Lambeck, U/T New York UGMA," which is acceptable.

A gift of money may be made by giving it to a bank or a broker to be credited to an account in the appropriate name of the custodian and the minor, *exactly* as stated above. If only the custodian's name is used without the balance of the necessary designation, you will *not* have made a gift under the UGMA. The same rule applies to life insurance and annuity contracts. Remember, this does not mean it is impossible to make a gift to a minor without designation of custodian under the UGMA, it merely means the rules of the UGMA will not apply to a gift that is not made in accordance with these requirements, and in such cases, you run the risk of expensive court action if a question arises.

Each gift under the UGMA may be made to one minor only, and only one custodian may be named for that gift. That is, you may not name two custodians on one gift to a minor, nor may you make a gift to a custodian for more than one minor, unless you separate the gifts. For example, you may make gifts to your spouse as custodian for each of your three children, but they must be three *separate* gifts and she or he must manage each one *separately*.

You certainly may name different custodians for different gifts, although there is no benefit to this unless you were not happy with a previous custodian. Further, no matter how you spread it out among custodians, your "tax-free" gifts are still limited to $10,000 per donee per year, and in this case, the *minor* is the donee. So, three $5,000 gifts in the same year to different custodians for the benefit of the *same* minor will exceed the $10,000 gift tax exclusion for that donee and result in a taxable gift as discussed in Chapter 4.

Use of the Funds

During the period that the custodian holds any property under the UGMA, he may use and apply the income earned by the property, as well as any part or all of the gifted property itself, for the benefit of the minor. The use and application of the funds by the custodian is always subject to review. However, as covered in detail in Chapter 3, if any of the income is used to satisfy an obligation of the parent, then that income will be taxed *to the parent*. Payments or "use" of the income for benefit of the minor *could* include such nonnecessities as vacations and musical instruments, but the UGMA states that it should be for the minor's "support, maintenance and education." Presumably private school costs are acceptable, but since our main objective here is to provide for college, you would probably have the custodian accumulate and reinvest any income until the time for college. During the years that the income is accumulated, it is taxed to the minor as discussed below.

Taxes

Gifts to a custodian for the benefit of a minor under the UGMA are deemed to be irrevocable gifts for the benefit of the minor, and as such, they fall under the gift tax rules discussed in Chapter 4. Because a completed gift has been made, there is a corresponding transfer of income tax liability on the income from the gift, and therefore, as soon as the transfer is completed, all income from the gifted property is *taxed to the minor*. This is a clear and easy way to shift income on the gifted property but as noted before, it is generally for smaller gifts of cash and securities.

Another income tax advantage under this arrangement, as it is with most of these income shifting arrangements where child dependents are involved, is that it does not affect the donor/parent's right to claim the child as a dependent and thereby enjoy an additional $1,000 income tax deduction for the dependency exemption.

During the period that the custodian is holding investments for the minor, either he or a parent of the minor will file any necessary income tax returns for the minor, showing the income from the custodial accounts together with any other income the minor had for the year.

There *is* an estate tax risk associated with the UGMA. It is a well-settled principle of tax law that if the donor names himself custodian, then the gifted property will be included in the donor's estate for federal estate tax purposes if the donor dies while serving as custodian. For this reason, it is advisable to name someone *other than the donor* as custodian (the donor's spouse is perfectly acceptable).

Accounting for Your Acts

A little-realized feature of the UGMA, designed to protect the interests of the minor, requires the custodian to "account" to the minor at the time the funds are turned over to him. An accounting is a detailed report, presented on an annual basis, of each transaction that took place in the custodial account from the time the custodian received the initial gift to the end of the accounting period. The account would show all funds received (from gift and income) and all amounts paid out (and why), and the balance should equal the balance presently held by the custodian. Once the minor reaches age 14, he or she can *personally* request an accounting from the custodian. If the account doesn't "balance," the custodian can be *personally* responsible for the difference.

As a practical matter, few individual custodians ever render an account unless formally called upon to do so. This may or may not be a favorable point, depending upon the amount of money involved and the family circumstances, or perhaps upon the relationship between the custodian and the minor. In the typical situation where Mom makes a gift of cash or securities each year to Dad as custodian for Daughter, when Daughter reaches adulthood, Dad simply turns over to Daughter the balance of cash and/or securities in the account and few questions are asked. There are situations, however, where Daughter may well be inclined to ask questions. In a case with very similar facts, Dad and Mom subsequently got divorced and Mom wanted to use some of the funds for Daughter's benefit. Dad (the custodian) refused, and Mom, on behalf of the Daughter, got a court to force Dad to give an accounting, since she thought he might be using the custodial funds for his own purposes.

Usually, the greater the amount of money or securities involved, the more activity there is and the greater the need to keep proper accounts. For these and other reasons, the UGMA should in most cases be restricted to comparatively small gifts.

Termination—You Have No Choice

When the minor reaches the age of majority, the custodian is at that time *required* to "terminate" the custodial account, and he must turn over any remaining custodial property to the child *regardless* of the child's situation. This is one of the major drawbacks of the UGMA and another reason that it is only suitable for small gifts. Once the child is given the money or securities, he may do with them as he pleases, and he may not necessarily spend the funds on education. Another problem could come about if the child dies before the age of majority. In this event, the custodial funds are paid over to the child's "estate." In most states this means that the parents of the child would "inherit" all or part of their gifts back from the minor; there is no provision in the UGMA which allows a parent or donor to name a beneficiary of the funds if the minor dies.

SUMMARY

The UGMA is an easy, efficient way to shift income on comparatively small gifts of money and/or securities. Once the gift is made, the income on it is taxed to the minor each year. The custodian can expend the funds for the minor's benefit or can simply accumulate income until the minor reaches the age of majority, at which time it must all be turned over to the child. Problems can arise, however, where the amounts get too large (as a rule of thumb, more than $10,000), since then the risks increase.

The major risks and drawbacks to the UGMA are:

- the minor must have access to the UGMA funds at a relatively young age and may decide *not* to use them for education;
- allowable investments are limited;
- if the donor is the custodian, the UGMA funds will be taxed in his estate;
- if the minor dies, the UGMA funds will pass through the minor's probate estate, then back to the parents;
- one cannot participate in sophisticated tax savings programs (such as gift and leaseback).

Generally, trusts are better if the gifts are of more than a nominal amount.

. . . .

Annuities, Insurance, and Zero Coupon Bonds— Are They Helpful?

Annuities and Insurance

As stated in the discussion of the UGMA above, a custodian may receive annuity or insurance contracts as a gift for the benefit of a minor. Of course, annuities and insurance may also be given to children who are not minors. Insofar as college education is concerned, proposals are often made to parents to take out a certain type of insurance or annuity contract to "fund" the child's education some number of years down the road. For reasons given below, I don't think that either of these alternatives is a particularly good approach when compared with the many others available. However, since it is a good bet that one or both will be offered to you, you should have a basic understanding of them to determine whether yours is one of the unusual situations in which they may be useful.

One alternative is to purchase an insurance policy, the other, to purchase an annuity contract, and in both cases you will be told that the arrangement will accumulate tax-sheltered dollars for the child's education. An annuity, by the way, is not life insurance; it is a legal contract, usually issued by a life insurance company, which is designed to produce, either immediately or at some future date, an annual payment to someone (the "annuitant") for life. There are other payment options, however, and one of them is a lump-sum payment at a future date.

The more popular annuity contract pitched for "college education" is the "single premium deferred payment" annuity. This type of contract calls for a single, lump-sum payment to the insurance company, and at some future date chosen by the owner of the contract, the insurance company returns the initial payment, together with interest (usually compounded) for the period they held it. There are certain restrictions, and often penalties, for cashing it in within the first several years, but the big tax advantage is that no taxes are paid on the deferred interest until you make a withdrawal or liquidate the contract. For income tax purposes, you will pay taxes plus penalties on any withdrawal within the first ten years, so that depending upon how much time you have between now and tuition day, you may be able to use this method to not only shift taxes but defer payment of them for a number of years. Whether this will actually save you money, however, is another question.

Here's an example of a typical annuity-for-education plan. You purchase a $10,000 single premium deferred annuity contract and give it to your spouse as custodian for your 12-year-old child. (Alternatively, you could give the custodian $10,000 and he or she could purchase the annuity.) The contract promises 12 percent interest, and in six years it will be worth about $20,000. Up to that point, no taxes will have been paid on the interest, since no money was withdrawn.

At age 18, your child becomes an adult and the custodian turns over the contract to the child, who thereupon cashes it in to use the funds for tuition payments. At that point, the child will have $10,000 of ordinary income ($20,000 received less $10,000 original investment) *on which a tax must be paid*, and under present tax rates (for comparison) the tax would be about $1,240. In addition, there would be a penalty of $500. This arrangement, in most cases, will only be helpful if the child himself was in a high tax bracket during the six years until the liquidation of the contract. Otherwise, it's a bad idea. Here's why.

If the same $10,000 were invested on a *taxable* basis at the same rate (12 percent) each year and the child had no other income, he would have paid total taxes of about $300, over the same period, or nearly $1,000 *less* than that produced by the deferred annuity contract, and of course, the penalty would be avoided as well.

Another seemingly attractive package which loses its luster upon closer inspection is the "educational" insurance policy. Generally, the pitch works this way: Dr. Socks has a 10-year-old daughter and he is told that if he pays only $100 each month, when his daughter is 18 she will receive $12,000 to use for college, and *further*, if Dr. Socks dies at any time before his daughter reaches 18, the policy will make up the difference, so there will still be $12,000 available for her college expenses. Attractive? Not really.

This is merely an endowment policy (one of the *most* expensive, least efficient types of insurance), combined with a decreasing term life insurance policy on the life of Dr. Socks. If Dr. Socks were merely to make gifts of the same $100 per month and supplement them with an inexpensive term policy for the decreasing difference, he and his daughter would be more than $2,000 better off at the end of the eight-year period. Decreasing term insurance to cover the $12,000 target would cost him an average of about $60 per year for a total of $480 over the eight years, but the $100 invested at only 10 percent over the same period would produce about $14,600. After allowing for the insurance cost, the advantage is about $2,100 over the "educational" policy.

SUMMARY

Annuities and insurance policies sold to "finance" education may produce some tax benefits but usually not enough to compare favorably with other approaches. Premature withdrawal of annuity funds can result in a penalty as well as a higher tax. Educational insurance policies are usually much more expensive than simply investing the cash savings portion and purchasing a decreasing term policy to cover the risk of death of the parent before the child enters college.

. . . .

Zero Coupon Bonds

A fairly recent investment product which was originally designed for retirement plans but has become quite popular in educational plans as well is called the "zero coupon bond." Whereas the traditional bond is issued (sold) at or near its face value and actually pays semiannual interest payments (the "coupon" rate) to the holder, the zero coupon bond (ZCB) is sold at a substantial *discount* from its face value, and *no* interest is paid on an annual basis (it has *no* coupon rate), but the full face value is paid at maturity.

For instance, not too long ago a $1,000 face value ZCB sold (at its original offering) at $560, to mature four years later for $1,000, giving rise to the advertised promise of nearly "doubling your money in four years—guaranteed!" Another ZCB sold at $167, to mature fifteen years later at $1,000!

For purposes of educational funds, it is easy to see that for a nominal present cost, a parent can use ZCBs to "insure" a substantial educational fund for a child at some future date. Under the second illustration, for example, a parent could purchase $50,000 worth of zero coupon bonds for $8,350 (i.e., 50 × $167 per bond), and place these in an educational fund for the child. In fifteen years, the child would be entitled to the full $50,000 at a "cost" to the parent of only $8,350.

The big advantages to the ZCB are the substantial discount from face value (but this is merely a factor of prevailing interest rates), and the fact that the "return" on the bonds is compounded. The compounding of interest is reflected in the discount. For example, an investment of $500 in a zero coupon bond that matures at $1,000 in six years reflects a compound interest rate of 12 percent over that period. The difference between the $500 investment and the $1,000 value at maturity is the compounded interest, paid in the form of the "maturity" value. As any high school math teacher will tell you, the effect of compounding the interest can be dramatic. For example, if the same parent in the above illustrations instead of purchasing the zero coupon bonds merely purchased $8,350 worth of regular bonds paying a current rate of interest, it would be difficult (if not *practically* impossible) to reinvest the semiannual interest payments so that they would compound at the same rate as the zero coupon bonds. In all probability, the result would be that the regular bonds and their interest would produce substantially less than the ZCB.

One potential disadvantage to the ZCB is that the tax laws require the holder (in our case, the child or the child's trust) to report a certain portion of the future interest *on an annual basis, even though no interest is actually received.* In other words, each year, the child (or the trust) may have to pay a tax on a portion of the interest, even though none is received. This could result in a tax due but no money to pay the tax (although once the problem is realized, it can be dealt with easily through small gifts of the amount of taxes due).

The taxable amount of income on a ZCB is based on a complicated formula that takes into account the "yield to maturity" on the ZCB (annualized compounded return from beginning to end). The effect of this formula is to include lower amounts of interest in the early years and larger amounts in the later years. For example, in the above illustration where a ZCB sold at $560 and matures four years later at $1,000, the interest income that must be reported under the formula ranges from about $87 in the first year to $135 in the final year for each $1,000 bond (it is not simply the total interest divided by 4). Therefore, if the parent had purchased twenty bonds, the child would have $1,740 interest "income" in the first year (20 × $87 interest per bond) and $2,700 in the last (20 × $135 interest per bond), with correspondingly varied amounts for the years in between.

The amount of tax that might be due on the unreceived interest would, of course, depend on the child's other income, but if there were none, the tax would only be about $200 in the last year (in this illustration). To cover this, the parent need only make a gift of that amount to the child or to the child's trust. Of course, if the cash requirements were much greater because of larger interest amounts, additional planning would be necessary.

There *is* an alternative, however, which in a sense gives you the best of both worlds, at least as far as the ZCB is concerned: you could purchase a zero coupon *municipal* bond. With a tax-free (municipal) ZCB there will be no federal income taxes on the bond interest during the term of the bond or at maturity. And although the municipal ZCB will usually pay a lower interest rate than a taxable one, it is interesting to note that long-term municipal ZCBs pay only about one percentage point less in interest rates than a taxable ZCB of comparable maturity.

Another potential drawback of the ZCB, and one which could thwart your entire educational financing plan, is its "call" feature. The call feature of a particular bond is that which allows the issuing company to redeem the bond, in effect call it back, *before* the bond's maturity date. Although with regular bonds this is not so disastrous, with a ZCB it can short-circuit your whole plan. For example, say that you pay $9,000 for a ZCB that will mature in 11 years at $40,000. Just enough (you hope) to pay for your 7-year-old child's education. Unfortunately, your child's bonds are called just after the first year. Of course, you will be paid something when the bond is called, but at best it will be your cost plus interest, plus a small premium (for your "trouble"). And what do you do then to replace the investment? It could be difficult.

There is nothing you can do to prevent a bond from being called if the terms of the bond issue allow it. Now that you are aware of this potential problem, however, you *can* be selective about the ZCB you buy and ask about the call feature of the bond. Some have call "protection" (i.e., they can't be called for a specified period of time, say 5 or 10 years), others are non-callable. On balance, you are usually better off accepting a slightly lower return in exchange for better call protection on your ZCB.

In addition to the risk of the ZCB being called, there is also the risk of wide fluctuation in the price of the bond between the time you purchase it and its maturity date. All bonds will fluctuate when the prevailing interest rate moves up or down. If you have a 10 percent bond, for example, and the going rate increases to 13 percent, the price of your bond in the market will drop considerably.

Fluctuation will be a problem only if the bond is sold within that period, but it is nevertheless a very important consideration, since ZCBs happen to fluctuate much more than conventional bonds. In fact, it is estimated that a 20-year ZCB will fluctuate *three times* more than a conventional bond, so if a sale before maturity is contemplated, a ZCB may not be the best investment.

Finally, an important consideration is the quality of the bond itself. Like other "traditional" bonds, ZCBs have certain investment characteristics and in most instances are "rated" from AAA, the highest, to DDD, the lowest. If you stick to a rating above BBB you will probably be okay. Just ask your broker for the rating before you buy. After all, you do want to be fairly sure that in ten or fifteen years the money will be there for your child.

SUMMARY

The zero coupon bond, if it is properly selected and if the "numbers" fit your family and educational needs, can be a very effective and economically attractive way to finance a child's education. In effect, the ZCB allows the education to be purchased at a discount, and little, if any, taxes are paid on the deferred interest (unless a large number of bonds are purchased). When the discounted bond matures, the full face value is paid to the holder, and so the bonds should probably be purchased by a child's educational trust rather than by the child directly, since it is seldom advisable for the child to receive thirty to fifty thousand dollars at age 18 or 19, as he certainly would if the bond was in his name or in the name of his custodian. So, if you can find a good zero coupon bond at a substantial discount (your broker can help with the selection), it would definitely be worth considering ZCBs to fund educational costs. The primary disadvantage is the requirement to report a certain amount of taxable income on the bond without the receipt of any cash, but this can usually be "covered" with additional small gifts from the parent, equal to the amount of the taxes due from the child or the child's trust, unless the child (or the trust) has its own funds to pay the tax or a tax-free (municipal) ZCB can be purchased.

· ·

Gifts and Borrowback

Under the typical use of the gift to shift income, the parent will make a gift of money to the child, and the child, either directly or through a custodian or a trust, will invest the money. The return on the child's investment is taxed to the child.

Depending on the situation, there can be two complaints raised about this arrangement—first, the parent loses the use of the funds, and second, the child may not always be able to get a good rate of return with a safe investment. Creative tax planners have come up with a solution to both problems—the *gift and borrowback*.

Under the gift and borrowback arrangement, the parent (or other donor) makes a gift of money to the child (or to a custodian or the trustee of a trust) and subsequently *borrows* the money back from the child at a specified rate of interest. The parent/donor now has the use of the funds and the child has "invested" the funds at a fair rate of interest. If the arrangement is properly structured, the parent will be able to *deduct* the interest paid on the loan each year and the child will show the same amount as income.

The keys to successfully structuring the gift and borrowback are, first, to be sure you have made a completed gift, and second, to be sure the loan is a legitimate, enforceable debt.

To make a completed gift, you must give up "dominion and control" over the gifted property. Placing funds in a joint bank account with a child, for example, will *not* generally be a completed gift. Transfer to a custodian, on the other hand, or outright to the child if he is old enough, or to an irrevocable trust, will all constitute completed gifts. The theory is that once your gift is complete, the donee is now the one in control of the funds and is under no obligation to loan them back to you.

If you try to take the loan without having first made a completed gift, the IRS will simply say you made a gift of the promissory note, which in most states is no gift at all. And even if the note were a gift, any interest paid would simply be an additional gift and not tax-deductible, so it is critical that a completed gift be made before the loan is taken.

After the gift, the donee may loan all or part of the funds to you, but it must be done on an "arm's-length" basis. That is, a genuine, enforceable debt must exist, at a fair rate of interest (prevailing rates), and this is best evidenced by a promissory note signed by the borrower and held by the lender until the note is paid in full. A promissory note is an unconditional promise in writing to pay a certain sum of money on a certain date (or on demand). In this case, it is important that the note bear interest, and to obtain the maximum deduction, the greater the interest (*within reason*) the better. The following is a very basic example of a promissory note:

> For value received, I, Maureen Belle, promise to pay to the order of Annie Bell, the sum of ten thousand dollars ($10,000), three years from this date, together with interest, payable annually, at the rate of fourteen percent (14%) on the unpaid balance.
> (signed) /s/ Maureen Belle.

An "arm's length" interest rate may vary according to the rates prevailing at the time the loan is made. The rate should not be substantially above the prevailing rates, since the excess could be deemed a gift by the IRS and would not be deductible by the parent. Similarly, if the rate is substantially below the market rate, the validity of the loan itself may be questioned or there could be adverse income tax consequences, as discussed in Chapter 7. Further, if the loan is made through a custodian or a trust, a low rate of interest could reflect on the performance of the custodian's/trustee's duty under the "prudent man" rule. Subsequent rate fluctuations after the loan is made will have no effect if the rate was reasonable at the time it was agreed upon.

Of course, for tax purposes, the parent is better off paying a higher rate of interest than a lower one. It appears, in fact, that it would not be unreasonable for a borrower to pay two or three points above the "prime" rate on borrowed funds. This would be supportable as a market rate, giving the parent a higher deduction and at the same time giving the child a better return than he would be able to get on most other "safe" investments such as Treasury notes or six-month money market certificates. Finally, the note should be written so that the parent pays *interest only* (no principal) during the term of the note.

Here's an example of how the gift and borrowback might work. Daughter is 18 and about ready to enter college, where her tuition and expenses are expected to be about $9,000 a year. Outside sources of aid will produce about $3,000, but she will have to tap Mom and Dad for the rest. In December, the parents make a gift to Daughter of $20,000 (the allowable "tax-free" amount) and then another $20,000 in January of the following year (again tax-free). In late January, Dad borrows the $40,000 from Daughter, giving her a promissory note due in four years with simple interest at 14 percent. In the fall, when tuition is due, Dad pays Daughter his first year's interest of 14% × $40,000, or $6,400, which daughter uses to pay her college expenses. Daughter, of course, will report the $6,400 interest income on her tax return, and, if this was her only income, she would pay a tax of about $600. Correspondingly, Dad takes a $6,400 deduction for the interest paid, and if he is in the 50 percent tax bracket, his effective "cost" is only $3,200. If Dad had to pay the same amount to Daughter on a *non*deductible basis, he would have had to earn $12,800 additional income in order to be left with $6,400 after taxes to give Daughter. The gift and borrowback, in effect, saved him $6,400 in costs (without taking into consideration Daughter's taxes of $600).

One drawback to this is that in four years (the term of Dad's note in the example), Dad has to pay back the $40,000 he borrowed from Daughter. There is, of course, the possibility that in the future, Daughter may decide to make a cash gift to her parents, but if this appears to be part of a scheme, the IRS certainly won't buy it.

Speaking of the IRS, they have tried to attack the gift and borrowback arrangement, and where the gift and borrowback followed the requirements set out above, they lost. Conversely, where the taxpayers did *not* follow the required steps, the IRS won. The following two cases illustrate both sides and the court's attitude toward this arrangement:

Mr. Gordon Todd of Cold Spring, N.Y., made certain "gifts" to his daughter and her three children. Todd operated a Wall Street investment firm and constantly used borrowed funds in his business. He felt it would be obviously beneficial to him and to his family if he could borrow (in effect, his own money) from them, and pay them deductible interest. He decided to make his gifts by "crediting" various accounts on his books in the names of his daughter and her husband and their children, then "borrowing" against those credits so he could pay interest on the borrowed amounts. No *funds* were physically placed in these accounts (which totaled well over $150,000); it was simply done by an entry in an account book. At the end of each year, however, Todd would actually *pay* interest to these accounts. From 1961 to 1964, Todd made total interest payments of over $62,000 which he deducted on his income tax returns.

The IRS disallowed his deductions on the basis that there were never any gifted funds from which to borrow. Todd argued that the "credited" amounts constituted valid gifts and that at the moment the entries were made, there was an "instant transfer of funds by gift,'' and that therefore his subsequent use of the funds was a valid loan.

The court didn't see eye to eye with Todd, observing that he never gave up dominion and control of any funds. The simple ''credit'' entries did nothing to divest Todd of the funds, and the fact that his books showed the family members as ''creditors'' was meaningless since *no funds had actually been given to the family.* Furthermore, even the interest that Todd paid went into the *same* accounts and therefore continued to be under his control. There was, then, no gift, said the court, which meant no subsequent loans, and which meant no interest deductions for Todd. Todd by the way, appealed this U.S. Tax Court decision to the Circuit Court of Appeals, and lost again.

In a similar case but with a different outcome, Dr. Avery Cook and his wife, Carolyn, of Louisiana, made gifts to their children by depositing funds directly into the children's bank accounts. After the gifts were made to the children, Dr. and Mrs. Cook borrowed some of the funds and signed negotiable promissory notes for the borrowed amounts, calling for the payment of interest. In 1971, they paid interest of $1,400 to the children and deducted the interest payment on their income tax return. The IRS balked.

In deciding in favor of the Cooks, the Tax Court noted that it was quite possible for a loan to have been made from funds gifted by the borrowers themselves. In fact, the court's instructions to the jury in this case speak for themselves on this point:

> Since the only source of funds loaned to Doctor and Mrs. Cook was the sums of money they themselves gave to their children, it is necessary that, before you can consider the question of whether the indebtedness was genuine, you first determine that bona fide gifts were made. If no bona fide gifts were made, no interest deduction is allowable, since there was nothing to borrow. However, if the transaction creating the indebtedness is a sham, that is, it was not genuine, then the deduction for interest is not allowed, even though money might actually have been paid. So the question here is for you to determine whether the transaction was, in substance, what it was in form.

Note the court's last comment, stating that the transaction must be ''in substance, what it was in form.'' This requirement pervades nearly every tax-oriented transaction and it is very important to keep it in mind. In this case it means, was there *really* a gift, and if so, was there *really* a loan, which at some point will be paid back? If there was both, then the interest paid will be fully deductible to the parents.

Other matters that must be taken into consideration are the "mechanics" of the transaction. How do you borrow, for example, from a 2-year-old? And how do you pay him or her interest? What if your 18-year-old demands his "money" back? Can he or she sue you? The answer to this last question is yes, and if this is a concern, the gift and loan should be made through a trust (see Chapter 6), where the trustee would not likely take such action except as a last resort. A trust can also be the answer to the other questions raised, but, as previously mentioned, a custodian, under the Uniform Gifts to Minors Act, can also provide some easy answers. Funds can be gifted to and borrowed from a custodian for the 2-year-old, and annual interest payments can be made to the custodian to hold for the minor.

Like all intra-family transactions, gifts and borrowback are subject to rigid and careful scrutiny by the IRS and the courts, and the burden of proof is usually on the family (the taxpayer) to show that the transaction was "in substance, what it was in form." As you have seen, however, the steps involved in planning a gift and borrowback are not that complicated, and if you follow them carefully, you can successfully generate an income tax deduction and shift income to a child to use for college expenses.

IMPORTANT REMINDER: Regardless of the plan you use, if any of the child's income, *whether from a trust or any other source*, is used to satisfy a parental obligation, *the income so used will be taxed to the parent*, despite the care taken with the rest of the plan. To avoid falling into this trap, be sure to review the discussion of this point in Chapter 3 (pages 26–33).

. . . .

Gifts of Appreciated Property

Another way of shifting income through gifts, but on a "lump sum" basis rather than through periodic income, is the gift of appreciated property. If, for example, you have some stocks that have appreciated in value and you need to raise money for tuition, you may decide to sell the stocks. In most cases, it would be better if you made a gift of the stocks to your child and let the *child* sell them, so that the gain will be taxed to the child instead of to you. If the gain happens to be very large, say $50,000 or more, then the situation would obviously require more sophisticated tax planning than a simple gift.

The reason that the potential gain on appreciated property is shifted to the child when the gift is made is that you, the donor, have not made the sale. You gave the property to the child and the child, as the new owner, made the sale. The reason the child will have a taxable gain on the sale is that he or she takes the property with the same "cost" that you had. (This is more thoroughly discussed in Chapter 4.) The only time this "cost" will be increased as a result of the gift is where you have actually paid a gift tax on the transfer.

Therefore, when you make a gift of property that is presently worth $10,000 for which you only paid $2,000, the child takes the property with a $2,000 cost basis, and a sale at anything over that amount will produce a gain to the child. The tax savings are realized because the child is presumably in a lower tax bracket than you.

Although the basic concept of gifting appreciated property appears quite simple, there are a few traps, and if you fall into any of them the gain will be taxed to *you*, not the child, even though it was the child who made the sale. This can happen, for example, if the gift is made at the same time as or just before a sale which has already been arranged. For example, say that John has a piece of real estate and after much negotiation has orally agreed to sell it to Frank. Immediately before the sale (or on the day of the sale) John deeds the property to his son, Jonathan, who makes the sale. Under these facts, the IRS could attack this transaction and claim that it was John (and not Jonathan) who made the sale, and the gain will be taxed to *him*. In addition, he will be treated as having made a *gift* of the net sales *proceeds* to his son Jonathan.

If the sale is not prearranged (such as a sale of securities in the open market), then, of course, this will not be a problem since it is difficult for the IRS to argue that any sale was prearranged when you don't know who the buyer is, nor the price that you will get, but under IRS attack, the burden would be on you to show that it was not a prearranged sale.

If you do contemplate a sale of property at a gain and consider using the proceeds for the child's education, the sooner the transfer is made to the child, the better. As mentioned above, this problem is not so common where publicly held securities are involved. More often than not, the IRS attack will apply to "private" sales of items like real estate or closely held business interests. If anything like this is the subject of your gift, be sure the donee owns the property for a reasonable period of time *before* the sale and is *not*, at the time of the gift, under any oral or written obligation to sell.

This doesn't mean that only publicly traded securities may be gifted, then sold. It simply depends upon the facts and whether it appears there was a prearrangement or an obligation to sell. It may well be that there is an *understanding* that the donee will sell, since the very idea is to shift the sales proceeds to the donee in his or her tax bracket. The Haley case provides a good illustration of this.

The Haley family of Georgia owned several closely held corporations. In an effort to consolidate some of the corporations and to shift control, James Haley made a gift of a number of shares of stock in some of these corporations to his wife as custodian for his six children. He filed appropriate gift tax returns, and because he exceeded the tax-free exclusion, he paid a gift tax. Some time after the gifts were made, Mrs. Haley, as custodian, sold the shares to other members of the Haley family at a gain. The gain was properly reported on the children's tax returns. The IRS later attacked the transaction as prearranged and charged James Haley with the tax on the gain. Unable to resolve it at the IRS level, Haley paid the tax and sued the IRS for a refund with interest. He won.

The court, in deciding in favor of Haley, noted that the gifts were valid gifts and that Haley retained no rights, directly or indirectly, to any of the proceeds. Haley himself gave up all dominion and control over the gifts, and Mrs. Haley, as custodian, was under *no* obligation to sell, even though everyone agreed that the sale was part of an overall plan to rearrange the corporate structures. Nevertheless, the court said, Mrs. Haley, as custodian, could have decided otherwise, and further, the proceeds of the sales were similarly subject to her use and control for the benefit of the children. The IRS was ordered to refund Haley's tax with interest, and the gain was appropriately taxed to the children.

A greater risk with a gift and subsequent sale of appreciated property will come about where there is an actual contract to sell the property in effect at the time of the gift. Even though the gift itself is valid, the IRS will tax the entire sales proceeds to you, since the sale was actually contracted and obligated *before* the gift was made. This will be attacked as an "assignment of income," as discussed in Chapter 1.

Finally, the gift and transfer must be "bona fide." If it is a "sham" or without substance, then the gain will be taxed to you even though it has the appearance of a gift. An example of a sham would be the transfer of property to a child, who sold the property, reported the gain, and then made a gift of the proceeds back to you. Although you might argue there is nothing wrong with making the gift and nothing wrong about the sale and nothing to prevent the child from making a gift back to you, when you put them all together they spell "sham" to the IRS, and under these facts, a court would probably side with the IRS.

Another point to remember is that outright gifts of appreciated property, at least for the purposes of saving money for educational expenses, are only a good idea if the intention is to *sell* the property and use the proceeds, in this case, for education. If the property is to be held for a long period of time, other factors must be considered before the gift is made.

. . . .

Gifts Through Joint Ownership

Still another tax-tested and surprisingly easy way (although not without its share of other risks) of shifting income to a child is through the ever-popular joint ownership method of holding property. To understand how it shifts income, you should understand a little about joint ownership of property. Joint ownership means that two (or more) people own the same item of property at the same time, with the understanding that on the death of either, the survivor will own the entire property. Real estate, stocks, bonds, bank accounts, or any other type of "property" may be held in joint names. It is often referred to as a "joint tenancy," and each of the joint owners is a "joint tenant."

When a joint tenancy is created, each of the joint tenants has an undivided equal interest in the jointly held property, regardless of the fact that they may not have paid in equal amounts, or any amount. Since this is a legal transfer of ownership of an equal share of the property, then each joint tenant is also legally entitled to an equal share of the *income* from the property, and therefore, the tax laws say, each will be taxed on his share of the income, according to his share of the property.

This general rule applies to just about every type of jointly held property except perhaps joint bank accounts. This is because jointly held bank accounts, in many states, are not considered equally owned by the joint tenants until there has either been contribution of funds to the account by both joint tenants or a delivery (completed gift) of a share of the account. Some states' laws (such as New York) provide a *presumption* of delivery or ownership so that as soon as the account is opened, each joint tenant has a legal right to an equal share of the account balance, and the income as well.

Therefore, if you want to shift half the income on $10,000 worth of 11 percent bonds, all you need to do is reregister the bonds in joint names with your child. Once the bonds are registered in joint names, your child will be taxed on his or her share of the interest income from the bonds, in this case, one half of $1,100 per year, or $550 per year. But don't forget that as soon as you have completed the new registration, you have also made a *gift* to your child of one-half the value of the jointly held bonds. Therefore, you want to be careful that you do not unintentionally exceed the $10,000 annual gift tax exclusion.

For example, say you have $40,000 of 10 percent Treasury bonds, paying $4,000 per year interest. When you register the bonds in joint names with a child, you have made a gift of

$20,000 to the child (one-half the value of the bonds at the time of the gift). If your spouse consents to the gift, there will be no taxable gift, since you are each allowed a $10,000 annual exclusion. After the gift, your child will receive and be taxed on one-half the interest, or $2,000 per year. Should your child die, you will get the bonds back; should you die, the bonds will belong to your child. Other than at death, however, you each have a right to only one-half the bonds. You have, in effect, *given away* one-half the bonds, and this is a very important point to keep in mind, as it could backfire on you.

For example, Morris had his 500 shares of telephone stock registered in joint names with his 18-year-old son, Philip, with the understanding that Philip would use the dividends to help pay for his college expenses. As it turned out, however, Philip decided not to go to college and simply began to spend the money from the dividends. Morris was understandably disappointed and demanded that Philip sign the stocks back over to him. Philip refused, and in a fit of rage Morris sued to have the other half of the stocks signed over to him, as they were his in the first place. The court agreed they were his in the first place, but disagreed that they should be returned. When Morris reregistered the stocks, the court said, he made a completed gift of one-half the shares to Philip, and Philip could not be forced to part with them without adequate payment for their value.

A transfer to joint names can also shift income on real estate, but with (in some cases) a slightly different twist. In these cases, although the law regarding equal reporting of the *income* still applies, the question of *deductions* may be different. Here, if one of the joint owners pays all the real estate taxes and mortgage interest, for example, then *that* joint owner will be entitled to those deductions and the other will not. For instance, say that Mom and Daughter own a four-family home that Mom recently placed in joint names with Daughter to shift some income to Daughter to use for college. The property produces about $15,000 per year gross rents. Real estate taxes and mortgage interest total $4,000 and other expenses are about $3,000 (assume that there is no depreciation). From some other sources of funds, Mom pays the taxes and interest, and the remaining property expenses are paid from rents from the property. Mom's share of the rents will be one-half of the net income on the property ($15,000 − $3,000 expenses ÷ 2), or $6,000. She can deduct the $4,000 of taxes and interest paid, so she will pay a tax on only $2,000. Daughter's share of the rents will also be $6,000 and she will *receive* and be taxed on this full amount. If this is her only income, she will pay a tax of only about $500.

You should note that in many cases, income from real estate is largely sheltered by depreciation deductions, and as a general rule, it is *not* beneficial to shift income that is already either sheltered or taxed in a low bracket. Depreciation deductions *cannot* be allocated unequally between the joint tenants as certain other expenses can (by payment), so if there are large depreciation deductions, you may not want to create a joint tenancy with a child in such property.

A gift into joint tenancy will also shift the income on a gain from a subsequent sale if the property has appreciated, but the same concerns apply in this case as outlined in the preceding discussion on gifts of appreciated property. The most prevalent argument, as noted, is the prearranged-sale attack. The Salvatore case and the Preebles case that follow illustrate a loss and a gain on the same point.

In the Salvatore case, Susie Salvatore inherited a Greenwich, Connecticut, gas station from the estate of her husband. Some years later, she decided to sell the station and in July 1963 she signed a written contract to sell the station to Texaco for $295,000. Prior to signing the contract she and her children agreed they would share the proceeds, but no formal action was taken at that point. In August 1963, she deeded a one-half interest in the station to her children, and immediately thereafter, the property was sold to Texaco and the proceeds divided between Susie and her children.

The IRS taxed Susie on the entire gain on the basis that the sale was prearranged and that Susie was under contract to sell. The transfer to the children just prior to the sale had no effect on the transaction, which was already destined to take place.

The Tax Court agreed with the IRS, and held that the children were mere conduits and that it was Susie who really sold the station. The sale was under agreement and the children had no power to change it. Susie was taxed on the entire gain.

In the Preebles case, more care had been taken to make the gifts prior to any written agreement and *prior* to final negotiations for a sale. In that case, Isaac Preebles owned 2,000 acres of timberland in Augusta, Georgia. In November 1941, Isaac offered the timber rights for sale to the Leigh Banana Case Co., but no agreement was reached.

In December, Isaac's tax advisor suggested that if Isaac made a gift of a portion of the property to his minor son, the proceeds would be taxed to his son and could also be used to pay for his son's education. Isaac agreed, and on December 8, deeded an undivided portion of the property to Mrs. Preebles as trustee for the benefit of their son. Shortly thereafter, because Isaac felt the outbreak of war on December 7 at Pearl Harbor would cause tax rates to rise, he insisted that the buyer conclude the sale by December 15. The sale was completed and the proceeds distributed to Mr. and Mrs. Preebles and to the trust for Preebles' son.

The IRS attacked this sale on basically the same argument as in the Salvatore case, but here the result was different. The court held for Preebles, noting that valid gifts had been made, that the sale might *not* have taken place (since no final agreement was reached at the time of the gift), and that Preebles was not entitled to nor had any control over the proceeds on the gifted share. Therefore, the portion of the gain attributable to Preebles' son was properly taxed to the son.

All these rules relating to shifting income through joint tenancy apply as well to a tenancy in common, but there are, of course, exceptions, which we will point out. There are two basic legal differences between a joint tenancy and a tenancy in common. First, the joint tenancy carries with it a right of survivorship (ownership to the survivor on death of the other), while the tenancy in common does not. That is, the share of a deceased tenant in common passes through his estate and not to the surviving co-tenants. The second distinction, and the one that changes some of the income tax considerations, is that the shares of tenants in common need not be equal, whereas the shares of joint tenants are presumed equal.

Therefore, a gift which creates a tenancy in common may, unlike a joint tenancy, create a gift of more or less than an equal share of the property. For example, if Dad makes Daughter a gift of a 20 percent interest as a tenant in common in his stocks and bonds, Daughter will be taxed only on 20 percent of all the income from the stocks and bonds. In many other respects, however, creation of a tenancy in common to shift income will carry the same risks as the joint tenancy. That is, the child can't be forced to give it back, and, in fact, could give his or her share away to someone else. Further, with a tenancy in common, in the event of the child's death the child's share will pass through his or her probate estate, rather than directly to the surviving parent/cotenant.

SUMMARY

This chapter covered some of the simpler ways to shift income by making gifts to minors and other children through various means, but each of these means involved an outright gift, with no strings attached. Gifts of income-producing property and appreciated property, gifts and borrowback of the funds, and gifts into joint ownership all involve some simple concepts and can successfully save taxes by shifting income, but each correspondingly has its own tax traps and you must be aware of them if you are to successfully use any of these maneuvers.

IMPORTANT REMINDER: Regardless of the plan you use, if any of the child's income, *whether from a trust or any other source*, is used to satisfy a parental obligation, *the income so used will be taxed to the parent*, despite the care taken with the rest of the plan. To avoid falling into this trap, be sure to review the discussion of this point in Chapter 3 (pages 26–33).

REFERENCES FOR CHAPTER 5

The Uniform Gifts to Minors Act
1. See State or Local "Uniform Gifts to Minors Act," Appendix C.
2. *Application of Muller*, 38 Misc. 2d 91, 235 NYS 2d 125 (1962), *aff'd* 18 App. Div. 2d 1067, 239 NYS 2d 519 (1962) (New York) (Custodian must account to minor).
3. IRC, Sections 2036 and 2038 (Estate taxation of custodial gifts).

4. *Gordon v. Gordon*, 70 App. Div. 2d 86, 419 NYS 2d 684 (1979) (New York) (UGMA gifts are irrevocable).
5. (UGMA included in Donor/Custodian's estate) *Stuit v. Commissioner*, 452 F.2d 190 (1971).

Annuities, Insurance, and "Zero Coupon" Bonds
1. IRC, Section 72 (Annuities).
2. IRC, Section 1232A (Zero Coupon Bonds).

Gifts and Borrowback
1. *Todd v. Commissioner of Internal Revenue*, 51 TC 987 (1969), *aff'd* 422 F. 2d 1322 (2d Cir. 1970) (New York).
2. *Cook v. United States*, 78-1 USTC Par. 9114 (W.D. La 1977) (Louisiana).
3. *Potter v. Com. of IRS* 27 TC 200 (1956).
4. *Linder v. Commissioner of Internal Revenue*, 68 TC 792 (New Jersey).

Gifts of Appreciated Property and Prearranged Sales
1. *Haley v. United States*, 400 F.Supp. 111 (1975) (USDC M.D. Ga) (Georgia).
2. IRC, Section 1015(d).
3. *Salvatore v. Commissioner of Internal Revenue*, 434 F.2d 600 (1970) (Connecticut).
4. *Preebles v. Commissioner of Internal Revenue*, 5 TC 14 (1945) (Georgia).
5. IRC, Reg. Section 1.301-1 (Distribution from a corporation).

NOTE:
IRC = Internal Revenue Code.
Regs. = U.S. Treasury Regulations.
RR = Revenue Ruling (by Internal Revenue Service).
Letter Ruling = Ruling for a Taxpayer by the Internal Revenue Service (not published in IRS Bulletin).
TC = U.S. Tax Court Decision (TCM = U.S. Tax Court Memorandum Decision, not the full court).
F. = Federal (U.S. Circuit Court of Appeals) Decision, (F.2d = Federal, 2nd series).
Cir. = Circuit (area of the U.S. served by that court).
aff'd = affirmed lower court decision.
rev'd = reversed lower court decision.
S. Ct. = U.S. Supreme Court Decision.
USTC = U.S. Tax Cases, Commerce Clearing House.

6

. . . .

Using Trusts to
Pay Educational
Expenses

. . . .

The Basics of Trusts

In the previous chapter we learned how income can be shifted quite easily to a child by simply making a gift to the child. We also saw that while the process is easy, the potential problems can be great, such as the inability to retain control over the funds, the inability to prevent the child from using the funds for something other than education, and in some cases, the lack of flexibility as to the type of property that can be used. Although trusts may be a bit more complicated, they can generally be designed to avoid all the shortcomings of the "simpler" ways to shift income.

This chapter will give you a brief overview of trusts, and then later a more detailed discussion of those specific trusts to use in providing educational benefits for children. Many of the specific trusts discussed will have more than one use and many can be designed to benefit more than one child. However, it is very important for you to understand the basics, just as it would be to learn the basic function of a piece of equipment which can be utilized in many different situations.

This chapter also gives some general rules on trust taxes, and how to avoid the more common mistakes in shifting income to a trust. We understand that you may never be (or want to be) a tax expert, but a knowledge of trusts and the tax laws will help you understand what you can or cannot do, and will help you decide which arrangement best suits your family needs.

Following the basics on taxes is a discussion of the three types of trusts best used in connection with educational benefits: *the minor's trust*—also called the 2503(c) trust—designed to provide for the child until the child reaches age 21; *the ten-year trust*—also well-known as the Clifford trust—designed to shift income on the trust property to the child, then return the property to you after ten years; and *the independent trust*—more commonly known as the "Crummey" trust, after the case of that name—which is "permanently" irrevocable and designed for a myriad of uses including the simple receipt of gifts for the child or children, with distribution to them at some future date selected by you.

The discussions of each of these trusts cover the necessary ingredients to qualify each for tax purposes, the legal and investment considerations (including the range of flexibility you may have in retaining control over the situation), and the various income, gift, and estate tax ramifications of the arrangement. The reason for this thoroughness is that the remainder of this book contains numerous ideas for tax-favored funding of educational costs which *require* the use of one or more of these trusts, and unless you are aware of the specific legal and tax requirements that must be met, as well as the certain characteristics peculiar to the type of trust you are using, you could lose the desired tax benefits or you simply would not have the true picture of how your trust would work out, or both.

The following chart gives you an overview of the several trust-type arrangements that may be created for educational purposes, and a comparison of their respective highlights:

	Possible Investments	Termination	Control	Income Taxes	Choice of Beneficiaries	Qualify for Annual Tax-Free Gifts	May Be Used to Provide Educational Benefits
Uniform Gift to Minors Act	Restricted by law	At age of majority (usually 18)	Custodian	Income taxed to child	Only minors, and only one minor per UGMA account	Yes	Yes
Minor's Trust [2503(c)]	No restrictions	At age 21	Trustee	Income taxed to child if paid out, to trust if not paid out	Child up to 21, only one child per trust	Yes	Yes
Ten-Year (Clifford) Trust	No restrictions	No less than ten years after the transfer of property to the trust	Trustee—generally should not be parent	Income taxed to child if paid out, to trust if not paid out	Anyone, no restrictions, any number of beneficiaries	Maybe, depending on terms of trust	Yes
Independent (Crummey) Trust	No restrictions	Any time that is provided in the trust	Trustee—generally should not be parent	Income taxed to child if paid out, to trust if not paid out	Anyone, no restrictions, any number of beneficiaries	Yes	Yes

What Is a Trust?

A trust is a legal arrangement whereby one person, called the *settlor* (or *donor* or *grantor*), transfers some type of property to another party (the *trustee*) to hold and manage for the benefit of one or more other individuals, called the *beneficiaries*. From the simplest to the most complex, every trust must contain these basic elements. If you create a trust while you are alive, it is called a "living" trust. For purposes of shifting income, all of the trusts we discuss will be *living trusts*. In addition, you will see that for purposes of saving income taxes, these trusts must generally be "irrevocable," at least for a period of time. An irrevocable trust is one which you cannot change or terminate at will. Such a trust must obviously be drafted very carefully and with all the necessary provisions, since once it is set up you cannot correct problems that may later arise. As you read about the different types of trusts, you will gradually understand more about trusts in general, and although the area is somewhat complicated, it will be worth your while to have this understanding.

Trusts and Income Taxes

The income tax laws surrounding trusts are quite complicated, but you should understand one general rule about shifting income through trusts. In order to successfully shift income, *you must give up the right to control the income and principal of the trust and the right to receive any benefit from it.* This is one reason, for example, why so-called trustee bank accounts are such a disaster from an income tax standpoint. If Mom creates a bank account in her own name "as trustee" for Daughter, Mom will be taxed on all the income earned in that account, since she not only has the right to control the funds, she also has the right to take the money back simply by withdrawing it. In effect she has shifted nothing. It makes no difference that Daughter's Social Security number is on the account, because the designation of a number has no legal effect whatever over ownership of the account or the income tax results. (See discussion of this in Chapter 3.)

In order for a trust to be taxed as a separate entity for income tax purposes, it must not be subject to control by anyone except the trustee, who in most instances must be someone independent of the settlor (the person who created the trust) and the beneficiaries.

For example, say that Jack, intending to shift taxable income to his children, transfers funds to a trust, naming *himself* as trustee and his children as beneficiaries. The trust is irrevocable, and the trustee has the power to distribute the income to the children in any shares he decides (that is, not necessarily in equal shares), or he may simply accumulate (hold) the income in the trust. Further, the trustee has the power to terminate the trust at any time and divide the balance among the children in any shares he decides.

Under this arrangement, even though the trust is "irrevocable" and cannot be changed, all the income earned by the trust funds will be taxed to Jack. Why? Because Jack named himself trustee, *and* as trustee he has the right to control and distribute the funds as he sees fit. This is not much different from the undesirable trustee bank account and would prove to be a waste of time and money for Jack as far as shifting taxable income is concerned.

If Jack had named an independent trustee such as a bank or trust company or other professional, or even an independent individual (not his spouse, for example) he could have succeeded in shifting the taxable income, because he would be considered as having given up control over the funds.

If it was very important to Jack that he be the trustee, it might be possible to arrange, but just about all trustee discretion would have to be eliminated. That is, the terms of the trust would have to *require* Jack as trustee to distribute (or accumulate) the income in equal or *pre*determined unequal shares among the children, and Jack could not have the power to terminate the trust. Giving up this flexibility is hardly worth the right to be the trustee.

If a trust is irrevocable and meets all the other requirements for shifting income, it will file its own separate income tax return and will pay a tax on any current income retained in the trust. A trust is taxed on its *undistributed* income (that which is kept in the trust), and the beneficiaries are taxed on the trust income that is *distributed* (paid out) to them. In effect, the trust gets a "deduction" for income that is passed on to the beneficiaries. For example, say that Jack created an irrevocable trust for the benefit of his three children, naming the New York Trust Company as trustee. During the year, the trustee received $10,000 in income and paid out a total of $8,500 to the three children for educational expenses. The New York Trust Company will file a trust tax return showing the $10,000 income, but will be entitled to deduct the $8,500 paid to the beneficiaries, and will pay a tax based on the $1,500 balance (less expenses). The trust will also be entitled to either a $100 or a $300 exemption, depending upon the type of trust. Each child will be given a statement from the trustee showing the amount of taxable income that he or she received during the year, and describing the nature of the income—that is, what portion is interest, dividends, capital gains, or some other form of income. This statement is called a "Schedule K-1," and the information contained on that schedule can be used in preparing the child's income tax return.

As noted at the outset, there are many different types of trusts that can be used in shifting income. Some are "standard" arrangements that have been tried, tested, and approved by the IRS, while others are more innovative but still quite legal—there is no limit to the plans that may involve trusts. Once you understand that an irrevocable trust can be a separate legal and tax entity, you will realize that it can be designed to accomplish almost any legitimate objective. You will see, for example, that a trust can purchase property in an installment sale, own an interest in a family partnership or corporation, own a tax shelter, or lease property to a family business. Whatever form of trust you use and for whatever purpose, you must be sure that it meets all the requirements to satisfy your tax and legal objectives. This is not to be taken lightly, because these trusts must usually be irrevocable to accomplish the tax savings, so extreme care must be taken to "get it right" the first time. For this reason, you should *never*, I repeat, NEVER use do-it-yourself form books, which cannot possibly have been written with your specific situation in mind. In the past, I have likened such form books to the mail-order purchase of a cheap suit—they both fit about the same way. Since the trusts we refer to may save you several hundreds or even several thousands of tax dollars over the years, it is foolhardy to get anything less than the best expert advice in structuring the plan and preparing the documents.

Trustee Fees

The trustee is the "manager" of the trust, whose job is to invest the trust funds and manage the trust property, and to collect and distribute the income to the beneficiaries as directed by the trust instrument. For this he is entitled to be paid a fee, but there is no fixed percentage or amount. Most states' laws require only that the trustee's fee be "reasonable under the circumstances." In just about every case, this means reasonable in the light of the amount of time, effort, and responsibility required of the trustee in carrying out the terms of your trust.

If your trust has a "professional" trustee (an attorney or accountant), or a "corporate" trustee (a bank or trust company), then the trustee should be able to tell you what the fee will be (usually on an annual basis) or at least how it will be computed. Many corporate trustees, for example, base their fees on the size of the trust (the amount of money or property) and the amount of "activity" (income and distributions) each year.

Most banks and trust companies have printed "fee schedules" which they will be glad to make available to you before they are appointed trustee. In some cases, a different fee, or a fixed fee can be negotiated if the trustee's duties are clearly limited. As with all costs, trustee's fees must be considered in determining the overall savings in your plan.

If you have a *qualified* relative or friend as trustee, he or she may charge you nothing at all, which is permissible, but not necessarily fair to the trustee, since administering a trust does require some time and effort. In this case, you should at least agree to review the situation annually to try to arrive at some "fair" compensation for his or her services to the trust.

In any event, you should get an estimate and you should also be sure your trust provides for removal of the trustee in case you are not satisfied with performance (*unless*, of course, your tax advisors tell you the power of removal may cause a loss of tax benefits). In most cases if the power of removal is accompanied by a corresponding power to appoint only an *independent* trustee, there should be no tax problem.

. . . .

Minor's Trusts

One of the simpler forms of trusts used to shift income to minor children is called a 2503(c) trust, in affectionate reference to the particular section of the Internal Revenue Code that allows such a trust and sets forth the basic rules which must be followed in establishing one. A 2503(c) trust, or minor's trust, has several advantages over use of the Uniform Gifts to Minors Act. Before I get to these, however, one major practical distinction between the two should be mentioned. While a UGMA gift simply requires a transfer to a custodian, a minor's trust requires the drafting of a written document as well as a transfer to the trustee. As a result, its creation will cost more than a gift under the UGMA. Section 2503(c) trust provisions are relatively standard, however, and the legal fees for preparing such a trust should not be particularly great. On the whole, the advantages of the minor's trust over a UGMA gift can make the additional costs of setting up the trust quite worthwhile.

Advantages over the UGMA

A minor's trust has a number of advantages that are not available to the same degree under a UGMA gift. For one, the minor's trust is a separate taxpayer, while the UGMA is not. That is, the income from the trust property may be accumulated in the trust and taxed at the *trust's* tax rates until the child reaches age 21. With a UGMA gift, all the income is taxed to the child each year, and all the property and accumulated income *must* be paid over to the child at age 18 in most states. Under a minor's trust, there is no additional tax to the child when he or she receives the accumulated income at age 21, even though the child never paid a tax on it.

There is also a great deal more investment flexibility with a minor's trust, and there is the advantage of retaining control over the funds for a much longer period of time, particularly at the ages in question, that is, 18 through 21. Further on the matter of control, a minor's trust can, in effect, provide for the funds to pass to other children on the death of a child who is beneficiary, whereas a UGMA gift cannot. Finally, there is flexibility in appointment of a trustee and a successor trustee with a minor's trust. In short, except for a few mandatory provisions to preserve the tax benefits, *you* may dictate the terms of your 2503(c) trust, but the terms of a UGMA gift are dictated by law.

Taxes

Under a direct comparison of income between a minor's trust and a UGMA gift, there will not be a big difference in the amount of taxes, because the child receiving or taxed on UGMA income will be able to use his $1,000 exemption against that income, whereas the minor's trust has only a $300 exemption. However, it is possible to use a UGMA gift *and* a minor's trust together, and save additional taxes by distributing each year from the trust to the child's UGMA account an amount of income equal to the exemption allowed to the child. The balance may be accumulated in the trust to use the trust's exemption as well, since the trust, itself, is a separate taxpayer. In fact, if the trust income is comparatively large, you could divide the income between the trust and the child in shares that would produce the lowest possible overall tax on the income for that particular year by using the lowest tax brackets available to the child and the trust.

For example, say that your minor's trust has income of $4,000. If the entire amount is retained in trust, the tax will be about $520; if you distribute only $1,000 to cover the child's exemption allowance and keep the balance in the trust, there will be a tax of about $385. If instead, you distributed $2,000 to the child and retained the other $2,000 in the trust, there would be a tax to the child of about $110, and to the trust of about $235, for a total of about $345. This is $175 and $40 less, respectively, than keeping the total amounts in trust, and although it may not be a big difference, it does illustrate ways to use the minor's trust and the child as separate tax entities to produce a lower tax. Remember, however, in making distributions *out of* a minor's trust to the child or to a custodian for the child, such distributions will then pass to the child at age 18 (in most states).

An additional tax characteristic of the minor's trust is that, like the gifts to the UGMA, gifts to a minor's trust will qualify for the annual gift tax exclusion (the "tax-free" gift) even though they may be held to age 21. In other words, a $10,000 gift to minor's trust will not be subject to a gift tax.

As with UGMA gifts and with all other trusts for minors described in this book, if any of the minor's trust income is used to satisfy a parent's legal obligation of support, then that portion of the income will be taxed to the parent. (This is discussed in more detail in Chapter 3.) To avoid this problem, many minor's trusts contain a provision stating that income from the trust may not be used to satisfy a parental obligation of support.

Trust Investments

Another major advantage of the minor's trust is the added investment flexibility it offers over the UGMA gift. Under the UGMA, for example, only certain property may be held by the custodian, while under the minor's trust virtually any type of property or investments may be held, including real estate or business equipment, as well as the usual investment vehicles such as stocks, bonds, or other securities.

The Trustee—The Person in Charge

Whereas a custodian under the UGMA is generally a member of the minor's family, there is no such tradition for selection of the trustee of a minor's trust. Just about anyone the donor chooses can be a trustee, but with certain exceptions if you want to preserve tax benefits. That is, the donor himself should not be a trustee or the estate tax benefits would be lost. The donor's spouse may be a trustee or a successor trustee if the trust provides that none of the trust income may be used to satisfy a parental obligation of support. Every trust should have clear provisions for the appointment of a successor trustee to automatically assume the position of trustee when the original trustee is unable to serve. Otherwise, costly court action to appoint a successor will be required. Other than these special concerns with the donor or his spouse, anyone else can be a trustee. Logical choices might include a bank, or an accountant, attorney, or other professional advisor, or even a capable family member.

Control of Trust Funds

The powers of a custodian under a UGMA gift are clearly defined and limited by law, while the powers of a trustee under a minor's trust may be broad, and may take advantage of certain options a donor has when creating a trust. For example, while in the minor's trust, the trust funds can be protected from lawsuits or attachments by creditors of the child until he reaches age 21 and receives the funds outright (a "spendthrift" provision).

A further advantage is the opportunity to keep the funds in the trust even *after* the child has reached 21. Although the law requires that the trust funds "pass to" the child at age 21, if the funds are made "available" to the child without restriction, that will qualify. The fact that the funds are only available for withdrawal for a brief period of time, say sixty days, will not disqualify the trust so long as the period for withdrawal is reasonable (she would have enough time to withdraw), and so long as she is notified of the right to withdraw. For instance, say that Patricia creates a minor's trust for her daughter, Katie, and the trust provides that Katie may withdraw the entire balance upon reaching age 21, but if she does not make the withdrawal within sixty days after reaching 21, then the funds will *remain* in the trust, for Katie's benefit, for an additional five years (the five-year period is simply an illustration—the period could be longer or shorter, and other *new* terms and conditions could be added—such specifics should be discussed with your lawyer).

In other words, if Katie fails to withdraw the funds within sixty days of her 21st birthday, she will have to wait another five years (or more, if you wish) to get full control of the funds. In the meantime, the trust will continue to pay her benefits during this extended period. There are *no* new tax benefits obtained by this extended period; the only advantage is the continued segregation and control of funds beyond age 21. After Katie reaches age 21, all the trust income will be taxed to Katie even if not paid out to her, because by allowing the sixty-day period to expire without withdrawal, Katie is treated as the new donor or grantor of her trust. Since she has, by failing to withdraw the funds, "created" a trust which may pay her income, she will be taxed on all the income received by the trust.

Death of a Child

If the child dies before reaching age 21, anything held in a minor's trust must be payable to the child's estate, or as the child directs in her will. It does not matter that the child is not old enough to make a will; under the terms of the 2503(c) trust instrument, she must nevertheless have the power to dispose of the trust property under her will. It is possible, however, for the trust to provide that if the child fails to make a will (and a minor cannot), then on the child's death the property can pass to another child or even to a trust for another child. This provides an important planning advantage that is simply not available under a UGMA.

A Review of the 2503(c) Rules and Ramifications

Briefly, the rules for a minor's trust are that:

1. The income must be accumulated or paid out for the benefit of a child under 21;
2. All accumulated income must be paid out or at least made available to the child upon reaching age 21;
3. On the death of the child before age 21, the child must have a right to dispose of the funds through his or her estate. (Failing this, however, other beneficiaries may be named.)

For gift tax purposes, it is critical that all the rules be followed to the letter. If a trust does not comply with each one, then it will not be a 2503(c) trust, and gifts to the trust will not qualify for the $10,000 annual gift tax exclusion for purposes of 2503(c). The remaining tax characteristics, however, will still be present (the trust will still be taxed separately, as described above in "Trusts and Income Taxes").

If you follow the rules, then:

1. The income will be taxed either to the trust (if accumulated) or to the child (if paid out);
2. Gifts to the trust will qualify as annual tax-free gifts (subject to the annual per donor limitation, currently $10,000);
3. You can keep effective control of the funds through the child's age 21, and even longer;
4. You can protect the funds in trust from reach by a child's creditors;
5. You can decide who will be in charge by naming your own trustee and a successor trustee;
6. The trust can invest in every type of property or investment;
7. You can name an alternate beneficiary of the trust funds in case the child dies.

SUMMARY

A 2503(c) minor's trust is generally more advantageous than a gift under the UGMA for use in providing funds for education, largely because of its added flexibility in investments and in distributions and accumulation of funds, as well as the ability to keep control over the funds to a later age. In addition, it offers income tax benefits that can be combined with the use of the UGMA to increase overall savings. It is not preferable, however, where relatively *small* amounts of money (say, under $10,000, cumulatively) are involved, since the costs of creating the trust and filing additional tax returns each year are generally greater than those for the UGMA gift.

. . . .

Ten-Year Trusts—
Mr. Clifford's Legacy

Making gifts to provide educational benefits may effectively shift income and save taxes, but there is one basic problem with gifts— the property you give away is gone forever. If shifting income is the "name of the game," there should be a way to do this without completely giving up the property. There is.

By far the most popular of the income-shifting trusts over the past forty years has been the "ten-year" trust. This type of trust is known by many different names—a short-term trust, a reversionary trust, a grantor trust, and a Clifford trust—but they all refer to a trust with the same basic characteristics: it lasts for ten years, shifts the income to someone else, and then returns the original gift to the creator. The name "Clifford trust" comes from the now-famous case in which Mr. Clifford tried to use a trust to shift income on certain securities to his wife (this was in 1940 before joint returns were allowed), and lost. In that case the U.S. Supreme Court said it would be possible to shift income this way, but Clifford hadn't gone quite far enough in parting with control and benefits, so he was taxed on the income.

Mr. Clifford didn't know it, but in his unsuccesful attempt to shift income, he set the stage for a change in the tax laws allowing the effective and legal shifting of income without (ultimately) giving away the property that produces the income. This, it appeared, was the best of all possible worlds—that is, this "new" law allowed you to give away the income without giving away the property—almost.

General Rules for Clifford Trusts

In developing the so-called "grantor trust" rules, which allow for the legal shifting of income, Congress wanted to be sure there was a sufficient parting with dominion and control over the property to justify taxing the income to someone other than the owner. As a result, there are several very specific and exacting requirements which must be strictly followed to successfully shift income in this way, but if done correctly, you *can* legally shift the income and get the property *back* after a period of time. Here are the general rules to follow for a Clifford trust, keeping in mind that, although not included in the general rules, having an attorney or accountant familiar with the tax laws to set up the trust is every bit as essential as any of the other requirements.

Benefits

The trust may not provide benefits (*income* payments) for the grantor or the grantor's spouse (the grantor is one who creates the trust and makes the initial gift to it). The grantor's right to get the property back after the prescribed period of time does not violate this requirement. Since this type of trust is more often used to shift income to a child for educational purposes, the grantor or his spouse would probably not want to receive benefits in any event.

Rights to Change the Trust

The trust must be irrevocable for a certain period of time. This means that during the prescribed period, as discussed below, *you may not change the trust in any way.* You cannot add or remove children as beneficiaries; you cannot later decide to give one beneficiary more than another; and you cannot decide to terminate or cancel the trust once it is created (although you can reserve the right to change trustees as discussed below). The trust must last for the prescribed period except in the case of death of the grantor or the beneficiaries.

Duration

The question of how long the trust must last and when you can get your property back is relatively simple, but simple as it is, it has caused a great deal of trouble through carelessness and a lack of understanding on the part of many professional advisors. You will read and hear that this type of trust must last for "ten years and a day," or ten years and one month. This is *not* the exact requirement at all! The actual requirement is that the reversion (the time when the property comes back to you) must not occur *before* the expiration of *ten years from the time that property was transferred to the trust.*

Lack of attention to this simple provision has caused many Clifford trusts to *fail* for tax purposes. The law means that regardless of what the trust says, you may not get the property back before ten years *after the transfer* of the property to the trust. Here is how your trust could flunk the critical test. Your attorney drafts the trust, which says it will terminate "ten years and one day" from the date of signing, at which time the trustee will return the property to you. On February 1, 1984, you sign the trust and the next day (February 2) you give your broker instructions to transfer certain securities to the trust. The transfer is carried out the very next day, which is February 3, 1984. We now have a Clifford trust that will *fail* for tax purposes, because ten years and a day from the *signing* will be February 1, 1994, which is *one day less* than ten years from the *transfer* to the trust which took place on February 3 (ten years from February 3, 1984, would be February 2, 1994).

In other words, the securities will revert to you one day too soon and on account of this slip-up, you will *lose* the entire tax benefits of the trust. Note that it does not matter that you do not actually receive the securities on that day. What matters is that you had a right to them *before* the expiration of ten years from the transfer to the trust. And remember, the trust is irrevocable; once you have made the transfer, the die is cast. To undo a "simple" mistake like this can be extremely costly and cumbersome, if it is possible at all. *The importance of dates and coordination of transfers in these cases cannot be overstated.*

There are numerous cases where the taxpayers have missed the ten-year period by a day, a week, or a month or more, simply through oversight, and have *lost* all the tax benefits of the trust, while being "stuck" with it, since the trust is irrevocable. Here's just one case:

C. O. Bibby and his wife, Marie, created a ten-year Clifford trust on September 3, 1957, for their daughters Kathy and La-Verne. The trust was prepared by their bank trust officer and it provided that C. O. and Marie would get the property back at the end of ten years and one day "from the date of the execution of the trust." Unfortunately, the deed to the property, which consisted of a 320-acre farm in Deaf Smith County, Texas, was not recorded until August 20, 1958. This clearly meant that C. O. and Marie would receive their property *before* the required ten-year period, and so the IRS taxed C. O. and Marie on all the trust income (even though they had no right to receive that income).

C. O. and Marie appealed the decision to the U.S. Tax Court, arguing it was clearly their *intention* that the property be transferred on September 3, and in fact they made an "oral conveyance" of the property. The court found this hard to believe, but held that even if it was true, an oral conveyance of real estate is not valid, so no transfer had been made to the trust until August 20, when the deed was recorded. Under these circumstances, the trust did not comply with the required ten-year period *after transfer of the property*, so the Bibbys had to pay the tax.

In some cases, the trust may terminate (and the property be returned to the grantor) prior to the ten-year period without loss of the tax benefits. This can happen, for example, if the terms of the trust provide for termination in the event of the death of a beneficiary, or the death of the grantor (the creator of the trust), provided the grantor's life expectancy (but not necessarily the beneficiaries') is greater than ten years at the time the transfer is made to the trust.

The Trustee—Who It Should Not Be

As a general rule, the grantor or his spouse should *not* be the trustee. If, however, the trustee is simply directed to pay out all the income each year in *equal* or predetermined, fixed shares to the beneficiaries, or to accumulate it in such shares, or if there is only one beneficiary to the trust, then the grantor or his spouse may be a trustee. In other cases it can easily cause the trust to run afoul of the tax laws—the risk is not worth it. Most professionals like to see an independent trustee in any case, just to be on the safe side. An independent trustee might include a bank or trust company, one of your professional advisors such as your attorney or accountant, or certain family members other than you or your spouse as defined below. You may reserve the right to remove any trustee and appoint a successor, but *if you appoint or have the power to appoint yourself, or anyone other than an independent trustee, you may lose the tax benefits* as well as some of the broad discretionary powers and flexibility that may be given an independent trustee.

For example, you may give the independent trustee the ability to pay out or accumulate trust income in shares—not necessarily equal—among all the beneficiaries of your trust. Where there are two or more children who will be attending college at different times, this power would enable the trustee to use income to pay the tuition and expenses of each child as his or her respective needs arose, rather than simply dividing the shares equally.

You may reserve the right to change trustees (and it may be a good idea to do this if you become dissatisfied with your independent trustee), but if you do reserve this right, you must be very careful that the trust provides that you may only appoint a successor *independent* trustee. If you can appoint yourself and such an appointment would adversely affect the desired tax benefits, this alone could cause a loss of those benefits, *even though you never made a change of trustee.*

Any of the following would NOT be considered an independent trustee: the grantor or his/her spouse (unless the spouse is not living with the grantor); the grantor's father, mother, children, grandchildren, brothers or sisters (but note that such relations of the grantor's *spouse* may qualify as an independent trustee. The grantor's brother-in-law, for example, would qualify); an employee of the grantor or a subordinate employee in a corporation where the grantor is an executive; or a corporation (or an employee of a corporation) in which the grantor has significant voting control.

Remember, this does not mean that none of the above parties could be a trustee; it merely means that if one of them is the sole trustee, there can be very little discretion as to distributions from the trust. It is possible to name one of the above parties as *co-trustee* with an independent trustee, but unless there is some special need to do so, *it should be avoided.*

If you, as grantor, must be the trustee, you must be careful that your trust follows the grantor trust rules discussed above, since, with one exception, if *any* of the rules are violated, *all* the income will be taxed to you, regardless of who actually receives it. The exception is when income is used to satisfy a legal obligation of the grantor. In this case, only the income actually used for that purpose will be taxed to the grantor (see the more detailed discussion of this in Chapter 3).

In addition to the requirements discussed above, *any of the following powers or rights in the grantor or his spouse will cause the grantor to be taxed on all of the trust income*:

- the power to revoke the trust;
- the power to add beneficiaries;
- the power to change beneficiaries;
- the power to withdraw funds;
- the right to receive income; or
- the power to make discretionary distributions (with certain exceptions as noted below).

This is not a complete list of prohibited powers, but simply the major restrictions you must be aware of.

Certain powers held by a grantor/trustee are permissible, such as the power to accumulate income to age 21 (similar to the minor's trust described above) and the power to temporarily withhold income during the child's disability or for some other reason, as long as the withheld income is eventually payable to that child. Further, the grantor may borrow from the trust with adequate interest and security, or even purchase property from it (but this can be very risky—more so than borrowing), as long as the transactions are truly on an arm's-length basis. If the grantor does borrow, the loan and its terms will be scrutinized *very* carefully. The loan should be collateralized with some asset of value equal to the borrowed amount, but if there is *no* such security for the loan, it must be repaid *with interest* before the beginning of the next taxable year. If a loan or purchase of trust property by the grantor is contemplated for purposes which will extend beyond one year, there *must* be an independent trustee, and there *must* be adequate security. (This is discussed in greater detail under "Borrowing from Your Clifford Trust," later in this chapter.)

You *may* also retain the following powers as trustee, without the income being taxed to you:

- The power to make distributions of principal (as opposed to income) if that power is limited by what is called "an ascertainable standard." This means the trustee's discretion is not absolute; it is limited by certain identifiable needs of the beneficiary, without leaving too much room for discretion. One frequently used ascertainable standard, for example, would be "health, maintenance and education," since these needs can be reasonably interpreted, whereas a standard of "happiness" can not, and would not qualify. Thus the inadvertent or careless addition of the one word "happiness" could cause all the income from this type of trust to be taxed to you.

- The power to accumulate income (as opposed to principal), provided that any accumulated income is added to the share of the beneficiary for whom it is being accumulated. For example, say you set up a Clifford trust for two children and the income from the trust property is $2,000 per year. From the fifth to the tenth year you pay one child $1,000 per year and the second child nothing. When the trust terminates, at the end of the tenth year, you will have to pay over the $5,000 accumulated income to the second child, since it was accumulated as a part of his or her share.

These restrictions or limitations on the discretion of a grantor trustee may or may not present a problem to you depending upon your particular circumstances. If, like many families, the objective is simply to accumulate income for a minor until he or she enters college at 18 or older, then the relative lack of flexibility is not a concern and you or your spouse or other close relation may be a trustee. In fact, a great many ten-year trusts are created for a single beneficiary just so the grantor *can* be a trustee. Correspondingly, if flexibility is important, as where one trust provides for several children, or where the nature of the property or trust activity actually requires an independent trustee (as with a "borrowback," or with a "leaseback" as discussed in Chapter 8), an independent trustee will be necessary, regardless of the other factors.

Trust Property

Generally, any type of property or investments may be transferred to a Clifford trust; one of the primary advantages to the Clifford trust is that you needn't transfer cash to it. In fact, it is one of the very few situations where you can use *existing* property or investments that are currently producing an income, without selling or otherwise affecting the status of that property.

For example, say that you have $20,000 worth of stock in a closely held corporation. You do not wish to sell it and give up your shares of the company, but at the same time you don't need the $3,000 per year income it provides. If you create a Clifford trust and transfer the stock to the trust for the benefit of your child, the $3,000 annual income will be taxed to the child or to the trust (depending upon whether it is paid or accumulated), and the stock will be voted by the trustee of the trust. If the voting of the stock is important, you may want to structure the trust so that you or your spouse could be trustee; however a "friendly" trustee would probably decide to vote in a manner that coincides with your wishes.

Sometimes a Clifford trust is used to hold income-producing real estate, but if the real estate is subject to a mortgage there will be tax problems, as discussed below. Further, if the real estate is providing you with depreciation deductions, you may be better off *not* putting it into a Clifford trust.

Business equipment may also be transferred to a Clifford trust and then leased back to the business (as discussed in Chapter 8), but this can be tricky from a tax standpoint and all the special requirements in this case must be considered carefully before such a transfer is made.

Obligations (promissory notes) under an installment sale may be transferred to a Clifford trust but care must be taken to avoid the "assignment of income" problems (discussed in Chapter 3) that could result in the grantor being taxed on all or part of the income despite the transfer to the trust. It appears that a Clifford trust may be used to shift the income tax on the *interest portion* of all the installment payments, but paydown of principal (the capital gains portion) will be taxed to the grantor, even though the trust is not presently receiving it. Ideally, an installment obligation that pays "interest only" with a balloon principal payment after the ten-year period would be best suited for the Clifford trust.

As a rule of thumb, only property that is transferable without tax consequences, that is producing a taxable income to the grantor, and that is not subject to a mortgage or other lien should be considered for transfer to a Clifford trust.

Once property has been transferred to the trust, it is the trustee's job to "manage" the property. Technically, this could include a sale of the property and reinvestment of the proceeds; however, since the grantor has a reversionary interest in the property, it is arguable (and quite customary, I might add) that the trustee should obtain the grantor's consent before any such sale. As a rule, if the "property" is anything other than cash, it would just be held in the trust for the required period and then returned to the grantor on termination of the trust. If a sale of securities is contemplated or becomes necessary during the term of the trust, any gain or loss produced by the sale could be offset by a corresponding loss or gain taken by the grantor outside the trust.

For example, if Oscar's Clifford trust sold securities at a $12,000 capital gain, Oscar should attempt to sell something outside the trusts which will create a $12,000 capital loss, if possible. Otherwise, as noted previously in this chapter, Oscar will be taxed on a $12,000 gain which he will not receive for several years.

Borrowing from Your Clifford Trust— Too Good to Be True?

Perhaps the most singular advantage and unique characteristic of the Clifford trust is the fact that at the end of the ten-year period your gift to the trust will be returned to you. It is this characteristic that makes the following tax plan almost too good to be true—but it *is*.

By arranging to borrow back funds you have given to your Clifford trust, you not only recover the use of those funds, but you can pay *tax-deductible* interest to the trust, which in turn may directly be used for your child's educational expenses. This has the effect of *converting nondeductible educational expenses into completely deductible expenses*. What's more, it can be used even when a family is "cash-poor." Here's how it helped one family.

Dr. and Mrs. Greenfield are in the 50 percent tax bracket but are simply unable to accumulate any cash. They have only a few thousand in savings and no other investments except their home, worth $200,000 with a $50,000 mortgage, and a summer home, worth $80,000 with a $60,000 mortgage. Their daughter, Cindy, will enter college in a year or so and they are somewhat concerned that they have done no planning. Cindy's college expenses are expected to be about $10,000 per year, and the Greenfields realize that in their bracket they have to "earn" $20,000 to have $10,000 left for college. They had been reading about tax planning for educational purposes, including gifts (but they have no assets to give away) and Clifford trusts to shift income (but they have no income-producing property to shift), but they simply didn't know what to do.

I advised them on how they could borrow on the equity on their home, make a gift of the borrowed funds to a Clifford trust for Cindy, then borrow from Cindy's trust to repay the bank loan. If properly carried out, the interest they paid to Cindy's trust would be tax-deductible and could in turn be used for Cindy's college expenses. Dr. Greenfield took the following steps:

1. He applied for (and was granted) a loan of $80,000 from his bank, using the equity in his home as collateral. The loan contains *no* prepayment penalty.
2. He immediately made a *gift* of the $80,000 to a Clifford trust (which he established at the same time he made the gift) for the benefit of his daughter Cindy.
3. The trustee of the trust invested the $80,000 in short-term Treasury bills, paying about 9 percent.
4. Some time later (say thirty to sixty days; *the longer the better*), the trustee, in search of a better return, agreed to *loan* the $80,000 to Dr. Greenfield at 14 percent, with payments of interest only, and the trustee took a second mortgage on Dr. Greenfield's home as security for the loan.
5. Dr. Greenfield used the $80,000 he borrowed from Cindy's trust to repay the bank loan.
6. Each year, Dr. Greenfield pays $11,200 interest ($80,000

× 14%) to the trustee. The trustee in turn uses these funds to pay for Cindy's educational expenses.

7. Each year, as he makes the interest payments, Dr. Greenfield takes an $11,200 tax deduction on his income tax return. In his tax bracket, Dr. Greenfield's net cost for these payments is $5,600 (50% of $11,200).

8. Since the $11,200 is paid out to Cindy after age 18, she pays a federal income tax of about $1,100, leaving over $10,000 to cover her college expenses.

When the ten years are up, Dr. Greenfield's note to the trust should be paid back. To do this, he will have to reborrow $80,000 from the bank and pay this amount to the trustee. The trustee, in turn, after canceling Dr. Greenfield's note, will terminate the trust (since the ten-year period—the term of the trust—has passed) and the principal ($80,000 cash) will be returned to Dr. Greenfield. On receipt of the $80,000 cash, Dr. Greenfield will repay the bank, and everyone (except perhaps the IRS) will be satisfied.

There is a diagram on page 106 illustrating the above steps.

The trust and borrowback idea is illustrated with a Clifford trust for a very specific reason. Where the family is cash-poor and has borrowed the funds, it is critical that these funds make the full circle back to the family. If Dr. Greenfield had simply made a gift to Cindy (or to a different type of trust for Cindy), he might still get the interest deduction but he would never get his $80,000 back. This means he would have to repay the $80,000 to the bank at some point, which is *not* a desirable result. Use of the Clifford trust will cause the $80,000 to be returned to Dr. Greenfield in ten years without adverse tax consequences. There *are* some risks, however, and before you consider the Clifford trust and borrowback idea, you should read and reread this entire section carefully.

For some families, the ten-year period is just too long, often because the age of the child (or children) and the projected educational periods do not require the full ten-year term. In those

Loan, Gift, and Borrowback from Clifford Trust

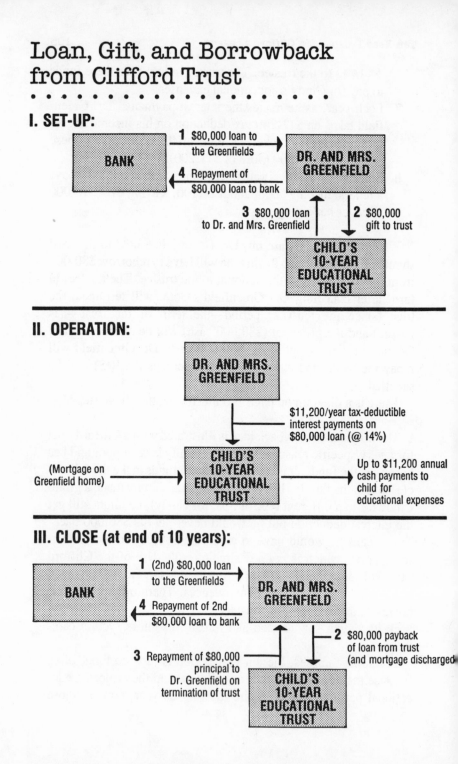

I. SET-UP:

BANK

1 $80,000 loan to the Greenfields

4 Repayment of $80,000 loan to bank

DR. AND MRS. GREENFIELD

3 $80,000 loan to Dr. and Mrs. Greenfield

2 $80,000 gift to trust

CHILD'S 10-YEAR EDUCATIONAL TRUST

II. OPERATION:

DR. AND MRS. GREENFIELD

$11,200/year tax-deductible interest payments on $80,000 loan (@ 14%)

(Mortgage on Greenfield home)

CHILD'S 10-YEAR EDUCATIONAL TRUST

Up to $11,200 annual cash payments to child for educational expenses

III. CLOSE (at end of 10 years):

BANK

1 (2nd) $80,000 loan to the Greenfields

4 Repayment of 2nd $80,000 loan to bank

DR. AND MRS. GREENFIELD

2 $80,000 payback of loan from trust (and mortgage discharged)

3 Repayment of $80,000 principal to Dr. Greenfield on termination of trust

CHILD'S 10-YEAR EDUCATIONAL TRUST

cases, there is *still* a way to accomplish the above maneuver, but the principal *may not* return to the grantor at the end of the trust period. For a more detailed discussion of this idea see "The Shortcut Clifford Trust," on page 121.

STRICT RULES TO FOLLOW

There are some very tricky steps to this borrowback arrangement which, if not followed precisely, could cause the whole plan to fail. The tax laws are extremely strict about when deductions will be allowed for interest payments in a borrowback situation such as this, but if done right, they *will* be allowed.

First, *the trust must have an independent trustee*, and the tax code is clear on who is "independent." It cannot be the grantor or a party who is "related to or subordinate to" the grantor. This means it cannot be the grantor's spouse (unless living apart) or the grantor's immediate family, including brothers or sisters, or an employee of the grantor, or other "business" associates who may be "subservient" to the wishes of the grantor. Generally, the grantor's banker or attorney or accountant are considered independent, and would therefore qualify as an independent trustee.

Next, *the loan from the trust must be at an "adequate interest rate."* "Adequate" basically means that the rate of interest must not be a bargain to the borrower. In most cases, this is not a problem, since the borrower (usually the parent) will want to pay as high a rate as he or she can afford (within reason) to get a larger tax deduction. A fair interest rate might be that which an independent lender would charge for a similar loan, easily determined by one or two phone calls to lending institutions. In practice, you will find that such rates are high enough to produce a good deduction.

Third, *the loan must be secured*. That is, there must be some collateral given to the trustee to protect the loan. *Without this, the interest payments will not be deductible.* Security for the loan may be stocks or bonds pledged to the trustee as collateral or, more commonly, a mortgage on the parents' (borrowers') home. The mortgage or pledge (sufficient in amount to cover the loan balance) would remain until the loan is paid in full; at that time the trustee can release the collateral.

In the event the parent wishes to *sell* the home and purchase another, the trustee's mortgage may simply be released on the home that is sold and another mortgage placed on the newly purchased home, so the proper collateral is still present. If a replacement home is not purchased, then some other collateral must be substituted, since the loan must remain adequately collateralized until repaid. Whatever the collateral, it must be worth enough to secure the loan or the plan could fail. If a grantor pledges a $50,000 home as collateral for a $100,000 loan, the IRS could disallow all or at least a part of the interest deductions since "adequate security," as *required* by the Internal Revenue Code, was not present.

In carrying out all of these steps, it is very important not to take any of them casually. Every move must be documented and every requirement fulfilled to the letter. Remember, this is a *ten-year* irrevocable arrangement and once put in place, it is difficult to go back to correct an oversight.

NONTAX RISKS

If the grantor/borrower dies within the ten-year period, the trust can terminate (if you provide for it in the trust) and the loan be canceled as explained above. However, if the grantor/borrower should become permanently disabled, a serious problem can arise, since the interest payments on the loan must still be met. One way to help would be extra disability insurance to cover the interest payments. If this is too expensive, you may simply decide to run the risk. But remember, if the trustee does not receive the interest payments on the note, he may be forced to *foreclose* on the collateral. A similar result could occur if the grantor/borrower were to become unemployed. This would obviously be a very painful result, so be sure you understand, plan for, and are able to handle the obligation to make these interest payments for the necessary period.

In the "worst case" situation, it would be possible to simply "fold up the whole show" by an early termination of the trust in the event of an unmanageable catastrophe (such as extended unemployment or uninsured disability) and simply suffer the tax consequences, which would be a loss of the tax deductions for (at worst) the previous three years. (It is difficult for the IRS to go back further than that.)

Usury laws may in some states present another concern in paying a high interest rate to your trustee on a borrowback. Although the majority of state usury laws allow fairly high interest rates (18–20 percent) as a maximum, a few states still have very low limits (Michigan's is 7 or 8 percent!). Before establishing a rate with your trustee on your borrowback, you should check the usury laws of your state to be sure you do not violate them.

If it turns out that yours is one of the low-limit states, check with your attorney to see if you can waive (disregard) the limit by an agreement between you (the borrower) and the trustee (the lender). If even this is prohibited, you could consider establishing the trust in another state where the interest limit is higher.

WHEN TO MAKE INTEREST PAYMENTS
Interest payments on your borrowback may be based on a schedule that is convenient to you and also suits the needs of the child. If you have plenty of time to accumulate funds for the child, the payments may be made according to your ability to pay them comfortably. For example, if the borrowback takes place when the child is 14 and no funds will be needed until she reaches 18, then it won't matter whether you make your interest payments monthly, quarterly, or even annually.

On the other hand, if this is an emergency measure that requires an immediate transfusion of funds to pay tuition, other tactics must be used. Legally, you may pay *any amount* of interest in advance. If you take out a three-year loan, for example, you may pay the entire three years' interest up front and the trustee (lender) will have the use of that money for the full three-year period. Unfortunately, the tax laws do *not* allow you to deduct the full amount, at least not "up front." Current tax laws only allow you to deduct prepaid interest that is attributable to the *current* calendar year. Any excess must be deducted in the year to which it applies.

For example, on January 1, 1985, you borrow $10,000 at 16

percent for two years. The total interest you'll owe is $10,000 × .16 × two years, or $3,200. If you pay the trustee the full $3,200 interest up front, you may only deduct $1,600 on your 1985 federal income tax return, which is the interest that applies to the current year (1985). The balance of $1,600 may be deducted in 1986, which is the year to which it applies.

Even though you cannot take an income tax deduction for more than the current year's interest payments, this does not prevent you from prepaying at least that amount to cover tuition bills that come due before you have time to accumulate adequate funds in your trust. For instance, in April, Sebastian creates a Clifford trust for the benefit of his daughter, and arranges for a loan of $50,000, which is contributed to the trust. On July 1, Sebastian borrows the $50,000 for five years at 16 percent interest. As is usual with such borrowback arrangements, the note calls for payments of interest only ($8,000 per year, or $666.67 per month), and at the end of the five-year term, the full principal balance will be due.

In August, however, Sebastian receives his daughter's tuition bill for $4,000 before he has had enough time to accumulate that amount in the trust. (The first thing he should do is return the bill to the school and have the school send a new bill to his daughter or to the trust.) He may then prepay the interest to the trust for the remainder of the current year, six months × $666.67, or $4,000, which will be fully deductible for the current year, and may be used to pay his daughter's $4,000 tuition bill.

If the amount of the tuition bill was in excess of $4,000, Sebastian could pay the excess to the trust, as interest, but it would not be deductible until the following year. The important point to remember, though, is that even though the interest payments must be deducted in a later year, they *are* deductible. If Sebastian simply paid the tuition directly, it would not be deductible.

TAX RISKS

Contrary to what others may tell you, the Internal Revenue Code specifically acknowledges borrowing from a Clifford trust and allows a tax deduction for the interest payments if the requirements enumerated above are met, so if these are properly carried out, there should be no tax risk in the arrangement *by itself.**

However, where the borrowback is clearly prearranged or where the initial funds contributed to the Clifford trust are themselves borrowed, gifted to the ten-year trust, then borrowed back, *there is the possibility that the IRS could attack the transaction as being "without substance,"* that is, a "step transaction." Step transactions are those in which although each individual step in the transaction is legal, when taken as a whole, they lack real "substance."

In my opinion, the Greenfield transaction described above is *not* "without substance": there is a positive, ten-year actual cash gift to the trust, the grantor had the financial capacity (the equity in his home) to make the gift, and the trustee was under *no obligation* to loan it back to the grantor. If the grantor had sold the home and then used the proceeds to carry out the same transaction, there would have been no tax risk. Conversion of the equity interest in the home to cash under a loan arrangement, then, should not prove fatal to the transaction.

The IRS has not yet ruled on this specific arrangement, nor are there any court cases with the *exact* same pattern of events. There are cases, however, which support the deductibility of interest on a loan from a trust, and it would appear that if every step is seriously and carefully followed and carried out at arm's length (that is, as if you were dealing with a stranger) the tax risk would be minimal and the deductions supportable.

Another problem arises when an independent trustee is not used. Some grantor/borrowers object to the use of an independent trustee. According to the Internal Revenue Code, a grantor may indeed borrow *without* the need for an independent trustee (and even without collateral) provided that the loan, together with the interest, is *repaid in full within one taxable year.* For example, a grantor could name his spouse as trustee of his Clifford trust, bor-

---

Caution. If the funds borrowed from the Clifford trust are used to make or carry an investment (other than paying off the loan on your home) there may be a limitation on the amount of interest payments you can deduct (see references for this chapter). If the loan is for a home mortgage there is no such limitation.

row (unsecured) the available funds on January 2, then repay the
loan with interest on December 31 of the same year. Assuming all
other aspects of the transaction were bona fide, he would be entitled to deduct the interest paid on the loan.

The problem with this arrangement, however, is that although
it seems permissible on an isolated or emergency basis, it will
probably *not* work if the loan and repayment are repeated every
year (as would be necessary to make college payments, for instance). As soon as this arrangement becomes a pattern, the IRS
could attack it as a step transaction, and in my opinion, it would
be much more vulnerable to such an attack than the properly secured loan described above. Since it would be so risky to use this
method repeatedly and since educational funds are usually required on a repeated or successive annual basis, this method does
not offer much attraction as a means of financing educational expenses.

Whatever your plan, if you wish to be positive about the outcome before you enter into the plan, *you can apply for a private
ruling from the IRS.* If you submit to them all the details of your
proposed transaction, the IRS will usually tell you how they will
treat it from a tax standpoint. Where "creative" ideas such as this
are involved, however, many advisors feel that applying for a ruling is something like telling the opposing team your surprise plays
and asking how it would react.

In any event, you should certainly get the advice and counsel of
a tax expert to guide you through the steps or at least help you decide whether an IRS ruling is advisable in your particular case.

COSTS VS. SAVINGS

As with any business or tax plan, the costs of implementing the
plan must be weighed against the projected savings. The start-up
costs of the Clifford trust and borrowback plan described above
will include the legal fees for preparing the trust, the mortgage
fees to the bank and to the trustee (although these should not be
duplicated), and the interest charges to the bank for the period (although brief) between the time of the loan from the bank and the
time of the borrowback from the trustee (do *not* agree to extra
"points," as this will be a short-term loan). Depending upon the

amount borrowed, these costs could amount to $2,000–$3,000, and the biggest portion of these costs is usually interest charges by the bank. For example, forty-five days' interest on $80,000 at 15 percent would be $1,500. Also, *be sure* that the bank loan allows for prepayment *without* penalty, as this penalty fee could be prohibitive, and a costly oversight. The fact that just about all of the costs would be tax-deductible, however, may ease the bite.

After the start-up costs, there are annual costs to consider, but these are usually nominal. They include the cost of an additional tax return for the trust and/or the child, and trustee fees for administering the trust. If you have a "friendly" trustee, he or she may forego a fee, but if you have a bank or other professional, there will be a fee and it will vary depending upon the amount of work to be done. Since the "management" of the trust principal is somewhat limited in this case (because the principal consists of the grantor's promissory note), the fees should not be excessive. One Boston CPA firm, for example, charges only $500 per year in such a situation, and this includes preparation of the trust's income tax returns. Separately, the tax returns could run about $150–$300 per year, again depending upon the activities within the trust.

Before your family decides to embark on this involved ten-year plan to make college expenses tax-deductible, all of these costs must be weighed against the potential tax savings. If you are in the 50 percent tax bracket and expect to pay $8,000 per year in interest payments, you'll save $4,000 in the very first year and this should well exceed your costs. However, you must also factor in any taxes that the trust and/or the children will pay on the $8,000 income. If all this produces a net savings to the family, then it will be worthwhile for you to implement the borrowback. After all, without it, you'll simply be paying the $8,000 or so each year, *after taxes*, without any help from anyone. If Uncle Sam is there to give you a hand—even a small one—why not take it?

A SAFEGUARD AGAINST AN IRS ATTACK
Due to the fact that this loan/gift to trust and borrowback arrangement could be considered "aggressive" tax planning by some of the more conservative advisors, and that the arrangement seems

to "lock you in" for ten years, we have developed at least one "safeguard" against a successful IRS attack. In legal jargon, it is called a "savings" clause. This is a provision in the trust which says that if the IRS or the courts make a ruling or decision which adversely affects the intended tax results of your trust, then the trust will *terminate* at that time (*despite* the fact that ten years have not elapsed). This provision is quite legal and prevents you from being stuck with a sour tax situation for the balance of the ten-year period.

In other words, say that you carry out this or some other "aggressive" tax plan in your Clifford trust and three years later the IRS audits the trust and disallows the shifting of income. That is, they tax you on all the trust income for the three-year period, because, they say, your plan was "without substance." This in itself is one problem, but the larger problem is that your trust has another *seven years* to run and there is nothing you can do about it! Well, almost nothing.

If your Clifford trust contains a "savings" clause, which allows the trust to terminate if an adverse tax result comes about, you can completely avoid this risk. If the necessary savings clause is present, the trustee, on notification of the adverse ruling, would simply return all the trust property to you, and you would then have the opportunity to start again with a new plan.

Here is an example of a typical savings clause:

> If the Internal Revenue Service finally determines that the Donor is to be treated as the owner of all or any portion of the income of this Trust under any of the provisions of Sections 671–679 of the Internal Revenue Code, this Trust shall thereupon terminate, and the trust principal together with any undistributed income shall be distributed to the Donor, or to his nominee as may be designated by him in writing, provided, however, that the provisions of this paragraph shall not apply if said provisions themselves would lead to such a determination by the Internal Revenue Service.

Remember, this is only *sample* language. The particular language used in your own trust should be reviewed and approved by your own advisors.

Tax Considerations

The primary benefit offered by the Clifford trust is a savings of income taxes by the shifting of income from the grantor to the beneficiary (or the trust), but there are also incidental gift and estate tax considerations that are worth noting, and that are outlined below, following a review of the income tax considerations.

INCOME TAXES

If the trust meets all the grantor trust rules under the Internal Revenue Code, then the income received by the trust will be taxed to the beneficiary or to the trust in the shares distributed or retained, respectively, by the trust. Remember that with only one exception (where trust income is used to satisfy an obligation of the grantor) if *any* of the grantor trust rules are violated, *all* of the trust income will be taxed to the grantor, even though he or she has not received it. Once the rules are understood and the trust properly set up, however, the tax consequences are fairly predictable, although not necessarily simple.

Under the basic explanation of trust taxation outlined earlier in this chapter, if the terms of the trust require that all the income be paid over to the beneficiaries, all distributions of income from the trust will be taxed to the beneficiaries in the beneficiaries' respective tax brackets. The trust, in effect, gets a tax deduction for amounts paid out and is not taxed on these amounts. The tax code calls this a "simple" trust.

Accumulations, however, can be a bit more complicated. A trust that accumulates part or all of its income is called a "complex" trust, and you'll see why. As a rule, accumulated income (i.e., income that is not paid to the beneficiaries in the year it is received by the trust) is taxed to the trust. However, when this accumulated income is ultimately paid to the beneficiaries in some future year, another computation becomes necessary. The objective of the computation is to determine what the tax would have been if, instead of accumulating the income, the trust had paid the income to the beneficiary in each respective year. In effect, each year's income is thrown back to the beneficiary—hence this accountant's headache is appropriately called the "throwback" rule. If the computation produces a higher total tax than has been paid, an additional tax will be due. Luckily, there are abbreviated averaging methods which may be used.

Fortunately for educational trusts, the throwback rule *does not apply* to accumulations made in a trust *while the beneficiary is under age 21*. In other words, trust accumulations for a beneficiary through age 21 may be distributed to the beneficiary at any time in the future with *no* additional tax. For purposes of college payments, this exception to the throwback rule allows substantial tax savings, since most payments are usually made between the ages of 18 and 21, and accumulations thereafter would only be subject to brief periods of accumulation, so should not produce a big tax.

For example, say that you place $30,000 of securities into an eleven-year trust for your 10-year-old child, with income to be accumulated during the period of minority. At age 18 the child enters college and the trust has accumulated income, to that point, of $25,000 after taxes. *The trustee may pay out all or any part of that $25,000 tax-free to the child.* In fact, the trust could continue to accumulate until the child reaches age 21, and distributions of accumulated income would similarly pass tax-free to the child. (Remember that the income has already been taxed to the trust.)

CAPITAL GAINS

One of the potential drawbacks of a Clifford trust is the treatment of capital gains realized during the ten-year period. For trust tax purposes, capital gains or losses are not considered "*income*" but rather a realization of changes in the value of the *principal*. For example, if a share of stock drops from $15 to $11, the *principal* has decreased in value by $4. Because of the fact that the underlying property in the trust (the principal) will come back to you at the end of the ten-year period, anything that increases or decreases the value of that property will logically carry through to you. For example, if you transfer $15,000 worth of Terminal Motors stock to a Clifford trust and by the tenth year the stock has dropped in value to $11,000, all you get back is stock worth $11,000 because the *principal* (the stock) in effect remains yours, while the *income* (the dividends) belongs to the beneficiary.

Since capital gains and losses are generally considered changes to the principal of the trust and since the principal belongs to the grantor, then the *tax effects* of any capital gains or losses will *pass through* to the grantor *in the year they are realized by the trust.* And this is so even though the grantor will not really feel the effect of the gains or losses until the trust terminates. Further, the basis or tax cost of the property is not affected by a transfer to the trust. The trust takes the property with the same basis as the grantor.

For instance, say that in 1984 Carolyn purchases $10,000 of stock and in 1985, when it is worth $11,000, she transfers the stock to a Clifford trust for her daughter, Danielle. In 1988, the stock has appreciated to $15,000 and the trustee decides to sell the stock and reinvest the $15,000 proceeds to produce a higher income for Danielle. In 1988, the year of sale, Carolyn will have to pay a tax on the *$5,000* capital gain ($15,000 proceeds less her cost of $10,000) even though she didn't receive any of it (it will stay in the trust until the trust ends in 1994).

The obligation to pay an immediate tax on such capital gains can produce quite a surprise for an unsuspecting grantor, so property that is likely to be sold at a gain during the ten-year period should *not* be your first choice for transfer to a Clifford trust. Of course, if it is your only choice, that is another matter. Further, there may be several different securities transferred to the trust, some with built-in gains, others with losses. In such a case, losses can be taken to offset gains, so the tax effect on the grantor would be negligible. And if the result is a net loss, the grantor may take the tax benefit of that loss in the year it is realized.

Some taxpayers have attempted to circumvent this "pass-through" rule by including in the trust a provision that requires capital gains to be distributed to the grantor, or alternatively, a provision that requires capital gains to be distributed to the beneficiary. *Either approach is risky.* In the first case, the IRS may treat a distribution to the grantor as "principal reverting to the grantor" within the ten-year period, which would *disqualify the entire trust.* In the second case, the IRS could argue that the capital gains as principal should still be taxed to the grantor, and that subsequently an additional gift (of the capital gains) has been made to the beneficiary. In my opinion, the best route is to avoid large capital gains, if possible, or if the trust has to sell at a gain, try to time the gain so that you can offset it with a corresponding loss.

IMPORTANT REMINDER: Regardless of the plan you use, if any of the child's income, *whether from a trust or any other source*, is used to satisfy a parental obligation, *the income so used will be taxed to the parent* despite the care taken with the rest of the plan. To avoid falling into this trap, be sure to review the discussion of this point in Chapter 3 (pages 26–33).

GIFT TAXES

Since a transfer to a Clifford trust is irrevocable for a prescribed period, the tax laws hold that a gift is made at the time of the transfer. If the terms of the trust provide that income is to be distributed currently to the beneficiary, or if the terms of the trust qualify under section 2503(c) explained earlier in this chapter, or if the beneficiary (even though a minor) has certain rights of withdrawal under the trust, then the gift to the trust will qualify for the $10,000 annual gift tax exclusion. Otherwise, it will not qualify for the exclusion and you will be required to use a part of your gift tax credit as discussed in Chapter 4. As will be seen, application of the gift tax to large gifts to a Clifford trust can be a drawback to these trusts in large estates.

The value of a gift to a Clifford trust is not equal to the amount of property transferred, because eventually that property will be returned to you. Rather, the gift is based on the value of the *income interest* in the amount transferred for the term of the trust. The tax regulations contain tables which must be used for valuing such income interests, and for a ten-year income interest the gift is considered to be worth just under 62 percent (.614457 to be exact) of the value of the trust property at the time of the transfer. (For gifts prior to December 1, 1983, the factor was approximately 44 percent of the gift.) For example, if you transfer $15,000 of securities to a ten-year Clifford trust (which pays out all income), you have made a gift of about 62 percent of the $15,000 or $9,300. Since $9,300 is less than the $10,000 exclusion, there is not only no gift tax to worry about, but no gift tax return to file. If both spouses "split" the gift, a little over $32,000 may be transferred to a ten-year trust (with one beneficiary) without exceeding the $10,000 annual exclusion for each spouse. This may be multiplied by the number of beneficiaries, if more than one is involved *and* the proper terms are included in the trust; so for two beneficiaries, the gift-tax-free amount would be about $64,000 if both spouses consent to the gift.

If you exceed the $10,000 gift tax exclusion in a Clifford trust and if you have a large estate, the effect can be to artificially increase the size of your estate as discussed below. In those cases, this is one of the potential disadvantages of a Clifford trust, but usually not such a sufficient disadvantage to warrant foregoing the income tax advantages it offers, especially where educational expenses are concerned.

ESTATE TAXES

It is fairly easy to understand that what you presently own will be included in your estate at your death for federal estate tax purposes. What you own may well include something that you are legally sure of getting at some point, such as a loan you have made that will be paid back to you next year, or in five or even ten years. Since you have a legal right to the money at some point, its present value can be determined. So it is with the Clifford trust. Even though you have "given away" the use of the trust property for ten years or more, you have retained a "reversionary" interest—the right to get it back—and the value of this right can be determined at any time. Therefore, if the grantor's death occurs during the ten-year period, the present value of his reversionary interest will be included in his estate for federal estate tax purposes. You should not view this as a serious problem, however, since you never intended to give away the principal itself, merely the use of it.

An estate tax problem can arise, however, if the transfer to your Clifford trust exceeds the allowable gift tax exclusion, or does not qualify for the annual exclusion (where trust income is to be accumulated, for example), *and if* you have a taxable estate (one that may be subject to a federal estate tax). The problem lies in the estate tax treatment of taxable gifts made during one's lifetime. The law provides that such gifts are *added back* to your taxable estate, and in the case of a Clifford trust, the effect can be to create a larger estate than you actually have. Here's how.

Jake made a $100,000 gift to a Clifford trust, which will *accumulate* income, so it will not qualify for the $10,000 gift tax exclusion. Using the 62 percent factor, he has therefore made a taxable gift of about $62,000. Ten years later, the trust terminates, Jake recovers his $100,000, and then dies. His estate will include the $100,000 he received from the trust *plus* the $62,000 taxable gift, which he doesn't have and never had, for a total of $162,000, which must, of course, be added to his other estate assets. If Jake's estate is not taxable anyway, it won't make a difference, but if it is, this can produce a substantial extra estate tax. The (questionable) reasoning behind this seeming inequity is that if Jake had kept the $100,000, the income he would have earned would have increased the size of his estate anyway. So, if you intend to make a large gift to a Clifford trust and you have a taxable estate, be sure your tax advisor structures it in a way to produce the least possible gift *and* estate tax exposure.

What constitutes a taxable estate depends for the most part upon whether you are single or married, and when you die. If single, a "large" estate is one over $400,000 for 1985, $500,000 for 1986, and $600,000 for 1987 and thereafter. If married, and your estate plan utilizes the maximum marital deduction (tax-free amount that passes to a surviving spouse), then the estate will *not* be federally taxable regardless of its size.

As to the estate of the beneficiary, his or her interest normally ceases on death, so there is nothing further of the trust to include in the beneficiary's estate except the income accumulated prior to his or her death.

SUMMARY

The Clifford trust will undoubtedly continue to be one of the more popular methods of shifting income for educational purposes since it allows the shifting of income on property or investments that you have at present, without giving away permanently the property or investments. However, it does have a few drawbacks, such as a required ten-year term, the capital gains tax problem, and the caution and restrictions necessary where the grantor or spouse is the trustee. Nevertheless, the issues and the guidelines are very clear, and if the requirements are carefully followed, income can be very effectively shifted with a minimum of tax risks.

NOTE: The general tax requirements and principles for shifting income with a Clifford-type trust will apply to every transfer in trust where shifting income is desired, no matter what type of trust is set up. For the most part, the only difference will be the "reversionary" interest. Other trusts, which do not provide for a reversionary interest but which are nevertheless designed to shift income, must follow much the same requirements to avoid taxation to the grantor.

The Shortcut Clifford Trust

In many family situations, the Clifford trust would be "perfect" were it not for the ten-year requirement. In such instances, the family has a definite need to shift income, but *not* for a ten-year period. These families will be pleased to discover there is a way to accomplish their objective in less than ten years, while enjoying all the same advantages offered by the ten-year Clifford trust, including the opportunity to borrow back all or part of the trust principal, as discussed above. There is a price to pay, but, in most cases, it can be quite affordable.

You recall I pointed out that a requirement of the Clifford trust is that the trust principal cannot revert *to the grantor* for ten years after he or she makes the transfer to the trust. In fact, the principal *may* revert to someone *other than the grantor* within *any* period, *and the grantor will still achieve the same tax benefits.* This means that a grantor may make a transfer to a trust that by all other indications is a Clifford trust, except for the fact that it does not last for ten years and that the principal does not revert to the grantor. That is, the trust is irrevocable, has an independent trustee, but at the end of the prescribed period the trust principal is paid to someone other than the grantor—i.e., the grantor "never" gets it back. But here is how such a trust could prove relatively painless.

Mickey, who is in a high tax bracket, has three children and two of them have already completed college. Unhappily, Mickey paid for their education with expensive, after-tax dollars. His third child, however, is ready to enter college at a cost of $8,000 per year, and he faces four or five years of such expenses. He has heard about Clifford trusts but cannot see entering into a ten-year commitment when only four or five years are needed. Happily, Mickey just finished reading this book and discovered he can use a Shortcut Clifford trust to meet his needs. He raises $52,000 and contributes this to a Shortcut Clifford trust for the benefit of his son. The trust is irrevocable, it has an independent trustee, and it is to last for five years. At the end of that period, the trust will terminate, and the $52,000 principal will be paid not to Mickey, but to Mickey's wife, Minnie.

Meanwhile, shortly after the trust is created, Mickey borrows the $52,000 from the trust at 16 percent interest. He uses his home as collateral for the loan and for each of the next five years pays the trustee $8,320 interest (i.e., 16% × $52,000), taking a tax deduction accordingly each year. At the end of the five-year period, Mickey repays the $52,000 debt to the trust, the trustee terminates the trust, and, as the terms of the trust direct, the trustee pays the principal ($52,000) to Minnie. Mickey, in the 50 percent tax bracket, has saved $4,160 per year (50% × $8,320) each of the five years, or $20,800 in federal income taxes. His son has paid about $4,600 in taxes for a net savings to the family of over $16,000 in federal income taxes over the five-year period! Looked at another way, had Mickey done nothing, he would have had to earn about $16,600 each year to have $8,320 left over to pay for his son's college education. With this arrangement he uses only $8,320 of earnings to give his son the same amount, and he has saved $8,320 each year (less the tax his son pays on the interest income).

Because the $52,000 principal does not revert to Mickey when the trust ends, the ten-year rule is not violated. Although Mickey, on creation of the five-year irrevocable trust, has technically made a *gift* to Minnie, there is no real problem, since the gift tax laws allow spouses to give an unlimited amount to each other tax-free (the gift tax marital deduction), so there will be *no* gift tax (for the gift to the spouse) nor any use of Mickey's unified credit as discussed in Chapter 4.

In addition, because the gift to his son is only a five-year income interest instead of a ten-year income interest (as it would be with the usual Clifford trust), the gift tax consequences will be substantially less (see "gift tax consequences of Clifford trusts," page 118).

The following table illustrates the amounts that may be given by one person to a Shortcut Clifford trust without exceeding the $10,000 annual tax-free gift amount:

For a trust which lasts	You may contribute (rounded to the nearest $100)
3 Years	$40,200
4 Years	$31,500
5 Years	$26,000
6 Years	$22,900
7 Years	$20,000
8 Years	$18,700

In other words, a gift of $26,000 to a five-year Shortcut Clifford trust is equivalent to a gift of just under $10,000 to the trust beneficiary. If the grantor's spouse consents to split the gift (see Chapter 4), then the allowable amount can be doubled, as it was in our example with Mickey and Minnie. Note that the terms of the trust *must* be such that a gift to the trust will qualify as a present interest gift to the beneficiary (see explanation of this under "gifts in trust" at the end of Chapter 4).

Any capital gains realized during the term of this trust will be taxed to Minnie (since she is the ultimate "owner" of the principal), but this is generally not a problem if known beforehand. Further, since Minnie and Mickey will probably file joint income tax returns, the tax would be the same as with a Clifford trust. As with a Clifford trust, the trustee must not use any trust income to satisfy Mickey's legal obligation of support as repeatedly noted earlier, or the trust income so used will be taxed to Mickey and Minnie.

In the Shortcut trust, if the reversion is to pass to the grantor's spouse, it is *very important* that *the spouse make no contribution to the trust,* otherwise a portion of the trust income attributable to her contribution will be taxed to her. This does not mean that she cannot consent to "split" the grantor's initial gift to the trust (for gift tax purposes) as long as none of the trust principal *actually* came from her.

Although the trust principal need not revert to the grantor's spouse (it could be anyone other than the grantor, his creditors, or his estate), the spouse would appear to be the most appropriate person if the husband and wife desire to recover the principal. And although there appears to be no specified minimum term for this type of trust, it would seem that a period of less than a few years would be "pushing it" in the eyes of the IRS. As to termination due to other contingencies, the trust may terminate on the beneficiary's death, but should not be affected in any way by the grantor's death, since the grantor has reserved absolutely no rights, benefits, or future interests in the trust.

There is an added benefit to this type of trust that does not exist with the standard Clifford trust where the principal reverts to the grantor. Since in the Shortcut Clifford trust the principal is paid to the grantor's spouse, the property in this trust will *not* be included in the grantor's estate, so there could be a savings of estate taxes as well.

Finally, there is at least one caveat. The grantor *is* in fact giving his property away. If, at the end of the term of the trust, he is not on good terms with his spouse (or is separated or divorced, or about to be), it could be tough luck for him. Nevertheless, in most instances it is a risk worth taking since the tax savings can be substantial without having to go the full ten-year route.

· ·

Independent Trusts—
Mr. Crummey's Legacy

Uniform Gifts to Minors Act gifts, the 2503(c) minor's trust, and the Clifford trust each have special characteristics which may make one or another more or less attractive in any given situation.

In fact, I have even suggested the use of two or more in combination. In planning to save taxes by shifting income, you must keep an open and creative mind, since many different tax "products" for this purpose have developed over the years. Therefore, it is up to you and your advisors together to determine the best products, since the IRS surely won't tell you.

The UGMA gift is simple and inexpensive, but presents problems for long-term planning and where larger amounts are involved. The minor's trust is a step better than the UGMA, but it, too, has a limited life and must follow certain IRS requirements to qualify for shifting income. The Clifford trust is an excellent vehicle, even for large investments, but only the "use" of the investments is given away, and in addition to certain restrictions on control over the investments and income, as a practical matter the life of a Clifford trust is limited to ten years or so.

In the continuing process of developing new and better tax products for your use, vigilant tax lawyers have refined another vehicle, the so-called "independent" trust, to the point where it can shift income, qualify for the gift tax exclusion, operate as well for small investments as for large, and last as long or as short as you like. Actually, this type of trust is not really new. It is simply an irrevocable trust, usually for the benefit of children, and designed to last considerably beyond age 21, or for some other specified term, giving the trustee discretion to pay out or accumulate funds in accordance with the child's needs, with emphasis, of course, on education. The recent development which has made this type of trust considerably more attractive for educational purposes is the decision in the Crummey case.

In 1962, D. C. Crummey and his wife created an irrevocable trust for the benefit of their four children. It was their intention that any gifts they made to this trust qualify for the gift tax exclusion (at that time, $3,000 per donee). With certain exceptions, gifts to a trust are considered a "future interest" as discussed in Chapter 4, and so usually will not qualify for this exclusion. To obtain the exclusion, the Crummey trust provided that each year until December 31, each beneficiary had the right to *withdraw* the lesser of $4,000 or that child's share of the amount contributed to the trust by the Crummeys. If a demand was not made by December 31, all amounts contributed to the trust in that year would *remain* in the trust and be administered according to the remaining trust provisions.

The Crummeys felt that the children's right to withdraw would give the children the present ability to *take* the funds currently, and thus qualify for the present interest exclusion. The IRS argued that the *minor* beneficiaries were not legally able to withdraw their shares, so the gift tax exclusion should not apply in this case, as the beneficiaries did not have a "present interest"—i.e., immediate enjoyment of the gift. The Crummeys argued that even as minors, the children had the right to demand their shares, that a guardian could be appointed to make the demand for them, and that if desired, even a parent, as natural guardian, could make the demand for the child. The court *agreed* with the Crummeys and *allowed* the gift tax exclusions for all the beneficiaries. This 1968 decision gave legal birth to what is now commonly known (at least among tax advisors) as a "Crummey trust."

The Crummey trust is basically an irrevocable trust with provisions allowing for withdrawal of certain amounts each year by the beneficiaries for the purpose of having gifts to the trust qualify for the annual gift tax exclusion (see Chapter 4). It does not matter that the beneficiaries are minors, so long as notice of the right to withdraw is properly given to the beneficiaries. The withdrawal provision should not be a major concern, since if a child exercises his or her right and actually withdraws the funds, then you need not make any future gifts for that child. Further, you can limit the amount of time a child has to make the withdrawal. For example, you can provide that if the child fails to withdraw the funds within, say, thirty days after the gift to the trust, then the right of withdrawal is lost for that year. This open period is sometimes called a "window."

The IRS formally approved a sixty-day window for withdrawal, but many tax advisors feel even thirty days is acceptable. A window of anything less than thirty days is subject to attack as not providing enough time for withdrawal and therefore negating the right to withdraw, which would cause a loss of the gift tax exclusion. Once the window is closed, the funds which are not withdrawn become a *permanent part of the trust* and are administered accordingly. The right of withdrawal will thereafter only apply to *new* funds contributed in a subsequent year. Funds that are not withdrawn are "pooled" in the trust and may be used for all the beneficiaries at the discretion of the trustee. It is this probable outcome (where there are no actual withdrawals) that makes the Crummey trust desirable from the perspective of providing educational benefits for two or more children who will enter college at different times, while still taking advantage of the individual gift tax exclusion for each.

The duration of the trust is entirely up to you. It need not last ten years, as the Clifford trust must, but it certainly should last for some period beyond the time the children reach age 21. If all you need is a trust to last until they reach 21, you would be better off with the minor's trust. Many Crummey trusts last to age 30 and beyond, some even for the child's lifetime. It usually depends upon your family's circumstances, the purposes of the trust, and the amount of property in it. Remember that funds or property in the Crummey trust will not revert to you, as they would in Clifford trust after ten years. A Crummey trust can certainly be set up to provide for educational benefits at appropriate ages. It is more flexible than a minor's trust, since it can provide for accumulation and distribution of funds after age 21, when the child may still be in college. Further, the same trust can provide for several children of differing ages (as in the Crummey case), so that each child can be provided for in accordance with her or his individual needs. This is especially helpful in cases where they enter college at different times.

Income Taxes

Subject to the tax effect of the right of withdrawal (described below), the income tax treatment of a Crummey trust will generally follow the same rules as those discussed previously for minor's trusts and Clifford trusts, except for the special capital gains rule on Clifford trusts. With a Crummey trust, *capital gains are taxed to the trust or to the beneficiary* (depending upon whether they are accumulated or distributed) and not to the grantor, because the grantor has no reversionary interest (he will not get the property back).

The right of withdrawal may cause the beneficiary to be treated as the owner of that portion of the trust that he or she could withdraw for that year, or at least for the period of the right of withdrawal. For example, say that on January 1, Rita makes a gift of $20,000 to a Crummey trust for her two children, when there was already $20,000 in the trust from previous gifts, which were not withdrawn. During the year, the trust realized $4,000 of income. In that year, the two children will *each* report $1,000 of income ($10,000 for each share that could be withdrawn, divided by the $40,000 total trust property, times $4,000 income), and the trust will be taxed on the remaining $2,000. Note that this is so even though the children did not withdraw the gift *or* the income. In the next year, if no further gifts were made, the children should be taxed only on income which was distributed to them.

Gift Taxes

As explained above, gifts to a Crummey trust will qualify for the $10,000 gift tax exclusion. There is, however, another gift tax consideration that often comes as a surprise. When the beneficiary allows his right of withdrawal to lapse, technically he may be considered as having made a gift. As a practical matter, if the same beneficiary will ultimately receive the trust property, this does not pose a serious problem.

Estate Taxes

If the grantor reserves no rights or benefits under the Crummey trust and retains none of the problem powers as trustee, then the property in the trust will *not* be included in the grantor's estate. Whether it will be included in the child's estate depends upon the rights and benefits of the child. In most cases, since the child is the ultimate beneficiary, it will be included in his estate, but unless huge amounts of money or property are involved or the trust continues for the child's entire life, this should not be a serious problem either.

SUMMARY

The Crummey trust is advisable where the circumstances involved or the amount of money or investments is sufficiently large as to make distribution to a child at age 21 undesirable. This type of trust can last well beyond age 21 and even for the life of a child, if necessary. In addition, transfers to the trust will qualify for the annual gift tax exclusion because of the annual withdrawal rights given to each beneficiary, although amounts not withdrawn become a permanent part of the trust. The Crummey trust is recognized as a very flexible trust for the purpose of shifting income for educational purposes in a wide variety of situations, as will be illustrated by examples in the following chapter.

This chapter outlined the basic principles of trust taxation and the fundamental types of trusts which may be used to shift income for educational purposes. You will and should be making constant reference to it since many of the maneuvers suggested in subsequent chapters will necessitate or at least suggest the use of one or more of the trusts described here to facilitate the transaction. A quick review of the chart on page 201 should help you put these important distinctions into perspective, since a basic understanding of trusts and trust taxation will help you get the maximum tax mileage out of each idea you may use to achieve tax-favored financing of educational costs.

IMPORTANT REMINDER: Regardless of the plan you use, if any of the child's income, *whether from a trust or any other source*, is used to satisfy a parental obligation, *the income so used will be taxed to the parent*, despite the care taken with the rest of the plan. To avoid falling into this trap, be sure to review the discussion of this point in Chapter 3 (pages 26–33).

REFERENCES FOR CHAPTER 6

The Basics
1. IRC, Sections 641–644 (Laws regarding taxation of trust income).
2. IRC, Sections 651–652 (Deductions for trust distributions).
3. IRC, Sections 661–663 (Throwback rule).

Minor's Trusts
1. IRS, Section 2503(c) (Definition/rules for minor's trust).
2. IRC, Reg. Section 25.2503–4 (Requirements for minor's trust).
3. *Ross v. Commissioner*, 71 TC 897 (1979), *aff'd* 81-2 USTC Par. 13, 424 (Fifth Cir. 1981) (Texas).
4. *Heidrich v. Commissioner*, 55 TC 746 (1971) (Restriction on Trustee's Use of Money).

Ten-Year Trusts
1. *Clifford v. Helvering*, 309 U.S. 331 (1940).
2. IRC, Sections 671–678 and Corresponding Regulations (Clifford trust rules).
3. *C. O. Bibby v. Commissioner*, 44 TC 638 (1965) (Texas) (Ten-year period not met).
4. IRC, Section 662 (When beneficiaries are taxed on trust income).
5. IRC, Section 665–668 (When trust distributes accumulated income).
6. RR 68-392, 1968-2 Cum.Bull. 284 (Capital gains taxed to grantor).
7. IRC, Reg. Section 25.2512 (Valuation of gift to trust).
8. Regs. Section 25.2512-1 (Tables for Valuation of Gift of 10-Year Income Interest).
9. *Preston v. Commissioner*, 132 F.2d 763 (2nd Cir. 1942), IRC, Section 675(3) (Trust and Borrowback).
10. *Potter v. Commissioner*, 27 TC 200 (1956). (Gift of patent rights, borrowback of income).
11. IRC, Section 163(d) (Limitation on Investment Interest Deduction).
12. IRC Section 461(g) (Deduction of prepaid interest).

Independent Trusts
1. *Crummey v. Commissioner*, 25 TCM 772 (1966), 397 F.2d 82 (Calif. ninth circuit) (1968) (Tax free gift to trust).
2. IRC, Section 671 (Income taxed to owner of trust).
3. IRC, Section 2514(e) (Power of appointment).

NOTE:
IRC = Internal Revenue Code.
Regs. = U.S. Treasury Regulations.
RR = Revenue Ruling (by Internal Revenue Service).
Letter Ruling = Ruling for a Taxpayer by the Internal Revenue Service (not published in IRS Bulletin).
TC = U.S. Tax Court Decision (TCM = U.S. Tax Court Memorandum Decision, not the full court).
F. = Federal (U.S. Circuit Court of Appeals) Decision, (F.2d = Federal, 2nd series).

Cir. = Circuit (area of the U.S. served by that court).
aff'd = affirmed lower court decision.
rev'd = reversed lower court decision.
S. Ct. = U.S. Supreme Court Decision.
USTC = U.S. Tax Cases, Commerce Clearing House.

7

Interest-Free Loans

Background and Tax Problems

One of the most popular methods of shifting income for college education in recent years has been the interest-free loan. One reason might be that it seems to be usable by just about any family that has any funds at all to loan; perhaps another is that its concept is so simple—loaning money without charging interest. Whatever the reason, it caught on like the hula hoop, but like the hula hoop, its time has come and gone.

Over the past several years, the interest-free loan became a simple and effective way of shifting income, giving the IRS growing concern. They simply refused to accept the concept and this tax indigestion caused them to attack it repeatedly on every conceivable basis and in just about every available court. For many years, the IRS was almost totally unsuccessful in these attacks, until February 22, 1984, when the U.S. Supreme Court decided the Dickman case, discussed later.

This review will deal primarily with the evolution of "intra-family" interest-free loans, as opposed to interest-free loans from a closely held corporation to a shareholder, because the intra-family loan has been used most frequently in educational programs. An intra-family loan is merely one that is made between members of the same or related families or to family trusts.

The numerous cases involving interest-free loans go back more than twenty years, and many of the key cases which solidly established the "legality" of interest-free loans have, in fact, involved corporate loans. These are significant because for the most part the courts continually held that, by itself, the interest-free use of money "results in no taxable gain to the borrower."

The primary objection the IRS has presented in arguing these cases where interest-free loans were made by businesses to their owners or employees was that the free use of money resulted in *income* to the borrower in an amount equal to the interest which the borrower would have paid if he had borrowed from an independent party. For example, if you borrowed $10,000 for one year at 10 percent, it would *cost* you $1,000 in interest. Therefore, the IRS said, if your business loaned you $10,000 without interest (using my example) that would be the same as if it gave you $1,000 as *income* (since you did *not* have to pay any interest). For nearly twenty years, the IRS had virtually *no success* with this argument in court.

As to *intra-family* loans, the IRS has been similarly unsuccessful in court with the *income* argument. But since the IRS continually failed in its attempts to impute any *income* to a family borrower, it concentrated its attacks instead on the basis that the interest-free *use* of money given to a family member is a *gift of the value of that use* for the period the loan remains unpaid.

The granddaddy of intra-family interest-free loan cases is the Crown case. That particular case received so much attention and coverage that interest-free loans are often referred to as Crown loans, and related trusts referred to as Crown trusts. Briefly, the Crown case involved about $18 million of interest-free loans from a partnership owned by Lester Crown and his two brothers to twenty-four trusts for the benefit of their fifteen children and certain other relatives (see how the rich do it?). The $18 million loan bore no interest and you can easily see why this made the IRS nervous. The IRS attacked the transactions not on the income argument, but on the basis that the interest-free *use* of the money was a *gift*.

The IRS initially lost this and numerous similar cases, paving the way for more and more professional as well as pubic acceptance of the interest-free loan as an easy means of shifting income.

Nevertheless, the IRS persisted in its attack. Then came the Dickman case.

In the mid-1970s, Esther and Paul Dickman of Florida made several hundred thousand dollars of interest-free loans to their son, Lyle. On discovering the loans, the IRS contended that the interest-free use of the money was a gift to Lyle and imposed a *gift tax* on the Dickmans. The Dickmans took their case to court and countered by simply referring to the long list of preceding court cases which said the IRS was wrong. This particular appeals court, however, didn't see it that way, and on November 1, 1982, it agreed with the IRS, holding that the free use of the money *was* in fact *a gift*. And as to the value of the gift, the IRS took the position that the gift should be valued by measuring the interest at the same rate that the IRS charges on delinquent taxes (and pays on refunds).

Because the appeals court decision in the Dickman case conflicted with the decision of the appeals court in the Crown case, the U.S. Supreme Court agreed to hear the case to decide once and for all whether the interest-free use of money was a gift from the lender to the borrower. And it did.

On February 22, 1984, the high court decided that the free *use* of funds was definitely a measurable benefit to the borrower and that a *gift* has been made in such cases. The amount of the gift, the court said, would be "the reasonable value of the use of the money lent" (although it did not decide how the reasonable value of this use would be measured). After that, however, it became academic, because Congress changed the law.

. . . .

Changes in the Law

The decision in the Dickman case, by itself, was *not* devastating to interest-free loans, and, as the saying goes, rumors of its death were greatly exaggerated. That is, until June 1984. In an obscure provision tucked into the major Tax Reform Act of 1984, Congress added some new sections to the Internal Revenue Code, which clearly spelled the death of interest-free loans.

In addition to confirming that interest-free loans are subject to gift taxes, the 1984 law causes the lender of an interest-free loan to be treated as if he had received an interest payment on the loan—*even though none was received.* In most cases, this will result in a *taxable income* to the lender each year that the interest-free loan is outstanding, as illustrated below. Correspondingly, the borrower will be entitled to a tax deduction for the "interest" he didn't actually pay even though it may be of no use to him. The amount of interest considered to be "received" and "paid," so to speak, is based on one of the variable rates used by the government for other purposes (referred to as the "federal rate," applicable to various types of loans and based on the average recent yields of U.S. government obligations). In addition, there *still* would remain the gift tax exposure whenever such a loan is made. In short, passage of this law has destroyed the effectiveness of interest-free loans where the primary objective is to shift income from the lender to the borrower.

There are *de minimus* exceptions to the harsh tax result—that is, cases where the law regards the loan as small enough not to make a difference. For example, a $10,000 interest-free loan *between individuals* is exempt from the new law, but this exception *will not apply if the loan is "attributable to the purchase or carrying of income-producing assets,"* and when wouldn't it be if tax planning for educational costs is the objective?

For instance, if Mom makes a $10,000 interest-free loan to Son, there will be no adverse tax benefits to Mom as long as the loan does not exceed $10,000 and as long as Son does not invest the $10,000 in income-producing assets. Apparently, if Son simply uses the $10,000 to pay his college expenses there is no problem—but there is also *no tax saving!* In other words, if the deal even smells of a tax-planning maneuver, there will be adverse tax consequences, regardless of the amount of money involved. And, of course, the more money involved, the harsher the tax consequences.

For example, say that Dad, who is in the 50 percent tax bracket, makes an interest-free loan of $100,000 on January 1 to Daughter (who has no other income), so that Daughter can invest the funds and use the income for college costs. Assuming the applicable federal rate is 11 percent, Dad will be treated as if he *received* an $11,000 annual interest payment from Daughter, *even though he received nothing!* This will cost Dad $5,500 out of pocket to pay the income taxes on the "phantom" interest payment of $11,000, and *each year* the loan remains outstanding he will be *taxed* on an additional $11,000 of interest (or whatever the "applicable federal rate" dictates) *which he does not receive!*

Daughter, who happened to invest the funds at 11 percent (and so actually received $11,000 of interest income) will be entitled to deduct the $11,000 of "interest" which she never paid to Dad, even though she does not need the full deduction. And if that is not confusing or painful enough, Dad would still be treated as having made a potentially taxable gift to Daughter of $11,000 *each year* the loan is outstanding.

This situation could present even more painful and inequitable results if Daughter earns less interest than is imputed to Dad under the law. For instance, supposing she only earns 8 percent on the money and the applicable federal rate is 11 percent. Is Dad taxed on even more than Daughter earns? He *could* be, unless the loan falls within the "gift loan exception" in the law. If the loan is a "gift loan" (where the forgiveness of interest is in the nature of a gift, which usually would apply to intra-family loans), *and if* the total of such loans between Dad and Daughter does not exceed $100,000, then the amount that Dad is treated as receiving will be equal to Daughter's net investment income on the $100,000. In other words, if Daughter receives (after related expenses) only 8 percent ($8,000) interest, then Dad will be taxed only on that amount. Remember, Dad never receives the $8,000, but he is nevertheless taxed on it. Further, this $100,000 gift loan exception will *not* apply if one of the principal purposes of the loan is to save taxes.

All of this means that if you make an interest-free loan *of any amount* to your child, and if the primary purpose (or even *one* of the primary purposes) of the loan is to save income taxes by having the child invest the loan proceeds to produce income for his or her education, then *none of the exceptions will apply, you will be taxed on interest that you do not receive,* and the interest charged to you will be at a rate prescribed by the federal government, *re-*

gardless of whether the child earns less than that amount on the borrowed money.

These rules apply to all interest-free loans outstanding after September 16, 1984, which have tax savings as one of the primary purposes, *even though* the loan may have been made before the law was passed. So goes the game called "close the loophole."

CHAPTER SUMMARY

Although for over twenty years the IRS has been only marginally successful in court in attacking interest-free loans, it finally won in the U.S. Supreme Court, which held in February 1984 that the free *use* of the borrowed money is a gift. But the gift-tax treatment was not enough for the IRS. It wanted to do away with interest-free loans once and for all, and with that victory in hand the IRS redoubled its efforts to change the law, and Congress was easily convinced.

In June 1984 Congress passed a law providing that the use of interest-free loans to shift income will produce *taxable interest income* to the lender, *even though no interest is actually received,* so that the mere existence of an interest-free loan between individuals can produce out-of-pocket tax costs to the lender each year the loan remains outstanding. In effect, intra-family interest-free loans to shift income are now a thing of the past.

REFERENCES FOR CHAPTER 7

Background and Tax Problems
1. *Hardee v. U.S.,* F.2d 661, (Fed. Cir. 1983) 83-1 USTC Par. 9353 (Interest-free loan from corporation to shareholders).
2. *Lester Crown v. Commissioner,* 67 TC 1060 (1970), *aff'd* 585 F. 234 (7th Cir. 1978) (Illinois) (Interest-free demand loan, not a taxable gift).
3. *Dickman v. Commissioner,* USTC Par.13,501 (11th Cir. 1982) (Florida), 104 S. Ct 1086 (1984) (Interest-free demand loan *is* a taxable gift).
4. *Estate of Meyer Berkman v. Commissioner,* T.C. Memo 1979-46, 38 TCM 183 (1979) (Texas) (Gift of twenty-year notes taxable).
5. *Estate of Grace E. Lang v. Commissioner,* 80-1 USTC Par.13,340 (9th Cir. 1980) (Washington) (Interest-free demand loan, a taxable gift).

Changes in the Law
1. PL 98-369, "The Tax Reform Act of 1984."
2. IRC Section 1274(d) (Applicable federal rate of interest charged on interest-free loans).
3. IRC Section 7872 (Income and gift tax treatment of interest-free loans).

NOTE:
IRC = Internal Revenue Code.
Regs. = U.S. Treasury Regulations.
RR = Revenue Ruling (by Internal Revenue Service).
Letter Ruling = Ruling for a Taxpayer by the Internal Revenue Service (not published in IRS Bulletin).
TC = U.S. Tax Court Decision (TCM = U.S. Tax Court Memorandum Decision, not the full court).
F. = Federal (U.S. Circuit Court of Appeals) Decision (F.2d = Federal, 2nd series).
Cir. = Circuit (area of the U.S. served by that court).
aff'd = affirmed lower court decision.
rev'd = reversed lower court decision.
S. Ct. = U.S. Supreme Court Decision.
USTC = U.S. Tax Cases, Commerce Clearing House.
PL = Public Law.

8

. . . .

Using Family Businesses to Pay for Educational Costs

Can you employ your child and get a tax deduction for it? If so, can you add things like vacation pay and travel expenses? Can you give a part of your business and profits to a child without losing control of the business? Can you lease business equipment from a child and deduct the payments? Can the child use any or all of this income for college or private school tuition?

If your family is connected with a business that is profitable, the answer to each of these questions is *yes,* and these are only a few of the ways you can save taxes and educational costs by taking advantage of clever (but legal) tax planning to get the most mileage out of your tax or tax-deductible business dollars.

Family businesses lend themselves to several tax-planning maneuvers largely because they are businesses. Although not every expense of a business is tax-deductible, every "reasonable" business expense is. If we can make a payment to a child as a legitimate business expense, we will be creating a tax deduction where there was previously none. For example, if a doctor earning $70,000 makes a gift of $5,000 to his child, there are no immediate tax advantages. If the same doctor pays his child $5,000 to render bona fide services to his business, the doctor gets a $5,000 tax deduction.

Except as otherwise noted, the business deductions and arrangements discussed in this chapter apply to any type or form of legitimate business, so it won't matter whether your business is incorporated, a partnership, or a sole proprietorship. What *will* matter is whether there really is a business. For example, if you simply *say* you are in a business without actually carrying on that business, then you can forget about any deductions, let alone those for the child. Further, the IRS says you must be in business to make a profit, and losses from what amounts to a *hobby*, rather than a business, are not tax-deductible. Finally, while in most instances you can decide for yourself what is reasonable as a business expense, if your business takes in only $1,000 but you pay your child a salary of $6,000, don't be surprised if the IRS balks at your $5,000 "business" loss. In this connection, business transactions among family members are always subject to close scrutiny by the IRS, so you should be sure to follow the rules carefully.

. . . .

Employing Your Child

One of the most important sections of the Internal Revenue Code to all businesses is section 162, which tells us that "There shall be allowed as a deduction all the ordinary and necessary expenses paid or incurred during the year in carrying on any trade or business." The section goes on to say that this includes reasonable salaries or other compensation for services rendered, and although the tax code doesn't say it, this has been clearly held to include payments for the services of a child. To deduct salary or compensation to your child, the three basic tests you must meet are:

1. You (or your corporation) must be in a trade or business;
2. The child must have actually rendered services to the trade or business; and
3. Payments to the child must be reasonable in relation to the services rendered by the child.

It is items 2 and 3 that generally give rise to questions and a possible loss of deductions. Many parents simply *say* the child is employed, making payments to the child, but in fact the child renders few or no services. Further, parents frequently have a tendency to pay their child more than they might pay another person doing the same thing. If the child is employed, it is very important that the child's duties be clear and that they are in fact performed. It is equally important that the child receive approximately the same amount of pay as an unrelated party would receive for the same services.

If these tests are met, the IRS *itself* has said in numerous rulings that the payments are deductible by the parent. In at least one case, they allowed a deduction even though the minor child's earnings were being used for his education and support. The facts of that particular (1959) ruling involved a parent who owned a drive-in restaurant. During the summer he employed his three children (two were minors) at the restaurant and paid them an hourly wage. In holding that the wages paid to the children were a legitimate business deduction to the father, *the IRS said*:

> "The facts in this case show that actual services were rendered by each of the taxpayer's children as a bona fide employee in the operation of the taxpayer's business, and that the compensation paid each child for such service was reasonable and constituted an ordinary and necessary expense of carrying on such business. Hence, *such wage payments are deductible* from gross income as provided in section 162 of the Code. To hold otherwise would be tantamount to penalizing the father for employing his own children, inasmuch as the deduction would be allowable if he had employed someone else's children under the same circumstances."

Keeping Records

It is important to note that the father in the drive-in case was able to document the employment of the children and show the IRS that they actually rendered services. Many such cases have failed because the parent couldn't show payment records or evidence.

In one such case, a Dr. Furmanski of Los Angeles, California, employed his son and daughter (who were in college) to answer his phone, perform "secretarial" services, and help with medical "research projects." Some of the payments were made to the children in advance of their services, and other payments—for answering the phone, etc.—were sporadic. Few records were kept for any of the services rendered, the time spent, or the results.

With such a lack of substantiation the IRS (and the court) had no choice but to disallow almost all of Furmanski's claimed deductions for compensation to his children.

You should, therefore, *keep detailed records* as to payments to and services rendered by the child. You should file the necessary wage or other statements with state and federal authorities and give the child a "W-2" or "1099" statement (reports of wages or compensation) at the end of the year. If withholding is applicable, you should do so, although if you are not a corporation, the laws provide that you do not have to withhold Social Security payments for a child (check with your accountant). In short, you must keep at least the same records and file the same reports as you would for other employees.

The Wrong Records

Substantiation and documentation *alone*, however, are not the deciding factors. In another case, Dr. M., a dentist, had his professional corporation enter into a written contract with his son, Charles, wherein M corporation agreed to pay all of Charles's expenses in obtaining his degree in dentistry. In return, Charles agreed to perform dental services on behalf of M corporation for a period of eight years *after* his graduation. M corporation took a deduction for all the college expenses paid on the basis that the payments were for services *to be* rendered (i.e., in the future).

The IRS quickly disallowed the deductions. In order to be deductible, they reminded Dr. M., an expense must be "ordinary and necessary." The contract between M and Charles and the payments to Charles did not fall into this category. The fact that M corporation would derive a benefit from the transaction does not, by itself, render the expense either ordinary or necessary.

In this ruling the IRS referred to other cases where the taxpayer tried to enter into an agreement with a child to have the business pay for college in return for the child's future services. It is puzzling that these taxpayers took such a roundabout, risky, and contrived approach to something that could have been accomplished directly, and with less tax risk, as explained on the next page.

The IRS and the courts have said time and again that it is permissible to employ the child. In those cases where the child was employed to pay for educational costs, the question of deductibility usually turned on whether the child actually rendered services and whether a fair value was paid for those services. If a parent runs a dental practice, the child certainly cannot practice dentistry until properly qualified. In the meantime, however, the child can certainly render other services, and once the child actually becomes a dentist, there can be little question about the deductibility of his compensation, if fair.

Instead of the elaborate but unsuccessful contractual scheme (illustrated above in Dr. M.'s case), all the parent had to do was have the child borrow the costs of the education (the loan could be guaranteed by the parent or could even come from the parent), then, after graduation, the child could pay off the loan with the salary *then* paid to him by the parent. The college costs, in effect, could be made tax-deductible as salary payments *after* the child graduates, without raising any of the questions involved under the other unsuccessful arrangement.

If You Don't Have a
Trade or Business

In some instances, employment of a child can take place where *investments* are concerned, as opposed to the traditional "trade or business." For example, if you own income-producing real estate, services are often required for such things as grounds maintenance, building repairs, janitorial services, showing rental property, snow removal, bookkeeping, or anything else that is reasonably related to the "management, conservation and maintenance" of the property, as the tax code puts it. But the same "ordinary and necessary" test applies to these expenses as to trade or business expenses and, like the trade or business expenses, they must also be substantiated with records or other documentation.

A case illustrating both points is that of Charles and Mary Tschupp of Long Island, New York. The Tschupps owned rental real estate and employed their two teenage sons to clean the halls and stairs once a week, and to do miscellaneous other janitorial services. The IRS disallowed the Tschupps' deductions for these services and the Tschupps appealed to the Tax Court. The Tax Court agreed that the payments should be deductible, but found that Mr. Tschupp could not show exactly what he did pay his sons—Tschupp had no records. His testimony that the payments were made in cash and the boys' testimony that they received "in the neighborhood" of $500 were not sufficient to convince the Tax Court, but they did allow him to deduct about half of what he had claimed—a liberal finding.

All these cases clearly point out that it is quite permissible to employ your child if you simply follow the rules. Done properly, you can get a full tax deduction for the payments made, *even though* the child uses the payments for college.

Tax Advantage of "Earned" Income

Another major tax benefit in the child's receiving compensation as opposed to other income, is that compensation is considered *earned* income while dividends, interest, and the like are considered *unearned* income. The difference is that the earned income of a single individual is *not* taxed unless it exceeds a certain amount ($2,300 for 1984). With unearned income, an individual is taxed on everything over $1,000. In addition to this earned income "allowance," the child may still qualify as your dependent if he is under 19, or if he is a full-time student and you contribute more than half his support. In other words, the child's earned income of $2,300, plus his personal exemption of $1,000, plus the dependency exemption which you could claim for the child would total $4,300 of *tax-free* income that could be generated each year.

Fringe Benefits to the Child/Employee

A further advantage to employment of a child in a family business is the child's eligibility for fringe benefits. The extent of these benefits which may be given to a child depends upon the size of the business, the number of employees, and the amount of money available; in a large business, there may not be as much flexibility as there could be in a much smaller one. One thing the IRS always looks for is whether your child is getting "special" treatment. If it appears you are paying your child more than a "reasonable" amount (including the value of the fringe benefits), the excess (the total minus what is considered reasonable) will *not* be deductible to you. One of the factors in determining what is reasonable is whether other employees are entitled to the same benefit. This may or may not present a problem, depending on the size of your business. In a larger business, it could cost you quite a lot to give everyone the same benefit as you give your child (if that is the issue), while in a smaller one, it may not make much difference.

For example, say you have a construction business and you adopt a policy to pay all "laborers" a $50 weekly allowance for work boots and gloves. If you have a hundred laborers this "benefit" could be costly. But if your son is one of only two or three such workers, it might pay you to do so. Other "extra" benefits can be approached in a similar fashion. Use your imagination.

In addition to extra benefits, there are traditional fringe benefits which are much less likely to be questioned by the IRS, largely because the laws already contain strict requirements that they be given on a nondiscriminatory basis. These would include things like vacation pay, retirement plans, life and health insurance, and medical reimbursement plans (for payment of out-of-pocket medical expenses not covered by insurance). An employed child may certainly be covered by all of these, particularly if the child is employed on a full-time basis. For part-time employment, some benefits may be restricted.

Generally, if a child works for you more than one thousand hours in a year, it is considered full-time employment. In most instances, under this definition it would be possible to work "full-time," while going to college.

If the child does qualify as a full-time employee, one of the more meaningful benefits from the standpoint of paying for education could be your business's retirement plan. These benefits may or may not be relatively large, usually depending upon the amount of salary paid to the child and the length of time the child has worked for the company. To collect benefits from such a plan, you need not necessarily be retired. Many plans allow benefits to be paid on termination of employment, at the discretion of the plan's trustees. In a small business the plan's trustees are usually the owners of the business, often the parents, who could "elect" to pay out benefits to a child who has terminated employment. Benefits paid out of retirement plans in a lump sum are themselves subject to special favorable tax treatment to the child.

A typical, easy-to-apply plan is one in which the company sets aside an amount equal to a flat 25 percent of employees' salaries to the plan. Note that these amounts are fully tax-deductible to the company and not taxed to the employee until the employee receives them sometime in the future, and that such a plan would no doubt benefit the parents as well. Once again, a small company could easily adopt or modify a plan to suit the family's needs, whereas a large company may find the costs prohibitive.

Under a "25 percent" plan, if you are paying your child $6,000 per year, you would contribute an *additional* $1,500 (tax-deductible) to the child's retirement plan. In five years, this would total $7,500 *plus* tax-sheltered interest, all of which could be paid to the child (if the plan allows) on his or her "termination of employment." At that time, the payment would be taxed to the child but may also be subject to the special "ten-year forward-averaging" tax break, which is like spreading the payment over ten years, and lowers the tax considerably.

You should keep in mind that retirement plans can be quite involved and certain types of plans become fixed obligations on the part of the company. There are rules prohibiting discrimination and penalizing "top-heavy" plans, which benefit only the owners or highly paid employees. Further, a plan cannot be adopted and then terminated at the drop of a hat, so that once one is adopted, you will probably be required to keep it for several years. As a result, you would *not* adopt one simply to help with college education, but rather, when it would benefit the family business as a whole and comply with the law.

Educational Benefit Trusts for
Children of Employees

The Educational Benefit Trust is a tax-deductible plan set up by your corporation to provide an educational fund for children of employees on a nondiscriminatory basis. Of course, if it so happens that most or all of the employees are also the owners of the business, it could be that their children are the primary beneficiaries of the plan. But don't rush to set one up for your corporation until you understand all the details—these plans are not as great as they sound.

In an Educational Benefit Trust (EBT), a corporation would contribute a certain amount of money each year to an EBT for the children of its employees. The trust would accept, hold, and manage the annual payment, and in the future would make the funds available to qualifying children for their educational costs. While the funds are accumulating in the trust, there would be no tax.

Corporations setting up EBTs have attempted to treat them like other fringe-benefit plans, where the deduction is taken at the time the corporation makes the payment into a trust but there is no income to the employee until he receives some benefit. The IRS, on the other hand, has resisted accepting these plans and has repeatedly disallowed deductions for contributions to the trust until benefits are paid, at which time the corporation would get a deduction *and* the employee (not the child) would be taxed on the income. This tax treatment is similar to that of a deferred compensation plan, which is exactly how the IRS treated the EBT. Now, however, they may have to treat it differently.

In a 1982 decision of the U. S. Court of Appeals for the Federal Circuit, the court held that if an EBT meets the criteria established by the court in that decision, it will qualify as a fringe-benefit plan, contributions to which are deductible by the corporation *when made* and not taxable to the employees until the benefits are paid. In that case, Greensboro Pathology Associates, a professional corporation in North Carolina, created an Educational Benefit Trust "as a means of attracting and retaining employees of high quality." Under their plan, *every* employee was entitled to benefits of up to $4,000 per year for up to four years, for each child of such employee between the ages of 18 and 29, for the purposes of undergraduate or graduate study at an accredited college or university. There were no other restrictions or qualifications on eligibility. There were, however, provisions requiring continued employment, except for retirement or disability, so that if a parent left the company, his or her child would immediately cease receiving any benefits under the plan. Finally—and these are two very important factors—the plan had a completely independent trustee to carry it out, and none of the funds could ever revert to the corporation or its owners.

At the time the EBT was adopted, Greensboro had six employees, four of whom were the physician/owners of Greensboro. Shortly after contributions were made to the plan, eleven children were designated to receive benefits, and of these, nine were children of the physician/owners. Over a three-year period, the corporation contributed (and deducted) nearly $35,000 to the EBT. The IRS disallowed the deductions.

In holding in favor of Greensboro, the court set forth several factors which will probably serve as guidelines in qualifying future EBTs for current deductions. Whether an EBT will qualify as a deductible fringe-benefit plan, the court said, will depend upon the answers to the following questions:

1. Is the plan concerned with the well-being of the employees?
2. Are the benefits provided the employees based upon the employer's earnings?
3. Are benefits greater for someone employed longer?
4. Are benefits provided to all employees?
5. Are the plan benefits merely a substitute for wages or other compensation?
6. Does the plan serve its stated purpose, or is it a sham?
7. Does the employer lose control of funds it gives the plan?
8. Is there any sort of reversion of funds to the employer?
9. Is the plan independently administered?

The Greensboro plan, the court said, (1) was not a substitute for compensation, (2) covered and was for the good of all employees, (3) ensured that the funds could not revert to Greensboro and no control of the funds was retained, (4) was controlled by a truly independent trustee, and (5) was not a sham.

It should be clearly noted that the effect of *an EBT is merely a device for tax deferral and not tax savings,* because the income is not shifted to a lower bracket (i.e., it is still taxed to the *employee*). When the contributions are made, a deduction is realized to the corporation and no one is taxed at the time. But when benefits are later paid out in accordance with the terms of the plan, the *employee,* not his child, is taxed on the amount paid out. The savings to the employee is in the deferral of the tax on the contribution plus the deferral of any tax on the income earned by the contribution until it is paid out. For example, if Greensboro contributed $10,000 to its EBT in 1980 and invested it at 12 percent, the additional $1,200 per year income would be received by the EBT and remain untaxed until paid to one of the employee's children for college. At that time, it would be taxed to the child's parent. If the parent terminated his employment (except for disability or retirement) before the child received any benefits, all the benefits would be lost for that parent's family.

As with every other tax-planning idea, if the idea fits into the family picture, it can be useful. In the case of EBTs, there may be a lot of tailoring necessary and, further, the IRS reaction to the Greensboro holding remains to be seen.

SUMMARY

Unfortunately, it may not be just the IRS we have to worry about. Though the 1984 Tax Reform Act did not outlaw the EBT, it changed the timing of the deduction to the employer. Now amended tax code section 404 provides that contributions to plans such as EBTs will not be deductible to the employer until actually paid to the employee or other beneficiary.

You can employ your child either in your business or in connection with certain income-producing activities and you can take a full tax deduction for the amount paid to the child, *provided* the services are ordinary and necessary to the business or investment, and provided the amount of the payment is reasonable under the circumstances.

Such payments are considered earned income to the child and if the child is legitimately employed, he or she can enjoy the *same* fringe benefits as other employees, including vacation pay, travel expenses, insurance coverage, bonuses, and even retirement benefits. "Retirement" benefits in many cases can be paid to the child when the child leaves the job. In all events, careful records must be kept of the services rendered and the amounts paid in case the deductions are questioned. As with all family transactions, the arrangement will probably be scrutinized very carefully by the IRS.

. . . .

Borrowing from Your Retirement Plan— A Private Tax Shelter

One of the most advantageous tax maneuvers available through a family business is to borrow from your pension and/or profit-sharing plan. This maneuver allows you, in effect, to borrow from "yourself" and pay yourself tax-deductible interest on the loan. There are some limitations, but to the extent permitted, the action is *legal and quite advisable.* And when combined with trust borrowback (discussed in Chapter 7), borrowing from your retirement plan can be used to provide educational funds taxed at the child's bracket. Here is how this works.

When contributions are made to certain retirement plans, a separate "account" is kept for each employee. The money is not usually physically separated into these individual accounts, but it could be, and it is when a particular employee wants his account managed in a particular way or wants to borrow from it. The balance in each account, after adjustments for increases and decreases from investments and contributions, is carefully monitored and reported annually to the employee involved.

Under most plans, the full account does not "belong" to the employee right away—he must work for the company for a period of time before he is entitled to the full value of the account. If he leaves the company before the prescribed period, he will forfeit a portion of his account, and, correspondingly, the longer he stays with the company, the greater the amount of the account that will be "his" and not subject to forfeiture even though he subsequently leaves. In some instances, for example, the amount an employee accrues is 20 percent per year, so that after five years (5 × .20), he is said to be 100 percent "vested" or fully "vested." His *vested* share is the share to which he is entitled (a nonforfeitable amount) regardless of when he leaves the company.

Under present tax laws (for retirement plan loans taken after August 13, 1982), you may borrow up to $10,000 from your retirement plan account (if the account totals at least that amount) *regardless* of how much is vested, but if you borrow more than $10,000 it may not exceed one-half your vested share. In any event, the *maximum* you may borrow is $50,000. These limitations apply to the total plan loans from all plans you have at a given time rather than on a plan-by-plan basis. In other words, if you have two plans and you have borrowed $50,000 from one, you may not borrow from the other.

Here is how the dollar limitations work. If your plan account totals $12,000 and you are only 20 percent vested, you may nevertheless borrow $10,000, as this amount applies regardless of vesting. If your plan account totals $40,000 and you are 40 percent vested, the $10,000 limit will still be better for you, since one-half your vested amount would only be $8,000 ($40,000 × 40% × $^1/_2$). If your plan account is $100,000 or more and you are 100 percent vested, you may borrow the maximum of $50,000.

There is also a time limit on the loan. Unless you or a family member use the money for the purchase or substantial improvement of a home, the loan *must* be paid back within five years.

The penalty for borrowing more than the allowable limits or holding the funds for more than five years is that the excess (or the whole amount if the five-year limit is exceeded) is treated as a *taxable distribution* from the plan. In other words, if you should have borrowed only $10,000 but instead borrowed $15,000, the extra $5,000 is taxed to you as a taxable plan distribution rather than a loan. If you borrow $50,000 for three years, then extend the loan for another three years for a total loan period of six years, you will be *taxed* on the entire $50,000 at the time of the extension (*not* after the five year run out). Similarly, if you borrow for three years but simply don't pay until shortly after the fifth year, you will be taxed as of the last day of the fifth year.

Once you borrow the money, you should sign a promissory note for the borrowed amount and the note should provide for a relatively high rate of interest since all the interest you pay is *deductible to you and simply goes into your own plan account*. In effect, *you are paying yourself deductible interest*. You will also be required to "pledge" the balance of your account as security for the payment of the note. There are no rigid rules regarding interest on the loan: you may fix the interest rate at a point or two over the prime rate, or it may fluctuate with the prime or some other interest rate standard over the five-year period. There seem to be no limitations on how high an interest rate you could pay, but if it is too high, the IRS could disallow the deduction for the excess over a reasonable rate.

The money you borrow from your plan may be contributed to a Clifford trust for the benefit of your child. Shortly thereafter you may borrow it back from the trust and invest the funds on your own. (See the rules on a "borrowback" in Chapter 6—they must be followed carefully.) In effect, you then owe interest to your plan account (for the money you borrowed from it) and you owe interest to the child's Clifford trust (for the money you borrowed from that). If done properly, both interest payments will be tax-deductible, one going to *your own* plan account, the other for *your child's education*. I call this my Doublemint gum plan—("double your pleasure, double your fun"). At the end of five years you must be prepared to repay your plan account loan, but as soon as you do, you can reborrow it for another five years. While you have use of the funds, you can invest in just about anything *except* tax-exempt bonds, as this could jeopardize your interest deductions. At the end of ten years you must repay the loan to the child's trust, but the trust will then terminate and return the funds to you. At that point you must again repay the loan from your plan account (i.e., this is the second five-year period). If you wish, you could reborrow the retirement funds once again, if you don't have a headache by that time.

This plan is illustrated in the following diagram:

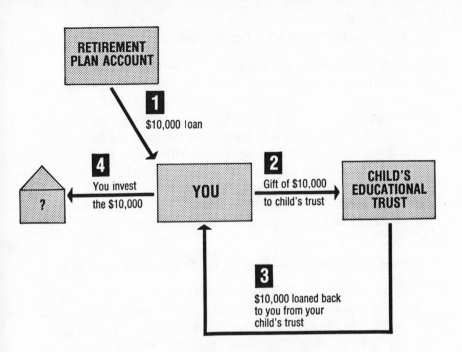

Result of: **1** You owe $10,000 to the Retirement Plan and the interest you pay on that loan is tax-deductible.

3 You owe $10,000 to the Child's Educational Trust and the interest you pay on that loan is tax-deductible.

You should note that not every retirement plan allows for borrowing. Some are restricted by their own terms while others are restricted by IRS regulations. Whether you may borrow from your particular plan can be easily determined by your professional advisor. If the plan does not allow borrowing, in many instances a simple amendment can add such a provision.

. . . .

Gifts and Other Transfers of Business Interests

In some cases, it is not convenient or appropriate to borrow from your retirement plan or to employ your child. Perhaps the child's income from family employment is not enough, or you simply want to take every conceivable opportunity to shift as much income to the child as possible through the family business. If any or all of these is the case, there are some additional ways that transferring shares of a family business can shift income. They include the family partnership, a corporation taxed as a partnership, and a recapitalization of your existing corporation. In all of these situations, income is shifted to the child through his *ownership* in the family business and would be *in addition to* any other income or compensation you might be able to pay him for services rendered to your business (or professional practice).

Family Partnerships—Sharing the Profits (and the Taxes)

If the family business is not incorporated, income may be shifted to lower-bracket children or trusts through the use of a family partnership. This is an arrangement where other members of the family (even *minors*) are made "partners" in your business and so are entitled to (and taxed on) a share of the business income. It's almost (but, of course, not quite) that simple.

A partnership itself does not pay a tax: the *partners* of the partnership are taxed on their individual shares of the partnership income. If the partners' shares (as established by the partnership agreement) bear a reasonable relationship to the corresponding investments made and services rendered by each partner (the IRS calls this "economic reality"), then the tax code allows each partner's share of the income (and losses) to be passed through to the respective partners proportionately. Each partner will then pay a tax on his share, along with income or losses he has from all other sources. In other words, a 22 percent partner will be taxed on 22 percent of the partnership's taxable income, and will likewise be entitled to deduct, on his personal tax return, 22 percent of the partnership's losses. Of course, there are some special rules that must be applied.

One of these "special" rules deals with income from services. As a general rule, you cannot create a family partnership where the partnership income is largely due to the *services* of the parent, or for that matter, whenever the partnership income is primarily attributable to the services of other partners. This is where the "economic reality" test of the IRS precludes dividing income among those who never rendered services unless there is some other sound "economic" basis for the division. For example, a physician or dentist cannot simply give a share of the income from his practice to a child merely because he has legally declared the child a partner or even if the child made a cash "investment" in the practice, since neither the child's services nor his investments gave rise to the income. The IRS (and the courts) regard this as an "assignment of income" (see Chapter 1) and the income would be taxed to the person who earned it, even though it may be paid to someone else. It is quite possible, however, to legally shift taxable income where "capital" (investment), as opposed to services, is a "material income-producing factor" (the IRS phrase) in the business.

Examples of businesses where capital would be a "material income-producing factor" are a hardware store, a construction company, a grocery store, an automobile dealership, or any other business where the equipment or inventory, rather than the services, plays a substantial part in generating the business income. This does not mean that services must be absent from the business. Rather, it means that the services, particularly the services of the partners, are not the *primary* factor in generating the income. If this is the case, then a portion of the income can be shifted to a child and used for education without the parent's losing control of the business.

Say that you run a small grocery store and net $50,000 per year taxable income. Your child is going to need about $5,000 per year for college but for some reason cannot work in the store. If you simply give your child the $5,000, you would use about $8,000 of your earnings since the gift is not tax-deductible. Therefore, the "cost" to you of the $5,000 college expenses would actually be $8,000 per year in your tax bracket. If instead you create a family partnership to run the store and make your child a 10 percent partner, he will "earn" 10 percent, or $5,000, as a partner and the $5,000 will be taxed directly to him. On that amount he will pay a tax of about $200. In effect, the family partnership will "save" nearly $3,000 in taxes each year, which can be used to pay college expenses.

THE RULES

To create a family partnership that will withstand IRS scrutiny you'll have to follow a number of rules. *First,* there must be a valid and complete transfer of the partnership interest to the child, or to a trust for the child. It does not matter whether the child's share was a gift by the parent or a purchase by the child. Some advisors feels more comfortable if the parent or some other party makes a gift of cash to the child, and the child then uses the cash to "purchase" a partnership interest. The IRS regulations clearly state that a *gift* of a partnership interest is perfectly acceptable, as long as the share of income distributed to each partner (including the child) is based on the share of capital owned by each partner *after* the partnership has made payment for services as discussed below. Whether the child's share is a gift or a purchase, all the other criteria must be met as well.

Second, as emphasized above, capital, rather than services, must be a "material income-producing factor" in the business. It is difficult to say exactly what constitutes a "material factor" since every case is different, but your advisor should be able to help decide in your particular case. Here is what the tax regulations themselves state on that question: "In general, capital is *not* a material income-producing factor where the income of the business consists principally of fees, commissions or other compensation for personal services performed by members or employees of the partnership. On the other hand, capital *is* a material income-producing factor if the operation of the business requires substantial inventories or a substantial investment in plant, machinery or other equipment."

Third, relative to the capital versus services test, it is clear that a business, although dependent on capital, cannot run on capital alone. Some services must be rendered. In this regard, the rules require that the share of the family partners bear a relation not only to the capital, but also the particular services rendered. In the grocery store example above, the parent would be required to first reduce the partnership distribution by the fair value of the parent's services in running the store. For example, if the profits were $70,000 and it would be fair to allocate a salary of $20,000 to the parent for running the store, then the balance of $50,000 would be attributable to partnership *capital* and would be distributed among the partners in accordance with their proportionate shares, so that a 10 percent partner would receive 10 percent of the $50,000 partnership profit, and so on.

In addition to the above requirements, the tax laws require that the partnership be real and that the child (or the trust) be the true owner of the partnership interest. *It does not matter that the arrangement was created purely to save taxes.* What matters is that it is a bona fide partnership and that a bona fide transfer to the child (or the trust) has been made. Normally, this would mean a written partnership agreement; records kept as a partnership would keep; filing with city or state agencies if required; filing a partnership tax return, etc. Here is a case that illustrates how *not* to do it.

Roy Acuff, a well-known country-and-western singer from Tennessee, and his wife, Mildred, created a trust for the benefit of their 9-year-old son. They then transferred a share of a music-publishing business to the trust and entered into a partnership agreement with the trust. So far so good; unfortunately, that's as far as they went. On IRS investigation of the facts, it turned out that they had kept no records for the partnership, no separate books of account or bank accounts, and there was no evidence of any business actually done by the new partnership. In fact, they continued to carry on business in the same way as before the partnership.

The U.S. Tax Court held that there was no partnership for tax purposes, that the trustee of the trust never became a bona fide partner, and that Roy and Mildred should be taxed on *all* the income from the business.

The requirement that the child (or the trust) be the true owner of the partnership interest does not mean that the parent cannot retain control of the business. It merely means that the child's share must have all the same rights attached to it as would an independent partner's share. For one, the child's share would be entitled to a proportionate share of the partnership income, and this may not be subject to the discretion of the parent. For another, the child (or the trustee of the trust) as a partner would have the right to an accounting from the partnership (financial reports) and the right to withdraw from (leave) the partnership without financial detriment, or the right to sell or transfer the partnership share, either back to the partnership or to a third party, depending on the agreement.

Most of these requirements will not pose a problem to the average family business and will not interfere with the ability of the "managing partner" to continue to manage and control the business, but they must nevertheless be met.

MINORS AS PARTNERS

Adult children as partners are usually not a problem since they are legally capable of acting on their own; minor children are another story. Although it has been held that a minor who is sufficiently mature to be capable of certain business dealings may be a partner, to be on the safe side, and in those cases where the minor is not capable of any dealings for himself, it is wise to have a "fiduciary" to act on behalf of the minor. The term fiduciary would include a *custodian* under the Uniform Gifts to Minors Act (if such an investment were allowed under that state's law), or a *guardian*, or a *trustee* under a trust for the minor's benefit. Normally, a trust is best.

A TRUST AS A PARTNER

Both the IRS and the courts have recognized that trusts (particularly trusts for minors) can be valid partners in a family partnership, *provided* the trustee truly represents and protects the interest of the beneficiaries. For this reason, although it is not an absolute requirement, it is best to have an independent party as trustee of the trust. If the trustee is not independent—that is, if he or she is the parent or is subservient or subordinate to the parent—then the arrangement will be more carefully scrutinized by the IRS to determine whether the minor's interests are being fairly represented. For example, if there are any funds left in the business after its reasonable needs are met, the trustee should see that such excess funds are distributed, so that the trust's share of partnership income may be used for the beneficiaries.

The types of trusts that can be partners include any of those previously discussed *except* the Clifford (ten-year) trust. Although there is at least one court case supporting the use of a Clifford trust as a partner, the IRS has taken the firm position that it will *not* recognize a Clifford trust as a partner for tax purposes. This is because the parents' reversionary interest in the trust makes the partnership interest "temporary," which does not satisfy the requirements in the tax regulations. Therefore, you may want to use a different type of trust, such as a minor's trust or an independent irrevocable trust (both covered in Chapter 6), but remember that for family partnership purposes, it is best to have an independent trustee. Once the transfer of the partnership is made to the trust, the *trust* (through the trustee) becomes a partner, not the child.

HOW TO DO IT
Once you have decided to use the family partnership to shift income, the first thing you must do is transfer a portion of the assets of your business to the child or to a trust for the child. For purposes of this explanation, let's say you choose a trust. The transfer may be by gift or by sale to the trust, but in either event, the fair value of the property transferred must be established so that any required reports (gift or income tax returns) may be made. If the assets are part of a going business, you may have to show a value which reflects not only the assets but also the "good will," if any.

Unless the business arrangement is extremely simple and easy to value, you would be best advised to get an independent appraisal or estimate of value. Your accountant or lawyer could give you an estimate or refer you to someone who can. If you are simply transferring one or more pieces of equipment, perhaps a dealer or manufacturer can tell you what they are presently worth. In any event, the appraisal should be in writing and kept with the rest of your tax records to support the transaction if it is questioned in the future. Once you have a value, you will know roughly what share you can give without running into a gift tax problem, as outlined in Chapter 4.

After a fair value is established, you will transfer the property or equipment or partnership share by a "deed of transfer." This is a legal term for a simple statement that basically says something like this: "For good and valuable consideration, I hereby irrevocably transfer all my right, title, and interest of every nature in and to one Jaguar double-dip ice cream machine, serial no. XJ6, together with a one-fourth undivided interest in all the remaining equipment, furnishings, and inventory situated at 11 Beacon Street, Boston, used in the business known as Bruno's Ice Cream Shop, to Don Corleone, trustee of the Bruno trust, dated 1/2/85, (signed) B. Bruno, (dated) date of transfer.''

If real estate is being transferred by itself, a special deed is required and it should be recorded (together with the trust). However, where real estate is held in a partnership, transfer of a partnership share does *not* require a deed transferring the real estate. That is, the real estate is an asset of the partnership and a transfer of an underlying partnership interest *carries with it* a share of the real estate without the need for a separate deed for the real estate.

If the business property is subject to existing liens or security interests, then approval must be obtained from the secured party (such as a bank holding a mortgage). In any event, it should be clear that you should not transfer property without proper professional assistance.

Once the trust owns the property the trustee will enter into a written partnership agreement with you for the operation of the business, and you and the trustee will each transfer your shares of the business property to the new partnership. As stated above, the agreement should provide that after payment for services (*including your own* if applicable) the net partnership profits will be shared in proportion to ownership, so that if the trust owns 30 percent of the assets it will receive, *after* payment for services, 30 percent of the profits. And learning by the mistakes of others, you will be sure to keep detailed partnership records, file all necessary reports, etc. as required.

If the business is already in the form of a partnership, it may simply be a matter of transferring a partnership interest, rather than partnership property, to the trust, and amending or at least reviewing the partnership agreement to be sure it complies with the family partnership rules. In any event, once the transfer is made, the trustee should act like and be treated as a partner. For example, in one case, a Mr. Hartman was the owner and managing partner of a ceramics-ware business, being operated as a partnership. He created trusts for his minor children, naming his attorney, his wife, and the children's uncle as trustees. He then made gifts of capital interests (partnership shares rather than transfers of machines or equipment) to the children's trust. As trustee, the uncle took an active role in representing the children's shares, kept careful records, and sometimes even influenced Hartman in business decisions. This was exactly what he should have done, and the court held that Hartman's trusts were valid partners and taxable on their shares of the business income.

If your business is incorporated, the process of using a family partnership is more complicated. One approach may involve dissolving the corporation and then running the business in the form of a partnership. In most cases, the question of a liquidation will depend upon whether it will be worth it to liquidate the corporation, or to "spin off" a part of the business and operate that separate part as a partnership. These are clearly complicated considerations. An easier possibility where a corporation is involved is to take advantage of a certain tax election (subchapter S) that allows you to keep the corporate form while being taxed like a partnership, as discussed below. In any event, expert advice will be especially necessary in these cases.

USE OF THE FUNDS

As the funds are paid out of the partnership to the child's trust, the trustee's use of the funds is directed by the terms of the trust. If the beneficiary is a minor, you should remember the discussion in Chapter 3 about using the funds to satisfy your obligations of support, because if any of the funds are used for that purpose, they will be taxed to you, even after all the trouble you went to in creating this elaborate partnership arrangement.

If your objective is to provide for the child's education with the cheapest dollars, your trust will accumulate and/or distribute the funds accordingly, and when the child is over 18 (the age of majority in most states), the funds may be applied from the trust, tax-free, to cover college costs. They may, of course, be paid out before that, but be sure to be careful that the funds are not used to pay educational expenses on which *you* have assumed personal liability.

SUMMARY

Since it generally does not directly involve a gift of money or the loss of investments by the parent, a transfer of interest in a family partnership is a convenient, relatively painless, but extremely effective way of shifting income and saving taxes.

Through the family partnership, income can be shifted from a family business in shares, which can be decided by the parent upon the formation of the partnership or the transfer of the shares. The IRS and the tax regulations contain relatively clear rules which, if followed, will result in a definite shifting of income from the parent to the child. Such income can later be used to provide for college expenses without further tax.

Another advantage is that the partnership interest may simply be gifted to the child or to a trust for the child, and the income-shifting benefits will still be realized. The parent can retain effective conrol over the management of the business, but the child or the trust must have control over its particular partnership share.

Corporations Taxed as Partnerships

If your business is already incorporated or for some other reasons you wish to do business in corporate form, it may still be possible to shift some of the business income to your children without losing control of the business, by making a special election to have your corporation taxed like a partnership. This is called a "subchapter S election," referring to a particular subchapter of the Internal Revenue Code.

Briefly, when a corporation elects to be treated as a subchapter S corporation, all the income after appropriate payment for services (the same requirement as with a family partnership) is taxed *not* to the corporation but to the shareholders in proportion to the number of shares owned by each, somewhat like a partnership. Therefore, if a corporation has $40,000 of profits left to distribute (after payment for services) and 20 percent of the shares are owned by a child, the child can receive and be taxed on 20 percent of the $40,000, or $8,000. Similarly, if the corporation has a

$20,000 capital gain, the child will be taxed on a capital gain of $4,000, since taxable income to shareholders retains generally the same character as that realized by the subchapter S corporation.

The subchapter S election must be made by the corporation during certain specified periods based on the beginning of its taxable year, and it must meet certain requirements to be eligible for the election. For example, the corporation cannot have more than thirty-five shareholders nor more than one class of stock. Until recently, a *trust* could not be a shareholder of a subchapter S corporation, a fact which seriously hampered the use of subchapter S corporations for funding educational costs. Now, however, certain trusts *may* be shareholders, as described below, and these trusts may be used to shift income *without placing the stock in the hands of a minor*. In terms of shifting income through a subchapter S corporation for the benefit of a minor child, a trust is just one alternative. You may also use a court-appointed guardian (which is seldom recommended) to hold the stock, or for simplicity you may wish to use a custodian under the Uniform Gifts to Minors Act. The potential problem with these alternatives is that in both cases the child will be entitled to take ownership of the shares at the age of majority, which is 18 in most states.

Nevertheless, income can be shifted by a gift of shares in a subchapter S corporation, but such gifts are always subject to careful scrutiny by the IRS. One of the first things they look at is the corporation's distribution of profits. You must *first* pay a fair salary for the services you (or others) render to the business, after which the excess "profits" may be shared according to ownership. Next, there is the question of the value of the stock you gave to your child or to his or her trust. Family businesses are always difficult to value for gift tax purposes, and the IRS will seldom accept an arbitrary approach, such as simple "book value" (i.e., total assets as valued on the "books," minus total liabilities). If the valuation is critical, you may ask your accountant, attorney, or banker to value the company. Finally, the whole transaction must be kept on an arm's-length (i.e., objectively fair) basis. If you organize the trust arrangement too casually, you could lose the right to shift the income and it will be taxed to you—the case of Henry Duarte is a good example of this.

Henry owned a profitable company and wanted to use some of the income to pay for his sons' college education. To do this on a tax-favored basis, Henry gave shares representing 25 percent of the corporation to each of two sons. Since both boys were minors, Henry registered the stock in his wife's name as custodian for each boy under the New York UGMA, and filed the appropriate gift tax returns. Henry then made the election to have his corporation qualify under subchapter S and be taxed like a partnership.

For the next three years the corporate tax returns showed a total of about $46,000 of distribution of profits paid to the two boys, and Henry filed tax returns for the boys reporting the income. But when the IRS asked where the money went, Henry could not respond. There were *no* actual records of payment to the boys, *no* custodial accounts established, and *no* bank accounts for the boys. In fact, neither the boys nor the custodian had ever received the distributions. The IRS and the tax court disallowed the shifting of income to the boys and taxed the whole amount to Henry since the transfers of stock were a "sham." Henry kept control and enjoyment of the funds and the whole arrangement lacked "economic reality." If you transfer subchapter S stock to a child, you should be careful to keep the necessary records and take all the necessary steps to show that the child is the real owner of the stock and enjoys all the benefits that any other stockholder would have. In other words, details, formal compliance with the law, and bona fide transfers are critical to the shifting of income.

ELIGIBILITY

To qualify for the subchapter S election, the corporation may have only one class of stock, which is usually common stock, although there may be different voting arrangements within a class. Even the stockholders must meet certain requirements (you can't be a nonresident alien, for example), and so the details of the election should be reviewed with your tax advisor. Another critical factor is that for the most part, subchapter S corporations must be "operating" corporations. An operating corporation is one performing a service or producing or selling a product. A company that derives its income solely from investments, for example, is not considered an operating corporation; its income is said to be "passive." If too much of the income (more than 25 percent) is "passive" income, then the corporation will not be eligible to make the subchapter S election. So you can't use the election if a substantial part of the corporation's total income is from things like rents, royalties, interest, or dividends, which are considered passive income.

Just because you have an operating corporation, however, doesn't mean you are "home free." The corporation must be legitimate and not a "sham" set up for the purpose of subchapter S, as a group of orthopedic surgeons from Alabama found out in a 1983 Tax Court decision. Drs. Horn, Hornsby, and Beck have a successful orthopedic practice in Huntsville, and in addition to surgery and medical consultations, their practice generated considerable income from related X-ray services. In an effort to find a way to set aside some of this income for their children's education, the doctors were advised to set up a separate corporation that would perform all the X-ray services for their professional corporation. The new separate corporation, they were told, could be a subchapter S corporation owned by their children, and all the net income from the X-ray services would be taxed to the children.

The new corporation was established, and purchased the X-ray equipment from the doctors' corporation with funds borrowed from the doctors' profit-sharing plan. The children's corporation took X-rays of the doctors' patients and received a percentage of the amount billed by the doctors' corporation. The X-ray corporation operated out of the doctors' offices, but paid no rent or costs other than X-ray technicians' wages. Over a three-year period the children received more than $50,000 of income from their corporation.

The IRS attacked the transaction as a sham and attempted to tax the doctors *directly* on all the income, not as salary, but as *dividends* from their professional corporation. (Dividends are not deductible to the corporation—as salary would be—and during the years in question, they were exposed to a tax of up to 70 percent to the doctors.) The Tax Court agreed with the IRS and held that the corporation was a sham, that it had no business purpose, and that the income received by the children should be taxed to the doctors as constructive dividends from their professional corporation. Here are some of the reasons the court gave for their finding (and these are good guidelines of how *not* to do it):

1. The new corporation did not hold itself out to third parties as a separate business, and did not obtain credit from a bank (it borrowed the funds from the doctors' profit-sharing plan);
2. It did not pay for its own rent, utilities, and other overhead;
3. It did not pay for its insurance coverage for liability arising from the X-ray services (it was covered by the doctors' insurance);
4. It did not maintain its own patient logs or records;
5. It did not notify the doctors' patients that the X-ray service was performed by a separate business;
6. It did not obtain a license in its own name for operating the X-ray equipment;
7. It used all the facilities of the doctors for its entire operation;
8. It did not advertise or list its services in the phone book (or other directory).

Although this was a harsh decision for the doctors, it seems apparent that had they gone somewhat further and attended to a few more details, the Tax Court could very well have found in their favor. The moral? *Uncompromising attention to details and the law are vital to the success of intra-family transactions, particularly those involving the use of separate subchapter S corporations.*

SUBCHAPTER S TRUSTS
Under a 1982 change in the tax law, stock of a subchapter S corporation can now be held in a trust for the benefit of a child, provided the trust meets certain requirements. The primary advantage of using a *trust* as opposed to a custodial or guardianship arrangement is that control of the stock can be held beyond the child's age of majority while the income from the distributions will still be taxed to him or her in a lower tax bracket.

The subchapter S law states that a trust will be a permissible shareholder if, among other things, the trust is one which will be treated as a grantor trust *with respect to the beneficiary.* A grantor trust in this case is one in which the child (even though a minor) is given the right to withdraw all the annual income, or which directs that all the income be paid annually to the child. In addition, *each trust must be for only one child.* If you want other children to benefit at the same time, you must have a separate trust to hold the subchapter S stock for each child.

The trust need not terminate at the age of majority, or at any age, for that matter. Although it could last for the child's lifetime, as a practical matter you would probably want it to terminate sometime after the child completes his education. If the trust *is* designed to last for a specific period, such as "until the child reaches age 25" or some other period tied to his education, then at that time *both the stock and any income* that has not previously been distributed must be paid to the child. Under this type of trust for subchapter S stock, *the only time the stock can be given to someone other than the child is in the event of the child's death,* so if stock ownership is important to you during the child's lifetime, then the trust could be designed to transfer the stock back to you or to someone else at a fair price. Thus under present law, a Clifford trust (a ten-year trust) as discussed in Chapter 6, should *not* be used to hold subchapter S stock.

Any distributions during the life of the child must be made to the child or to the child's legal representative (i.e., a guardian or custodian). If the trust terminates during the life of the child, both the stock and any remaining income must be distributed to him or her, as stated above. It is very important to note that in all other respects, the subchapter S trust should not violate any of the Clifford trust rules discussed in Chapter 6, as we do not want the income taxed to the parent.

Another important requirement where a trust is holding subchapter S stock is that the *beneficiary* must consent to the subchapter S election after or when it is filed by the other shareholders, including the trustee of the child's trust. If the beneficiary is a minor, the consent form would have to be signed by the parent, custodian, or guardian. A slip-up here could be disastrous, as it could cause you to fail to qualify for the subchapter S election. If this happens, *all* of the corporation's income—not just that of the child—would be taxed to the corporation instead of the shareholders, so attention to detail is critical.

Here are some examples of how the subchapter S trust might work. Judy transfers 15 percent of the stock in her subchapter S corporation to a trust for the benefit of her 8-year-old daughter, Alyssa, and the appropriate tax election is made. The trust provides that all the income is to be paid each year to Alyssa and that it will terminate when Alyssa reaches the age of 25. If Alyssa should die before that, the stock will revert to Judy; otherwise, both the stock and any remaining income will be turned over to Alyssa at age 25. After the transfer to the trust, the corporation has annual profits of $20,000, and 15 percent, or $3,000, is paid each year to the trust. The trustee of the trust then places the $3,000 in a separate account to invest in Alyssa's name or, in the more desirable alternative, the trustee pays the funds to Judy's husband, Richie, as custodian for Alyssa. As custodian, Richie may accumulate and invest the funds for Alyssa until she reaches the age of majority. In ten years when Alyssa begins college, the $3,000 annual distributions will have grown to about $52,000, assuming a 10 percent interest rate on the funds (and assuming a constant tax rate). All or part of these funds may be used (*without* further tax on the distribution) for Alyssa's education, but as pointed out in Chapter 3, none of the funds should be used in the meantime for Alyssa's support (i.e., those items which a parent is obliged to provide—food, clothing, health care, etc.) while she is a minor, since that would cause the income to be taxed to Judy.

In another case, Catherine transfers twenty shares of her subchapter S stock to a trust for her 17-year-old son, Christopher, and an additional fifteen shares to a separate trust for her 9-year-old daughter, Gina. Because Christopher is presently able to use the funds for education, his trust provides that all the annual income is to be paid to him, but Gina's trust provides that all the income shall be paid to her "upon her request." It so happens that she makes no such request until age 19, when she enters her first year of college. During the ten-year period, all the annual income will be taxed to Gina, since she had the "right" to take it, but until withdrawn the trustee may hold and invest it for her. Of course, she could request all or part of the accumulated amount at any time under the terms of the trust, but it is unlikely she would do so, since it would be against the wishes and instructions of her parents. The practical advantage is that the funds may be held and invested for her benefit by the trustee until they are withdrawn.

While the stock is in the trust, the trustee of the subchapter S trust will vote the stock. This should not be a problem since the trustee would normally be a "friendly" trustee (though it should not be a "subservient" one) and would in most cases have only a minority interest. If the trust provides for final distribution to your child at a certain age, then he or she will own the stock and have the vote at that time, and you should be prepared to deal with this. One way to do so is to have a "buy back" agreement, allowing you or the corporation to buy back the child's stock. However, there are some tricky tax rules governing this, so it should only be done with expert advice.

SUMMARY

It is possible for certain corporations to qualify for special tax treatment by making what is called a "subchapter S election." This election will result in the net profits of the corporation being taxed only once, at the shareholder level, in proportion to the number or percentage of shares owned by each shareholder, much like what happens in a partnership. In utilizing this election to shift income, a parent/owner could make a gift of shares of a subchapter S corporation to a child, or to a custodian for a child, or to a special trust for the benefit of the child. In each of these cases, the child would be taxed on the gifted share of the profits from the business. The election is somewhat complicated and the qualifications must be satisfied at all times, not just when the election is made, so constant awareness of the requirements and attention to detail is necessary. Nevertheless, if the family business is already incorporated and the corporation can meet the subchapter S requirements, it is an effective and "approved" way of shifting income for college education.

Recapitalization
(Gifts of Dividend-Paying Stock)

Some corporations cannot or simply should not, for various tax and legal reasons, make the subchapter S election. In these cases, an alternative way to shift income to a child is the use of a "recapitalization.'' The "capital" of a corporation consists of the investments and assets contributed to it. The capital structure is generally referred to in terms of the various designations of ownership and control, and the most popular is that in which the ownership of the entire corporation is in the form of common stock. If we change this for any reason, such as issuing another type of security (preferred stock or bonds), we are changing or reorganizing the capital structure, which is more commonly referred to as a reorganization, or a *"recapitalization."* So, if in the context of tax- or estate-planning you hear the term recapitalization, it usually means the type of stock presently outstanding is being restructured to accomplish some tax or legal purpose. One method of recapitalization often used for tax purposes involves the issuance of dividend-paying, nonvoting *preferred* stock.

It might work this way: Dad owns one hundred shares (which is 100 percent) of the common stock of Money, Inc. His son, Genius, is too young to be employed in the company and Dad does not want to make a subchapter S election (as explained above), because Money, Inc. does not want to have all its profits taxed to the shareholders, and Dad does not want to take in any more income personally. He decides to recapitalize the company so that Money, Inc. issues Dad an additional one hundred shares of stock. (Dad can do this since he owns all of the stock already and simply having more shares will not change that; i.e., he can't own more than 100 percent.) The new stock, however, is nonvoting "preferred" stock paying dividends of $25 per share.*

Dad then makes a gift of the one hundred shares of nonvoting preferred stock to an irrevocable trust for the benefit of Genius. Each year, Money, Inc. pays a dividend of $25 per share on the preferred stock, so that Genius' trust receives $2,500 each year, taxed to the trust or to Genius if paid out. Since the stock is nonvoting, Dad does not have to worry about losing control of the

---

*"Preferred" stock is so called because it gets preference in payment of dividends and in payment of its share of ownership before common stock in the event the business is liquidated. It usually has a stated par value, such as $100 per share, which will be paid if the corporation redeems it—buys it back—or if the corporation is liquidated.

company, or even having to deal with a minority vote. That's the good news.

The bad news is that the corporation does not get a tax deduction for the dividends paid on the preferred stock, and if Genius or the trust sells the stock, chances are the proceeds will be taxed as ordinary income rather than capital gains. These are just two of the many complicated tax and legal considerations when dealing with recapitalizations. Another involves valuation of the stock for gift tax purposes. When Dad gave the stock to Genius's trust, he made a gift, which must be valued for gift tax purposes. Valuation of stock in a closely held business is difficult, at best, and the IRS seldom agrees with the taxpayer's value. In the typical recapitalization where large gifts are to be made, the business owners will often get an outside professional appraisal of the value of the business.

Because of the nondeductibility of dividend payments and the legal and tax complexities associated with a recapitalization, it is not as popularly used to shift income as the other methods described here, although in addition to its limited income tax benefits, it can result in substantial estate tax benefits since the amount of stock owned by the children will reduce the value of the business left in the parents' estates. For instance, in the above example, Dad gave away the one hundred shares of preferred stock and his estate will be reduced by some or all of the value of that stock since he would not own it at the time of his death.

. . . .

Paying Tax-Deductible Rent to Your Child

If you have any real estate or any type of personal property (equipment, machinery, automobile, etc.) that you use in your business or profession, you may be able to transfer that property to a trust for your child and pay rent for its use. The rental payments will be fully deductible to you and, of course, become income to your child, but at his lower tax bracket you can quickly accumulate funds for education. There are two basic ways to accomplish this transfer and rental agreement. One is called a "gift and leaseback" and the other, a "sale and leaseback," although as you will see, applications of the latter are very limited. In both cases, strict rules must be followed if you want to qualify for the deductions, and the property involved must be property the use of which is *clearly* connected to a business, professional, or legitimate investment activity. Renting a personal residence from a child, for example, is of no real help since you get no deductions for rent paid on your personal residence. Similarly, renting your automobile from a child is of no benefit unless the automobile is used in connection with some business activity.

There are no restrictions on the type of property that may be leased from a child as long as its use gives rise to a tax deduction. In addition to the traditional leaseback of office or professional buildings and medical or dental equipment, it has been suggested that a leaseback can also be used for such items as furnishings and other office accoutrements, libraries and professional reference books, copyrights, patents, and office equipment, such as copy machines, typewriters, and computers, keeping in mind, of course, that as with all family transactions, it will no doubt be looked at carefully by the IRS.

Whatever the property, and whether the transfer is made by a gift or by a sale, the subsequent arrangement is the same (although greater tax savings will result from the gift and leaseback arrangement as you will see). Basically, once the child's trust has the property, it will enter into a written agreement with you for the use of the property for some period of time at an agreed rental. The rent payments to the trust are deductible to you and income to the trust.

In almost every case, *it is best to use a trust* as the lessor rather than the child, and therefore, the entire discussion that follows on gift and leaseback as well as sale and leaseback will refer to the child's trust rather than to the child individually. The types of trusts that may be used for a leaseback fall into two basic categories (both discussed in Chapter 6): the reversionary or Clifford trust, which lasts for ten years, after which the property returns to the parent/creator or to someone designated by him; and the independent (Crummey) trust, which can last for any predetermined amount of time, after which the property is distributed to the child or to someone other than the grantor. Both are *irrevocable* trusts, and you will see that in both cases, the leaseback trusts *must have an independent trustee*, so even though you may already have a Clifford trust or an independent trust, it will not be usable if it does not meet the requirements of these cases. If it does not, it may be worth it to create a new one, since the tax savings can be substantial.

Here's how the arrangement can save literally thousands in taxes and generate tax deductions where none previously existed. Malcolm owns a successful magazine publishing company and his earnings keep him well into the 50 percent tax bracket. One of the assets of his company is a printing press, currently worth about $60,000. Despite its value, however, the press has been fully depreciated by Malcolm, so it no longer gives him any tax benefit. As part of a plan to create new tax deductions and generate funds for the education of his grandchildren, Malcolm makes a gift of the printing press to a trust for the benefit of his three grandchildren. Since Malcolm's wife consents to the gift, there is no gift tax due on the $60,000 gift, nor any loss of their gift tax credit (three grandchildren × $10,000 each × two donors, Malcolm and his wife, = $60,000; see Chapter 4). After the gift to the trust, the next step in Malcolm's plan is to have the trust lease (rent) the press back to Malcolm's company. It is agreed by the company and the trustee of Malcolm's trust that a fair rent would be $2,500 per month ($30,000 per year) for the use of the press.

On paying the rent of $30,000 per year, Malcolm's after-tax cost (in the 50 percent bracket) is $15,000. If the full amount of the $30,000 rent is taxed to the grandchildren, they will pay a total federal income tax of about $3,500, which leaves $26,500 *after taxes* to use for their education. If Malcolm had to give them the same amount of nondeductible dollars for education, he would have had to earn $53,000 ($26,500 × 2). In effect, it only *cost* him $15,000 out of pocket to give his grandchildren $26,500 after taxes. The next two sections explain exactly how this sort of arrangement is done.

Gift and Leaseback

The gift and leaseback is the easier of the two leaseback arrangements in terms of transfer of the property, and, as will be seen, it is the more desirable since all it requires is a gift of the property by the owner to the trust. The property must be fairly valued at the time of the transfer, and a gift tax return must be filed. Frequently the property selected is used property, and therefore not susceptible to as high a value for gift tax purposes as new property would be.

As noted in the discussion on gift taxes in Chapter 4, the value for *gift tax* purposes will be the fair value of the property on the date of the gift. However, the value or tax cost to the trust for *income tax* purposes will be the basis, or tax cost of the property in the hands of the donor, increased by gift taxes actually paid. This is a very important point, since it has a bearing on the amount of taxable income realized by the trust.

For example, say that Dr. Pullemout has some dental equipment that he bought several years ago for $10,000. He has been depreciating it each year and now the remaining "cost" on his books is $2,000. His dental-equipment salesman tells him the fair value of the equipment is about $3,500. Dr. Pullemout creates a trust and transfers the equipment to the trust to provide for his children's education. On making the transfer, Dr. Pullemout has made a *gift* of $3,500, the fair value of the equipment. The trust, however, takes the equipment with a "cost basis" of $2,000, the same basis that Dr. Pullemout had when he made the gift. This means that once the equipment is leased back to Dr. Pullemout, the trust must use $2,000 as its base for depreciation or subsequent sale, or for any other income tax purposes.

Sometimes the equipment is purchased new by the trust, for example, where the trust is set up to purchase equipment which is to be used by the parent. Since a bank would probably not make an unsecured loan to a "poor" trust (one without substantial assets), the loan for the purchase price of the equipment is usually guaranteed by the parent. This is a loose form of gift and leaseback and (like the sale and leaseback) not quite as effective because of the lower cash flow to the trust. The lower cash flow is due to the fact that the trust must pay off the loan from the bank (used to purchase the equipment in the first place) and therefore some or all of the lease payments received by the trust will have to be paid to the bank to pay off the loan.

If new equipment must be bought, the "numbers" should be carefully worked out both ways (with and without the leaseback) since it could be that with tax credits and high depreciation allowances the parent/owner would be better off owning the new equipment rather than leasing it from the trust.

In most cases, then, the gift and leaseback lends itself best to transfer of *existing, low-basis equipment or property*. In fact, where the property has been fully depreciated or nearly so, it can actually create a deduction where previously there was *none*. For example, say that Dr. Cuttemup has medical equipment that has been depreciated to zero. Since he is no longer getting any tax benefit in using this equipment in his practice, he creates an independent trust for his children, making a gift of the medical equipment to the trust. The trustee then negotiates a lease for the equipment with the doctor at a rental of $1,000 per month, which is agreed to be reasonable. Dr. Cuttemup now gets the benefit of a tax deduction of $1,000 per month, whereas just prior to the leaseback arrangement he had *none*.

Usually, the gift to the trust can be structured so as to avoid paying a gift tax or using part of your gift tax credit. If a Clifford trust is used, the value of the gift, as explained in Chapter 6, will be about 62 percent of the value of the property when the transfer is made. You should note that although the courts have approved the use of a Clifford trust in a gift and leaseback situation, the IRS is reluctant to agree and may question it if you keep a reversionary interest. To get around this potential problem, you could simply have the interest in the equipment or other property revert to your spouse or children instead of to you.

Once the transfer of the property/equipment is made to the trust, the parent/owner should enter into negotiations with the trustee for rental of the property from the trust. The amount of the rental payments must be fair and reasonable in light of the circumstances and the nature, condition, and use of the property. A fair rental where used property (other than real estate) is involved is sometimes difficult to establish. One way is to get an independent appraisal or to determine what dealers are charging for rental of similar property. In the case of real estate, establishing a fair rent is usually much easier since a great many similar comparisons can usually be made to establish the prevailing rates for similar property in the area. *Be sure* to document (keep records of) all appraisals and exactly how you arrived at the rental amount.

In any event, the lease agreement must *not* be prearranged. It must be negotiated with the independent trustee *after* the transfer is made, and it must be in writing. Further, it should contain all the provisions that a truly independent party would normally include, since if it is clearly written in favor of the parent, the IRS could ignore it for tax purposes. For example, the lease should provide for reasonable increases due to things like tax escalation, increased maintenance or insurance costs, cost of living increases, etc., and, if possible, it should not be for a term exceeding the term of the trust. All rent or other payments should be faithfully made according to schedule, and, as always, thorough records should be kept.

Although they may seem to be little more than "window dressing," these details, as well as the others outlined later, are vital to the success of your gift and leaseback. On the matter of terms of the agreement, for example, the IRS and the court must be satisfied that the independent trustee did his best to negotiate the best terms for the beneficiaries. It was this fact, among others, that saved the case for Richard Quinlivan, in one of the landmark gift and leaseback cases.

Quinlivan, an attorney in Saint Cloud, Minnesota, transferred his interest in the building in which he practiced law to a Clifford trust for the benefit of his children, naming a bank as trustee. Immediately after the transfer, the bank negotiated a three-year lease with Quinlivan and his partner for rental of the property. When the IRS tried to disallow the rental deductions, Quinlivan took the case to the Tax Court and the court held that Quinlivan and his partner *were* entitled to the deductions for rent.

In its opinion, the Tax Court noted that the independent trustee had the power and the opportunity to negotiate terms favorable to the beneficiaries rather than to Quinlivan and his partner and that in fact it did so, and the rent was *not* prearranged.

Constant reference has been made in this discussion to an "independent" trustee, another critical requirement of the gift and leaseback. If you do not have an independent trustee, the IRS can show that you still have control over the property, and this will be fatal to the leaseback arrangement. In no event, therefore, should you or your spouse or any other "related or subordinate party" be a trustee of the leaseback trust. *You must have an independent trustee.* (See the discussion of the independent trustee under Clifford Trusts in Chapter 6.) An independent trustee is one who can represent the beneficiaries' interest without being influenced by you, and who has no interest of his own in the trust. In addition to the trustee's independence, his responsibilities and powers should extend beyond the mere collection of rent and distribution to the beneficiaries. He must have adequate powers to deal with the trust property and to negotiate on behalf of the beneficiaries, as noted in the Quinlivan decision.

The leaseback arrangement must also have what the courts call a "bona fide business purpose." In other words, you can't simply lease your living room furniture from your children and get a tax deduction for it. Sometimes the business purpose is not so clear, however, so whenever possible you should state it in writing. For example, if your business needs new office space and you intend to rent from a child's trust, you should recite the fact that your existing space is inadequate and that the president of the company is authorized to negotiate for new space. Self-serving? Yes. Helpful if you are audited? Definitely. For the most part, if the leased property is used in your business, a bona fide business purpose will be suggested by the very fact of the business use. (However, as noted below, some circuit courts have differed on this point so you should check with your advisor as to the opinion in your particular area.)

Finally, you must not retain any "ownership" in the property, at least during the term of the trust. What is meant by ownership (the IRS calls it a "disqualifying equity interest") is not entirely clear, and different courts have interpreted it differently. In some cases, it was held that the mere presence of a reversionary interest (getting the property back in ten years) disallowed the deductions. On the other hand, the Quinlivan case involved a Clifford trust where Quinlivan got back his property after ten years, and this was allowed. If the reversionary interest is a concern to you or your advisor, you may circumvent the problem by having the property revert to your spouse or to your children.

Mortgaged property can present another problem. It seems clear that if there is a *mortgage* or other secured loan on the property and if you are liable on the mortgage, then any payments by the trust which go toward reducing your liability (on the mortgage) will be taxed to you. If there is a mortgage and you are *not* liable but the trust is a Clifford trust which will return the property to you within ten years, again you may be taxed since part of the income of the trust is being used to pay off a mortgage (and thereby increase the net value) of property that will return to you. In general, it is best to avoid using mortgaged property for a gift and leaseback where you retain the right to get the property back after a period of time.

Some advisors' concern with the gift/leaseback is that the courts have not been consistent in their positions. In some areas of the country the courts have been reluctant to allow the deductions on the grounds that there is no real business purpose to the arrangement, while in others the attitude is that as long as the criteria discussed above are met, the arrangement will be upheld. The U.S. Tax Court, on the other hand, has consistently held in favor of the taxpayer where the tests are met. Here is a recap of the four tests applied to the gift and leaseback arrangement:

1. You must not retain substantially the same control—even as a trustee—over the property that you had before you made the gift (hence the requirement for an independent trustee).
2. The agreement to lease the property back to you or your business should be in writing and should provide for a reasonable rent.
3. The leaseback (but not the original gift) must have a bona fide business purpose.
4. You must not retain any ownership in the property (a "dis-

qualifying equity interest''), *at least* during the term of the trust. (It seems that if the leaseback is to a *corporation* as opposed to an individual or a partnership, there is less exposure to this problem.)

These requirements were established by the court cases on gift and leasebacks and not by the IRS. The IRS's attitude in some respects depends upon the part of the country you are in. For the most part it seems that if you rigidly adhere to these requirements, your chances of success are quite good, but remember, the requirements must be met at all times during the term of the trust and leaseback, not just when the trust and leaseback is created. This point is clearly illustrated in the case of Dr. Hobart Lerner.

Dr. Lerner is an ophthalmologist from Rochester, New York. In the early seventies, he incorporated his practice and shortly after that created a Clifford trust for the benefit of his three minor children to help provide funds for their college education. His attorney was named as trustee. Dr. Lerner then made a gift to the trust of all his medical equipment and office furnishings, and subsequently entered into a written agreement with the trustee to lease back the property for use in his practice. The lease provided for rental payments of over $8,000 per year, which was paid by Dr. Lerner and for which he took a full tax deduction. The IRS disallowed the deduction on the basis that the payments were not ''ordinary and necessary'' business expenses of the corporation. In holding for Dr. Lerner, the Tax Court noted that the rent was reasonable and the lease in writing, the trustee was independent (even though a friend of Dr. Lerner), there was a bona fide business purpose for the lease, and Dr. Lerner had no disqualifying ''ownership'' in the property.

The court went on to observe in considering the trustee's independence, that he was given sufficient powers to act for the trust, that he obtained several appraisals to determine the fair rental of the property, that when new property was purchased (by the trust) the rent was appropriately increased, and that, at times, the trustee resisted the purchase of new equipment and resisted Dr. Lerner's requests to borrow funds from the trust.

It was also noted in the Lerner case that the purchase of new equipment by the trust, which would later revert to Dr. Lerner, gave the court some trouble. Unfortunately (for the IRS, fortunately for Dr. Lerner), the IRS did not raise this issue in time, so the court did not rule on it. However, you may take it as a warning *not* to purchase additional property with trust income during the term of the trust if the property will revert to you when the trust terminates. With the potential for huge tax savings offered by the gift and leaseback, it would seem silly not to carefully follow the prescribed requirements to the letter.

TURNING YOUR CAR INTO A TAX SHELTER

Although the more common gift and leaseback arrangement usually involves a professional building, or valuable business (or professional) equipment, it is important to understand that the same principle can apply to just about *any* type of property or equipment used in a business or profession. Such items could range from a vacuum cleaner to a typewriter, and even to a car. In fact, a car used in business can be used very effectively as the subject of a gift and leaseback since its depreciable life is so short, while its rental value can continue to remain relatively high.

For example, due to IRS guidelines, most people depreciate their autos (used in business) over a three-year period. After that brief period the car is fully depreciated and there is no further tax benefit (other than the maintenance and operating expense). If the auto were transferred to a trust, then leased back as described in this chapter, the parent could create a *new* tax deduction in the form of lease payments to a child's trust for the rental of the car. (The maintenance and operating expense for the car will continue to be deductible in any event.)

Here is how it could work. Early in 1982 Dr. Smart paid $12,000 for a new Oldsmobile for her professional use. Over the next three years she deducted $4,000 each year as depreciation on the car ($12,000 ÷ three years). Beginning with 1985, however, her tax benefits of ownership cease, since the car has been fully depreciated. She would like additional tax benefits, but would rather not spend the money on a new car, as she is faced with non-deductible educational costs for her daughter. Instead, Dr. Smart creates an irrevocable trust for her daughter (either a Clifford trust or an independent trust could be used, or even a minor's trust, all discussed in Chapter 6). After creating the trust and naming an independent trustee, Dr. Smart makes a gift of the car to the trust, then negotiates a lease of the car from the trustee. It is agreed that a fair lease payment will be $190 per month, or $2,280 per year, and Dr. Smart will pay all other costs associated with the car— i.e., maintenance, insurance, etc.

If the car is used exclusively for business Dr. Smart may deduct the full lease payments plus all other costs. The lease payments received by the trust may then be used for her daughter's education. In effect, through this gift and leaseback of her fully depreciated car, Dr. Smart has created a $2,280 annual tax deduction for educational expenses, where before there was none.

Sale and Leaseback

Compared with gift and leaseback, the sale and leaseback has somewhat limited application because of the fact that, as the term implies, it involves a *sale* of property, which in turn suggests payments to the seller. If the child's trust is obliged to make payments on the purchase of property from you, it will not only produce potential adverse tax consequences to you (such as a *gain* on the sale to the trust), but it limits the amount that may be accumulated and used to provide for the child's education, since the trustee must use some of the trust income to pay for the property purchased from you.

Like the gift and leaseback, the sale and leaseback is subject to strict rules and scrutiny by the IRS, particularly where family transactions are involved. The biggest risk here is that the IRS will simply say the whole arrangement is a sham, designed for no other purpose than to avoid taxes. The next concern is that there are a number of specific tax laws designed to discourage sales between related parties. One, for example, provides that sales of depreciable property between family members will automatically be treated as ordinary income rather than capital gain. For this reason, the occasions where the sale and leaseback can be beneficial to the family are few.

The problem of exposure to taxable gain on the sale of the property to the trust (which is another reason the gift and leaseback is more desirable, as there is no gain to report) is difficult to deal with. If you sell business property to a family trust at a price in excess of your tax basis (your original cost less tax deductions plus improvements), you will not only have a gain, but it will be an *ordinary income* (i.e., taxed in full) as opposed to a *capital gain* (i.e., usually only 40 percent taxed), since the tax laws provide that you must "recapture" the amount of the tax benefits you previously took on the property. There are, of course, exceptions to this rule, but you should be aware of the problem. For example, if you have an automobile (used in your business) that cost you $8,000 but has been depreciated to $2,000, and you sell the car to a children's trust for $5,000, you will have a $3,000 *ordinary income gain,* fully taxable at your regular tax rates. The effect of this combined with the leaseback is simply to produce taxable income to yourself when you don't want it. For this reason, the sale and leaseback consequences should be carefully considered *before* the transaction. There may be some cases, however, where it may at least *defer* taxes while providing educational benefits to children. Here's one possibility.

Attorney Chargialot has a small professional building that he purchased years ago for $35,000, but is now appraised at $80,000. He sells the building to a trust for his children for $80,000 and the terms of the sale provide that no payments will be made for ten years, at which time principal will be paid in full, and accumulated interest will be paid in annual installments over another ten years. He rents the building for his law practice and pays the trust a fair rental, which he may deduct. The trust uses the accumulated funds to provide for the children's education, and at the end of ten years applies for a mortgage to pay off the $80,000 purchase price. At that time, the rent has increased sufficiently to carry the mortgage and the subsequent interest payments. The problem is that Chargialot will then have to pay a tax on the gain and the interest as he receives it.

But the ending could take other shapes. An alternative would be for Chargialot to *forgive* (as a gift) the $80,000 debt over a period of time. He would *still* report the capital gain, but the trust would not have to come up with the money since the payments were forgiven. Interest could be handled the same way. Still another alternative would be for the trust to sell the property after the ten-year period, pay off the debt and interest, and allow the balance, if any, to go to the children. Once again, however, Chargialot would pay a tax on the gain.

On close inspection, none of these scenarios really offers much appeal over the gift and leaseback of the same property. In the case of the real estate, for example, Chargialot could have accomplished the same objective (providing tax-favored dollars for the children's education) without the complicated procedure of the sale, mortgage, interest, taxable gain, and so on. About the only time the sale and leaseback seems to be desirable is when the owner really wants to sell the property to obtain the funds and possibly realize a higher deduction for rent than he would have had for depreciation, where he doesn't care about the taxable gain, and where the buyer can get some new tax benefits due to the increased cost basis of the property.

SUMMARY

Paying rent to your children through a trust for property you use in your business is an *excellent* way to provide deductible funds for education. It is accomplished through a *gift* of the business property to the trust and a subsequent *leaseback* of the property to your business. Strict and careful procedures must be followed, however, and an independent trustee is a must. A sale and leaseback is also possible, but its disadvantages generally outweigh its advantages.

If you are in business for yourself, whether a sole proprietor, a partner, or a stockholder in a small corporation, chances are you are overlooking ways to fund your child's education with tax-deductible dollars. There are many ways to do this, including employment of the child, making the child a partner, and leasing business property from a trust set up for the child. All of these have survived IRS and court review, so you can use any one or more of them to save substantial tax dollars, *provided* you understand and carefully follow the necessary guidelines.

IMPORTANT REMINDER: Regardless of the plan you use, if any of the child's income, *whether from a trust or any other source*, is used to satisfy a parental obligation, *the income so used will be taxed to the* *parent*, despite the care taken with the rest of the plan. To avoid falling into this trap, be sure to review the discussion of this point in Chapter 3 (pages 26–33).

REFERENCES FOR CHAPTER 8

Employing Your Child
1. IRC, Section 162 (Ordinary and necessary business deductions).
2. *Terrell v. Commissioner*, T.C. Memo 1979-222 (1979) (Texas).
3. RR 59-110 (Wages paid to child are deductible).
4. *Furmanski v. Commissioner*, T.C. Memo 1974-47 (1974) (California) (Importance of records when employing child).
5. IRS Letter Ruling 8248019, August 26, 1982.
6. IRC, Section 212 (Expenses to produce income are deductible—including wages).
7. *Tschupp v. Commissioner*, T.C. Memo 1963-98 (1963) (New York) (Employment of child—importance of records).
8. IRC, Section 63 (Taxable income defined).
9. IRC, Section 402(e) (Distributions from pension plans).
10. RR 75-448, 1975-2 CB 55 (Educational benefit trust—old rule).
11. Greensboro Pathology Assoc., P.A., 83-1 USTC Par. 9112, rev,g C&CIs, 82-1 USTC Par.9157 (Educational benefit trust).

Borrowing from Your Retirement Plan
1. IRC, Section 72(m), 72(o) and 72(p).

Gifts and Other Transfers of Business Interests
1. IRC, Sections 703–709 (Taxation of partnerships).
2. IRC, Section 704(e) (Family partnerships).
3. IRC, Reg. Section 1.704.1 (Partner's share of income).
4. *Acuff v. Commissioner*, 35 TC 162 (1960) (Tennessee) (Sham family partnership).
5. IRC, Reg. Section 1.704-1(e) (2) (vii) (Trustees as partners).
6. *Hartman v. Commissioner*, 43 TC 105 (1964) (New York).
7. IRC, Sections 1361-1379 (Subchapter S corporation to shift income).
8. *Duarte v. Commissioner*, 44 TC 193 (1965) (New Jersey) (No follow-through on tax plan—disallowed).
9. *Horne v. Commissioner*, 45 T.C. Memo 1982-741 (1982) (Alabama) (Sham corporation not recognized for tax purposes).
10. IRC, Section 1361 (Subchapter S trusts).
11. IRC, Section 368. (Recapitalizations).
12. IRC, Section 301.
13. IRC, Section 302. } (Tax treatment of corporate stock and distributions).
14. IRC, Section 306.

Paying Tax-Deductible Rent to Your Child
1. IRC, Section 1015 (Cost basis of gifted property).
2. *Quinlivan v. Commissioner*, 37 T.C. Memo 346 (1978) (Minnesota) (Gift and leaseback—real estate).
3. *Butler v. Commissioner*, 65 TC 327 (1975) (Gift and leaseback).
4. *Skemp v. Commissioner*, 8 TC 415 (1947), rev'd 168 F.2d 598 (1948) (Wisconsin) (Gift and leaseback—patents).
5. *Lerner v. Commissioner*, 71 TC 290 (1978) (New York) (Gift and leaseback—independent trustee).
6. IRC, Section 267 (Sales between related taxpayers).

NOTE:
IRC = Internal Revenue Code.
Regs. = U. S. Treasury Regulations.
RR = Revenue Ruling (by Internal Revenue Service).
Letter Ruling = Ruling for a Taxpayer by the Internal Revenue Service (not published in IRS Bulletin).
TC = U. S. Tax Court Decision (TCM = U. S. Tax Court Memorandum Decision, not the full court).
F. = Federal (U. S. Circuit Court of Appeals) Decision, (F.2d = Federal, 2nd series).
Cir. = Circuit (area of the U. S. served by that court).
aff'd = affirmed lower court decision.
rev'd = reversed lower court decision.
S. Ct. = U. S. Supreme Court Decision.
USTC = U. S. Tax Cases, Commerce Clearing House.

9
. . . .

Shifting
Tax-Shelter Income

Most of the plans for shifting income for education involve the investment of, or at least the use of a substantial part of the parents' capital. For instance, the Clifford trust will tie up your money for a while, and with outright gifts, of course, you will part with the funds forever. There is one approach that considerably reduces your "investment" in college funds while ultimately resulting in a shifting of income to the child—the use of certain "tax-shelters."

. . . .
The Tax Effect of
Shifting Shelter Income

Let us suppose that early in 1984, Alexander makes a $25,000 investment in the Strikealot oil program, which intends to develop oil and gas wells in Ohio. The developers project that Alexander can write off 100 percent of his investment in 1984, and that if successful, the wells should begin producing income in 1986. They look for a return of about two times Alexander's investment. Alexander takes the $25,000 write-off on his 1984 income tax return; since he is in the 50 percent tax bracket, this saves him $12,500 in taxes. Sometime in 1985 he makes a gift of his interest in the oil program to a trust for his daughter, Andrea, who expects to begin college in 1986. It so happens that in 1986 the oil program begins to produce a cash flow of about $500 per month, and this will be taxable to Andrea or to her trust if kept in the trust. At a onetime cost of only $12,500, Alexander has transferred about $6,000 per year in income to his daughter to use, in *her* tax bracket, for college expenses.

. . . .

Shelters in General, Educational Shelters in Particular

Over the past several years, tax shelters in general have become an accepted form of deferring income, and as readily saleable products, they have taken the financial field by storm. This is by no means to say that every "shelter" is a good investment, but they all have some things in common, one of which is to take advantage of certain tax laws that allow you a tax deduction or tax credit based on the amount of your investment in the shelter. Depending upon the amount of deductions and the level of your tax bracket, it could turn out that you would realize "a profit" just by making the investment, even though the shelter activity itself did nothing. For example, certain "book deals" offer you a "5 for 1" write-off on your investment, meaning that a $10,000 investment would generate a $50,000 tax write-off. This is called "leverage." If you are in the 50 percent tax bracket, the $50,000 leveraged write-off would save you $25,000 in taxes for a $15,000 "profit" over your $10,000 investment. Sound as if there's something wrong? There is.

The IRS has come down on these "abusive" shelters like the proverbial ton of bricks. As a result, the more exotic shelters like book and record deals, Mexican vegetable deals, Panamanian gold dredging, and diamond mines generally spell nothing but trouble for the investor, since you can not only lose your investment *and* your deduction but you can now be penalized by the IRS just for trying to take the deductions. So much for the sour deals. There are, in fact, many legitimate shelters that produce not only a supportable tax write-off but potential future income as well. These shelters, specifically, shelters in oil and gas programs and in real estate programs, may lend themselves well to planning for college education, as suggested in my example above. Let's look at oil and gas, for example.

By its nature, exploration for oil and gas is risky, and in order to induce investors to invest in programs to discover and develop this natural resource, the tax laws provide certain incentives when you make an investment in such programs. The incentive is in the form of a direct tax write-off for amounts spent on certain drilling expenses and a further incentive in the form of a tax break on the income from the wells. As a general rule, your write-off on an oil and gas investment will not exceed 100 percent of the amount you invest plus any other amounts advanced on which you are *personally* liable (borrowed funds). For the purpose of their use for educational plans, you should only consider those programs in which you have *actually made investments* as opposed to the use of borrowed funds. The reason is that under present tax laws, if you transfer an interest in a tax shelter in which you still have some liability, *you could trigger taxable income to yourself merely by making the transfer.* As a result, *you should only use "nonleveraged" shelters for this maneuver*, that is, those shelters which give you *no more than* a dollar-for-dollar write-off on your *actual* cash investment.

Oil and gas shelters in particular lend themselves to this arrangement because they are usually "nonleveraged." A $10,000 cash investment will bring only a $10,000 tax write-off. In the eyes of the tax law, this means that the investor's cost basis after the write-off is zero ($10,000 cost minus $10,000 tax write-off) and so a gift of the investor's share will produce no immediate income tax consequences to the investor.

Contrast this, for example, with a shelter in "leveraged" real estate where the investor has put in $5,000 in cash and realized a $15,000 tax write-off (because of the high mortgage on the real estate). This is "leverage." When a taxpayer obtains leverage on his investment, he can get a tax benefit that *exceeds* the amount of actual cash that he invested. For example, say that Rupert purchases a $100,000 condominium (for investment) by paying $5,000 cash and negotiating a $95,000 mortgage. The rental income just covers expenses so he has no taxable income, but he is entitled to a depreciation deduction. In this case, let's say it is $15,000. His "write-off" (tax deduction) will be $15,000; this is *three times* his investment. How is this reconciled for tax purposes? Under the tax laws, Rupert's cost basis after the write-off is a "negative" $10,000 ($5,000 investment *minus* a $15,000 tax write-off equals negative $10,000). The negative amount is due to the investor's share of the *liability* for the additional debt (the mortgage) on the property. But if Rupert then makes a gift of this shelter, the IRS will say he is being relieved of this $10,000 "liability" and treat it the same as *income* to him. Therefore, he would be subject to an *income tax* by the simple act of making a gift of this "negative basis" shelter. This is why only nonleveraged shelters such as oil and gas investments should be used under this particular plan for educational funds.

If you decide to proceed with an oil and gas program, you should try to stick with developers that have a good track record, and preferably with those programs that are in a proven area (where oil or gas has already been discovered). These ingredients will help you select a program that has a better chance of producing future income for your child to use for college. As it is, exploring for oil and gas is risky, and a strictly exploratory deal (one that drills in new, unproven areas) could result in a total bust, which will result in a loss of your investment (or 50 percent of it, allowing for the tax savings) and no future income. On the other hand, developmental programs, although by no means guaranteed, stand a better chance of producing some income, since they are structured to drill in proven areas where oil and/or gas has already been discovered. For good developmental programs, a return of one to two times your initial investment over a period of time is not considered unusual.

. . . .

You Can't Rely on "Projections"

The example I used at the beginning of this chapter projected a very neat income of $500 per month beginning in 1986 as projected. As you can guess, things seldom go as "projected," and in fact one of the problems with banking on this method of shifting income is that it is not at all predictable and not at all regular. Income *could* be $500 per month, but then it may more likely be $380 one month, then $680 the next, depending upon which wells begin producing, when the oil or gas is sold, and when the proceeds are finally distributed to the partners, as well as other matters that can affect the time and amount of the payments. The other side of this example, however, is the fact that Alexander would have had to invest a lot more than $12,500 in other investments to produce a $6,000 annual return for his daughter. Whether or not the monthly payments are regular should not really concern you, since, if your objective is to provide for education, it is the total *annual* amount that is important. If, however, it is necessary for some reason to have regular monthly payments, perhaps some other investment should be considered, or perhaps the child's trust could borrow the necessary funds (you could guarantee the loan) and when the irregular payments come in, the loan could be paid off. One potential advantage that oil and gas income has over other investments is that the amount of income to the child's trust can increase as the cost of oil and gas goes up.

· ·

Preserving the Tax-Free Depletion Allowance

Once the payments begin, they will be taxed to your child or to your child's trust, as the case may be, on an annual basis. Although oil and gas payments are normally subject to the "depletion" allowance (up to 22 percent tax-free), this allowance would probably *not* be available to your child if the underlying interest you have given her is considered "proven" property, and with developmental programs it probably would be. Nevertheless, unless the payments are huge (which would mean a big strike!), the absence of the depletion allowance will not make a substantial difference, as her lower tax bracket will still leave most of the funds available for college use. For example, if the payments were $6,000 per year and she had no other income and was not entitled to the depletion allowance, she would pay a tax of only about $680, leaving over $5,300 to use for college.

However, if the wells are expected to produce considerable income, it may be helpful for you to *preserve* the tax-free depletion allowance and it seems it is possible to do so. In a 1983 private ruling, the IRS held that it is permissible for the grantor to retain the right to the depletion allowance and give away only the taxable portion. In that case, Dad transferred his interests in an oil and gas partnership to a Clifford trust for the benefit of his children, but the trustee of the trust was required to *set aside* each year a portion of the income equal to the depletion allowance. These "depletion" amounts were to be accumulated and distributed to Dad when the trust terminated ten years later.

Because some of the income was accumulated for Dad (rather than for the children), the laws provide that those funds would be taxed to him. However, the IRS ruled he would at the same time be entitled to apply the depletion allowance and so the result was a "wash," that is, the funds would in effect be tax-free to Dad. For example, say that the total income to the trust from the wells was $10,000 and according to the prescribed split $1,600 was for Dad, and the balance of $8,400 held for the children. Although the $1,600 would be "taxable" to Dad, it would at the same time qualify for the tax-free depletion allowance, which would render it nontaxable. The $8,400 could be held in the trust for the children or used for their education as needed. In either event the $8,400 would not be taxed to Dad.

. . . .

Timing and Value of the Gift

The timing of the gift is somewhat important, since you do not want the value of the gift to exceed your $10,000 annual exclusion. If you make the gift just after the drilling is completed but before the wells are producing, the interest should have a relatively low value for gift tax purposes. The value of these interests is based on the (discounted) present value of the proven oil or gas reserves, which should be low or even unknown at the time of the gift. If you wait until the wells are actually producing, the value of your interest will be much higher and you might have gift taxes to contend with.

Even though the estimated value of your interest is less than the allowable $10,000 gift tax exclusion, I suggest you still consider filing a gift tax return to formally establish your gift and its purported value, as well as to begin the running of the period of limitations within which your return can be questioned. If you file no return and, as a result of a successful strike which years later produces large cash distributions, the IRS later questions the value of your gift, you could be vulnerable to additional gift taxes.

. . . .

Keeping an Interest in Future Profits

If you feel lucky and want to keep an interest in those future oil reserves that someday will produce millions, you may use a Clifford trust for your child, which, as described in Chapter 6, will return the interest to you after a ten-year period. Your child will get the income for ten (or more) years during which time her education should be completed, and the trust can then terminate and the partnership interest in the oil and gas program (if it still exists) will be returned to you.

SUMMARY

This is a brief and somewhat general explanation of how an investment in an oil and gas program can not only shelter some of your own income but also produce additional income which can be shifted to a child for educational expenses. The idea suggested here *can work* and *has worked* in numerous cases, but the taxation of oil and gas programs and the effects on investors *can be extremely complicated*. A maneuver like this, as with most others discussed in this book, should only be carried out with the best expert advice.

IMPORTANT REMINDER: Regardless of the plan you use, if any of the child's income, *whether from a trust or any other source,* **is used to satisfy a parental obligation,** *the income so used will be taxed to the parent,* **despite the care taken with the rest of the plan. To avoid fall-**

ing into this trap, be sure to review the discussion of this point in Chapter 3 (pages 26–33).

REFERENCES FOR CHAPTER 9

1. IRC, Section 38 and Sections 46–50 (Investment tax credit).
2. IRC, Sections 611–617 (Oil, etc. depletion allowance).
3. *Tennyson v. USA*, 76-1 USTC Par.13,128 (1976) (Arkansas) (Gift of partnership interest).
4. IRS Private Letter Ruling 8320012 (Retention of depletion allowance by donor).
5. *Malone v. U.S.* 326 F.Supplement 106 (N.D. Miss. 1971), *aff'd* 455 F.2d 502 (1972), also Regs. Section 1.1011-2(a) (3). (Gift of Negative Basis Shelter)

NOTE:

IRC = Internal Revenue Code.

Regs. = U.S. Treasury Regulations.

RR = Revenue Ruling (by Internal Revenue Service).

Letter Ruling = Ruling for a Taxpayer by the Internal Revenue Service (not published in IRS Bulletin).

TC = U.S. Tax Court Decision (TCM = U.S. Tax Court Memorandum Decision, not the full court).

F. = Federal (U.S. Circuit Court of Appeals) Decision, (F.2d = Federal, 2nd series).

Circ. = Circuit (area of the U.S. served by that court).

aff'd = affirmed lower court decision.

rev'd = reversed lower court decision.

S. Ct. = U.S. Supreme Court Decision.

USTC = U.S. Tax Cases, Commerce Clearing House.

10

. . . .

Coordinating Your
Estate Tax Planning
with Your Child's
Income Tax Planning

The primary objective throughout this book has been to outline the major (and some of the minor) ways to shift income from the parent to the child for the purposes of paying for educational expenses. Structuring and carrying out the various maneuvers suggested have the effect of creating and building assets either in the name of the child or which will ultimately pass to the child. In the unfortunate event of the child's disability or death, these assets must be dealt with, not only from a legal, but also from a tax standpoint. This chapter suggests ways of avoiding the potential problems in those cases.

. . . .

The Child's Estate vs.
the Parents' Estates

Except for those rare situations where huge amounts of money (several hundreds of thousands) have been accumulated by the child, the child's estate generally does not present an estate tax problem. Rather, it is the parents' estates that suffer because most of the assets remain with them, even after many of the tax-planning strategies discussed in this book. Under a Clifford trust, for instance, the property is returned to the parent when the trust has ended; and where a family business is involved, control (and majority ownership) usually rests with the parent. This is perhaps as it should be, but we do *not* want to make this situation a burden to the parents.

In fact, many of the shifts of income suggested in this book can serve a dual purpose. In addition to providing income tax savings in generating funds for education, they also can provide estate tax savings by reducing the parents' taxable estates. That is, in the event of the child's death or disability the parents' taxable estates will be reduced by the value of the gifts given to the child as well as by the income generated from those gifts. As stated above, the plan must be followed through, since all these estate tax savings could be lost if the property and assets accumulated by the child are passed back to the parent on the child's death (unless, of course, there is no one else to leave them to).

If the child dies, his or her property will pass in one or more of the following ways:

1. according to the child's will, if the child was old enough to have one and if there was one;
2. under the laws of "intestacy," if there is no will or if the deceased child was a minor; or
3. according to the terms of a *lifetime* disposition (such as a trust).

A minor cannot legally make a will. When a child dies without a will (whether or not a minor), his property will first pass to his parents (unless he is married), if either parent is alive. And even if a child makes a will, unless he is married, he will usually leave his property to his parents. In these cases, it means that all the property that was shifted to the child for the child's educational use will simply come back to the parents (on the child's death) to be later taxed in the parents' estates.

In addition to the potential tax problems, there may be *administrative* problems to deal with. If the child's property passes under either of the routes described in one or two above, the parents will be required to undergo considerable administrative trouble and expense before the child's property can be transferred. That is, in the majority of instances they will have to engage an attorney to see that the proper probate papers are filed and the necessary time-consuming procedures followed to settle the child's estate.

In most cases, there are ways these problems, delays and expenses can be avoided, and we will examine each of the different suggested vehicles to see whether and how it can be done in each case.

The Uniform Gifts to Minors Act

The UGMA was created by state law to provide an easy way to hold property for a minor, and it provides that property held this way will pass *to the minor's probate estate* on death. In this case, you have no other choice or ability to plan, which is another reason that use of the UGMA should be restricted to *small* gifts. There is, however, a way to deal with this problem *after* the fact. If a minor has died and funds from a UGMA account are to be distributed to the parents under state law, the parents could "disclaim" (refuse) their rights to the minor's estate and the property or funds would then pass *as if* the parents had predeceased the minor. This would be desirable if there were other children in the family, since the parents' disclaimer would then cause the property in the minor's estate to pass to the other children. If there were no other children, however, the disclaimer would probably *not* be a good idea.

Each state has its own specific laws stating how a disclaimer is to be carried out, but usually it involves a written statement by the heirs (in this case, the parents) disclaiming the inheritance. The statement must be filed with the administrator of the child's estate and the court, and it is generally required to be filed within a specified time (usually nine months) after the child's death. Before any disclaimer is made, however, the parents should be sure that it will produce a desirable result. In some cases, it may be better to simply take the property (by inheritance from the child's estate) and then carry out some *new* plan in favor of other children. Each situation must be considered on its own merits.

Outright Gifts

If you make outright gifts to a child and these gifts grow to a substantial amount, the *child* (if he or she is not a minor) should consider creating his *own* living trust (see Chapter 6). The primary difference between a trust created by the child (for himself) and a trust created by you for your child is that the child is not trying to shift the income taxes to someone else. In the case of the child's own trust, it is purely a matter of planning for smooth handling and disposition of the property in the event of the child's disability or death. In any event, you should *at the very least* have the child make a will (if he or she is not a minor). If there are other brothers and sisters, the child's trust (or will) could leave his property to them, or even to a trust for their benefit if they are minors. It would also be possible for an adult child to leave his property to a trust which is already in existence, such as an educational trust you may have previously created for that child and/or others. This could be done simply by having the child's will name the desired trust as a beneficiary—a simple matter for your attorney to handle. If the child is a minor, however, he or she cannot make a will, so it is *important* that you attempt to structure and coordinate your gifts accordingly, as described below.

Minor's Trusts

Since this trust will be created by you, it can contain the necessary provisions to avoid the problems we are considering here. Although one of the IRS requirements of this trust is that the principal and accumulated income pass "to the child's estate" on his death, it also suggests an alternative. That is, the trust will still qualify if the child has what is called a "general power of appointment." This means that the child can direct in writing where he wants the property to go at his death. When a power of appointment is given, it is customary (and good practice) to state what will happen if the power is not exercised (this is called a "default"). So, your minor's trust will give the child a general power of appointment, but it will go on to say that if the child does not exercise the power (and if he is a minor, he cannot), then the remaining property will pass to the child's brothers and sisters, or to their trusts. This way, the property will *not* return to the parents and will *not* pass through the child's probate estate, but will be coordinated to pass smoothly to brothers or sisters or to trusts for their benefit. If there are no brothers or sisters or children of the child, then of course some other beneficiaries must be chosen.

Clifford Trusts

By its own terms, the *principal* of a Clifford trust will revert to the parent/grantor (or someone designated by the parent/grantor) when the trust terminates, which is ten years after the property is transferred to the trust. The *income*, however, is either accumulated for the child or paid to the child. To avoid payment of any accumulated amounts of *income* to the child's estate, the Clifford trust should provide that if the child is deceased at the time of the required payment to the child and if the child does not dispose of his or her share by will, then such payment shall be made to other children or to their trusts, as the case may be.

Independent Trusts

These trusts, which are most frequently used for outright gifts, will almost always contain provisions that safeguard against payments to the child's estate, but you should double-check them, just to make sure.

Family Partnerships

Where an interest in a family partnership is owned by a child or even by a trust for the child, the partnership agreement will usually provide for a buy-out of the child's interest on the child's death. If it does not, then the child's estate or the trust will be entitled to an accounting (a determination of value of the child's share of the partnership). In *either* event (whether or not a buy-out occurs), the value attributable to the child should *not* be left to pass through the child's estate.

A better way to handle this is to hold the child's partnership interest in a *trust* and have the trust provide for the disposition of whatever value remains after the child's death. Otherwise, the parents and the other partners will have to deal with the executor or adminstrator of the child's estate. This could be time-consuming, expensive, public and quite inconvenient for the partnership. In short, it is almost always better to hold the child's partnership interest in a *trust* and provide in the trust for the disposition of assets on the child's death.

Stock in Family Corporations

The problems associated with these transfers are somewhat similar to those of the family partnership, except that the estate of a deceased stockholder is not entitled to an accounting as is the estate of a deceased partner. There can be restrictions on transfer of company stock (and there usually are), but these seldom extend to the death of a stockholder. If a child is a stockholder, the child's death will not usually interfere with the continuation of the business, as the child will most likely have a minority interest. Nonetheless, dealing with the child's estate can still be time-consuming and expensive. It is possible to have a buy-out provision on death, but this may not be desirable from a cash standpoint and there are potential tax problems as well. It will usually prove better all around if the child's stock were held in a trust, and then if a buy-out were undesirable, the trust could continue to hold the stock for other children. In that case, a buy-out may be required (see Chapter 8). Except in the case of subchapter S corporations, stock in a family corporation may be held in any of the trusts previously discussed, viz. a Clifford trust, a minor's trust, or an independent trust. Stock of a subchapter S can only be held in trusts which qualify as subchapter S trusts (see Chapter 8 for specific rules relating to these trusts).

Tax Shelters

Most tax shelters are held in the form of "limited partnerships." Briefly stated, a limited partnership is simply one where the liability of the limited partners is limited to his or her individual investment in the partnership. From the standpoint of ownership and transfer of the partnership share itself, it would generally be the same as that of the family partnership, except where the partnership agreement contained special provisions relating to transfers. In any event, if a tax shelter of this type is owned by the child, the child's estate will be entitled to an accounting for the child's share, as it is with the family partnership discussed above. In most instances, tax shelter interests should be held in a *trust* for the child, rather than by the child individually. If they are not, they will, like other assets in the child's name, pass through his probate estate either according to his will, or according to state law if he has no will, which means it will probably pass back to his parents after unnecessary time and expense involved in settling the child's estate. With a trust, it could easily pass to other children immediately upon the child's death, avoid most, if not all, of the delays, trouble, and expense.

Employment Benefits

The fringe benefits we would be concerned with here normally consist of insurance and retirement payments. In both instances it is possible to name a beneficiary in the event of the death of the employee/child, and this should certainly be done. If no beneficiary is named, then the insurance and plan benefits would be payable to the child's estate, *which we want to avoid.* This is done simply and easily by naming one or more "contingent" or successor beneficiaries who would receive the benefits if the child were deceased. The contingent beneficiaries could include the child's brothers and sisters, or the proceeds could be paid directly to *trusts* for their benefit. If there are any other company death benefits in addition to these, they should be handled in a similar fashion.

Child's Power of Attorney

As an additional safety measure in giving the parents flexibility in dealing with a child's assets and keeping them out of the probate court, a child who is not a minor should consider giving one or both parents a Durable Power of Attorney. This is a document that would give the parents the right to deal with the child's property in the event of the child's legal disability or incompetence (but *not* in the event of the child's death). The instrument is fairly standard and should be relatively inexpensive to obtain (perhaps $25–$50). Be sure it is a "durable" power.

The word "durable" indicates that the parents (called the "attorneys in fact" under the power) could still act, even though the child may be legally unable to act for himself. With this power, parents may be able to make changes or transfers of property that the child should have made but failed to do prior to a disability (i.e., name beneficiaries, transfers to a trust, etc.), and thereby avoid costly probate proceedings. The durable power of attorney is accepted in various forms in all fifty states.

The following chart will give you a quick review of the above points:

If the child owns or is a beneficiary under:	*Then to avoid probate in the child's estate, you should:*
Uniform Gifts to Minors Act	Nothing you can legally do until child reaches age of majority (but if the child dies before this and there are other children, the parents should "disclaim").
Minor's Trust	Provide in the trust for a successor beneficiary to receive the funds on the minor's death.
Clifford Trust	Provide in the trust for a successor beneficiary to receive the funds on the minor's death.
Independent Trust	Provide in the trust for a successor beneficiary to receive the funds on the minor's death.
Family Partnership Interest	Provide in the partnership agreement for a buy-out of the child's interest on his death, or, *better still*, hold the interest in a trust naming a successor beneficiary if child dies.
Stock in the Family Corporation	Provide in the corporate articles or in an agreement for a buy-out of the child's interest on his death, or, *better still*, hold the interest in a trust naming a successor beneficiary if child dies.

If the child owns or is a beneficiary under:	*Then to avoid probate in the child's estate, you should:*
Tax Shelter	Place the child's share in a trust for the child, with provisions for transfer or successive ownership on the child's death.
Employment Benefits	Be sure to provide for a contingent (successor) beneficiary if the child dies.
Outright gifts (or other accumulated funds and investments in the child's name)	Have the child, if not a minor, create his or her own living trust for his/her own benefit, and on the child's death the funds would pass to beneficiaries named in the trust. As an addition or an alternative, have the child give one or both parents a *durable* power of attorney for emergency changes or transfers. (If the child is a minor, this can't be done by the child.)

SUMMARY

These are simplified directions for the handling of a child's assets and accumulations in the event the child's death (or disability) occurs before the assets can be used for the intended educational purpose. The two principal objectives in making these recommendations are to avoid having the property tied up in the child's probate estate in the event of the child's death or disability, and to avoid having the property return to the parents and thereby increase the size of the parents' estates. In any event, a child who is not a minor should consider giving a power of attorney to one or both parents to enable them to deal with his or her property in emergencies. No mention is made of estate taxes in the child's estate since the child's estate would presumably be small enough, even with gifts from the parents and accumulations or growth on these amounts, so as not to be subject to a substantial tax, if in fact there is any tax at all. If the child does have a large taxable estate, the advice you get should go well beyond that in this book.

11

. . . .

Putting It All Together

One of the important principles to remember in successful tax planning is that you should seldom rely on just one idea to save your money. The expression "using every trick in the book" is quite appropriate when you are speaking of arranging your personal and business situations in a way to produce the *least possible tax*. For this reason, you should review every one of the "tricks" in this book with your advisors to be sure that you have taken advantage of all that apply to your particular situation.

. . . .

Developing the Best Plan

Our presentation has been on a chapter by chapter, subject by subject basis, and unless you are a tax-planning professional, it is easy to latch on to one particular idea and lose sight of the larger picture, where a number of different approaches may be combined to your benefit, not just for tax purposes but also for common-sense planning purposes. For example, in order to qualify for the $10,000 gift tax exclusion with a Clifford trust (Chapter 6) you must provide that the income must be currently paid out (or made available) to the beneficiary. In many cases you may not want to do this, such as where the beneficiary is a minor, or where he or she simply cannot handle the funds.

An alternative would be to have the Clifford trust income paid over to a minor's trust for the benefit of the minor, or to have your attorney include the necessary 2503(c) provisions in the Clifford trust itself. This can give you the benefit of having an additional taxpayer and possible additional tax savings. That is, the child is one taxpayer and the minor's trust is another, so income can be allocated between the two to save more in taxes (see Chapter 6). It may sound a little complicated, but it really isn't (and remember, once you commit yourself to tax planning, you might as well do it right). Both types of trusts have been "tried and tested," are of relatively standard format, and are relatively easy to deal with. All of the income from the Clifford trust could accumulate in the minor's trust until the child reaches college age (or until age 21), at which time it could be paid out with little or no tax consequences.

The importance of examining *all* of your alternatives cannot be overemphasized. To help you see the overall picture, take another look at the chart, which first appeared in Chapter 1:

If your family has:	Then for a tax-favored educational plan you should consider:	You will find this thoroughly covered in:
Savings	Gifts	Chapter 4
	Custodial gifts	Chapter 5
	Gift & borrowback	Chapter 5
	Clifford trust & borrowback	Chapter 6
A home, but no substantial savings or other investments	Clifford trust & borrowback	Chapter 6
Income-producing securities	Minor's trust	Chapter 5
	Clifford trust	Chapter 6
	Gifts	Chapter 4
	Custodial Gifts	Chapter 5
Low-cost securities with a high current value	Gifts	Chapter 4
	Custodial gifts	Chapter 5
	Minor's trust	Chapter 5
Income-producing real estate	Clifford trust	Chapter 6
	Employment of child	Chapter 8

If your family has:	Then for a tax-favored educational plan you should consider:	You will find this thoroughly covered in:
A family business	Employment of child	Chapter 8
	Clifford trust	Chapter 6
	Family partnership	Chapter 8
	"Subchapter S" corporation	Chapter 8
	Gift & leaseback	Chapter 8
	Educational benefit trust	Chapter 8
A professional practice	Employment of child	Chapter 8
	Gift & leaseback	Chapter 8
	Educational benefit trust	Chapter 8
Tax shelters that will produce income	Clifford trust	Chapters 6 & 9
	Independent trust	Chapters 6 & 9
Access to loans or gifts from family members or other "friendly" sources	Clifford trust & borrowback	Chapter 6

. . . .

Creating Your Own Private Tax Shelter

The chart above should help illustrate that several ideas may apply to a given family situation. In some instances you may be able to combine the tax benefits of more than one of these ideas to create your own tax shelter that previously didn't exist. Here's an example: Say that you have a business and your business needs some new equipment costing $10,000, but it does not have the cash to buy it. The business also lacks the cash to make the $10,000 annual profit-sharing contribution to your account. You happen to have $10,000 in savings that you were about to set aside for your daughter's college expenses. Instead, you make a short-term loan to your corporation of $10,000, which it uses to make the tax-deductible contribution to your profit-sharing plan. After the contribution, you borrow the $10,000 from your profit-sharing plan at an interest rate of, say, two points over prime, which will be tax-deductible to you, even though you are paying it to your own "account" (see Chapter 8). You then contribute the $10,000 to a Clifford trust for the benefit of your daughter, and your daughter's trust purchases the $10,000 piece of equipment for your business. The business then enters into an agreement to lease the equipment from the trust. At some future date, when the business can "afford" it, it could pay you back your initial $10,000 loan, at *no* tax consequence to you except for any interest that must be paid.

The lease payments for the equipment rental are deductible to the business and, of course, income to the trust, but the trust will be entitled to take a depreciation deduction on the equipment, which will have the effect of reducing the tax on this income. It may also be possible to pass certain tax credits (on the equipment) through to your business for an added benefit. The lease (rental) payments could accumulate in the trust to build a fully tax-deductible fund for your daughter's education—all for a $10,000 loan to your business. Here are the steps again in itemized form, followed by a diagram illustrating the steps:

1. You loan $10,000 to your business (and defer receipt of the interest payments to some future date; you could charge interest if you wish).
2. The business uses the $10,000 as a tax-deductible contribution to the profit-sharing plan (you are the only employee—if there are other employees this could still be done, but you cannot borrow back the same amount).
3. You borrow $10,000 from your profit-sharing plan at an interest rate of two points over prime; the interest payments are fully deductible to you.
4. You use the $10,000 borrowed funds either as a gift or to a trust for your daughter.
5. Daughter's trust uses the $10,000 to purchase the equipment needed in your business.
6. The business leases the equipment from Daughter's trust at a fair rental.
7. Daughter's trust accumulates the rental payments received to pay for Daughter's educational expenses.
8. At the appropriate time, the trustee pays out some or all of the funds for Daughter's educational costs.

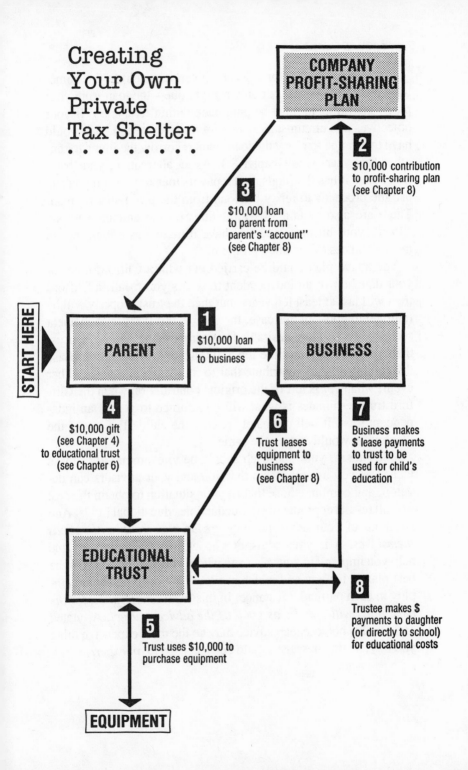

Creating Your Own Private Tax Shelter
. . . .

COMPANY PROFIT-SHARING PLAN

2
$10,000 contribution to profit-sharing plan (see Chapter 8)

3
$10,000 loan to parent from parent's "account" (see Chapter 8)

START HERE ▶

PARENT

1
$10,000 loan to business

BUSINESS

4
$10,000 gift (see Chapter 4) to educational trust (see Chapter 6)

6
Trust leases equipment to business (see Chapter 8)

7
Business makes $ lease payments to trust to be used for child's education

EDUCATIONAL TRUST

8
Trustee makes $ payments to daughter (or directly to school) for educational costs

5
Trust uses $10,000 to purchase equipment

EQUIPMENT

There is a "catch" (or at least a potential catch) to this somewhat convoluted plan, but only a slight one—the loan from your profit-sharing plan must be paid back within five years. If your objectives and circumstances require a longer period, you would have to arrange to repay the loan, then reborrow the funds for another five years (see Chapter 8.). As an alternative, your business, once it has the funds, can repay its loan to you and you can use the proceeds to repay the loan from the profit-sharing plan. There are also certain IRS limitations on the amount you can "loan" your business and still have it treated as a loan, but in most instances this is not a problem.

The above plan could be carried out with a Clifford trust for your daughter or an independent trust. As you recall, a Clifford trust will last at least ten years, but then the trust property will be returned to you—in this case, the equipment. If this arrangement seems better or more desirable for your particular circumstances, then you would contribute the $10,000, or you would purchase the equipment and contribute that to the Clifford trust. In either event, whatever is left of the original contribution when the Clifford trust terminates is what will be returned to you; if an independent trust, it will ultimately pass to the child. The rest of the illustration would remain the same.

Once again, your approach should be to examine *all* of these ideas, as well as any others that you and your advisors can develop, and combine those that fit your situation to obtain the best overall result for producing tax-deductible educational funds. And speaking of your advisors, *they are as important as the ideas themselves*. It is your advisors who will formally develop and help you implement your plan and whom you should ask what the best plan is for you and which available options you should employ in each particular instance. In this regard, *your plan, for the most part, will only be as good as the advice you get*. As stated early in this book, cheap advice may be the most expensive thing you buy, so the message should be clear—*go to an expert*.

. . . .

Getting the Best Advice

Once you recognize the sense in providing educational funds through some tax-favored arrangement, your first impulse might be to call your attorney and/or your accountant to get his or her opinion. This may or may not be a good idea (but it *is* the logical place to begin). Not every attorney and accountant is familiar with the plans suggested here. This, however, is not in itself the problem. The real problem is that many won't tell you that they aren't, which will lead to one of two possible results. Your attorney or accountant may say that the idea is risky or that it won't work for you or that it's only for the rich, so you'd better forget the idea and just do it the "safe" (and more expensive) way as you always have; or, without knowing exactly what he is doing, he may simply go ahead with the plan *you* suggest.

As illustrated in Chapter 6, I have seen many Clifford trusts fail, for example, because the attorney did not realize that it is the *transfer of the property* to the trust that starts the ten-year clock running, and *not just the signing of the trust*. As a result of this lack of expertise, the property is often put into the trust a day or two late, which will cause the parent/grantor to be *taxed on all the income*, and not the trust or the child as intended. As a general rule, it pays to go to an expert and it is silly to shop around for the cheapest advice. Once again, bad or cheap advice is often the most expensive thing you can buy.

If your attorney or accountant is honest with you, he will tell you right away whether or not he is capable of this type of work, and, if not, he is in the best position to bring in an expert from his own profession. It is usually quite difficult for you to find an expert on your own, since, unlike physicians and dentists, attorneys and accountants generally are not classified or certified as specialists. While there are many who are "de facto" specialists, the trick is to find them. Bar associations or accounting associations are of limited help. The best referral to an expert is an intraprofession referral, since most lawyers and accountants are aware of who in their profession is good at tax law or tax planning, and, if not, they are in the best position to find out. The fact that your attorney or accountant may refer you to another attorney or accountant does *not,* by any means, suggest that you should then change advisors, any more than you would stop seeing your family doctor because he or she referred you to a specialist for a second opinion. If you have established a good, long-term, trusting relationship with your attorney or accountant and you have confidence in him or her, that relationship should definitely be maintained before, during, and after the expert comes into the picture.

Once you do find your expert, try to get an estimate of what the work will cost you. This amount will have to be measured against the projected tax savings to be generated by your particular plan. If it is simply to make a custodial gift, there would, of course, only be a nominal cost, but the savings might also be nominal. On the other hand, if the plan involves a family partnership combined with a gift and leaseback trust, the costs will be greater, but *so will the savings*.

Tax planning for education is not easy. Of the many ideas and principles involved, some are fairly direct, some fairly complicated, but none will come by itself or be suggested to you by the IRS. *You* must do some studying and some analysis of your own situation to determine, at least on a preliminary basis, which of the ideas apply to you; then *you* must seek out the best advice for the implementation of your plan. If this is carefully done, you can reduce the burden of your children's educational expenses by as much as *half,* and *keep the rest of the money in the family,* with my and Uncle Sam's blessings.

Appendix A

**Ages of Majority in the Various States
(as of September 1, 1984)**

State	Age of Majority
1. Alabama	19
2. Alaska	18
3. Arizona	18
4. Arkansas	18
5. California	18
6. Colorado	21
7. Connecticut	20
8. Delaware	18
9. District of Columbia	18
10. Florida	18
11. Georgia	18
12. Hawaii	18
13. Idaho	18
14. Illinois	18
15. Indiana	18
16. Iowa	18
17. Kansas	18
18. Kentucky	18
19. Louisiana	18
20. Maine	18
21. Maryland	18
22. Massachusetts	18
23. Michigan	18
24. Minnesota	18
25. Mississippi	21
26. Missouri	18
27. Montana	18

State	Age of Majority
28. Nebraska	19
29. Nevada	18
30. New Hampshire	18
31. New Jersey	18
32. New Mexico	18
33. New York	18
34. North Carolina	18
35. North Dakota	18
36. Ohio	18
37. Oklahoma	18
38. Oregon	18
39. Pennsylvania	21
40. Rhode Island	18
41. South Carolina	18
42. South Dakota	18
43. Tennessee	18
44. Texas	18
45. Utah	18
46. Vermont	18
47. Virginia	18
48. Virgin Islands	18
49. Washington	18
50. West Virginia	18
51. Wisconsin	18
52. Wyoming	19

Appendix B

**Ages of Majority in the Various States
for Purposes of Distribution under the
Uniform Gifts to Minors Act***
(as of September 1, 1984)

State	Age of Majority
1. Alabama	19
2. Alaska	19
3. Arizona	18
4. Arkansas	18—females
	21—males
5. California	18
6. Colorado	21
7. Connecticut	21
8. Delaware	18—but donor may provide for continued custodianship until age 21
9. District of Columbia	18
10. Florida	18
11. Georgia	21
12. Hawaii	18
13. Idaho	21
14. Illinois	21
15. Indiana	21
16. Iowa	21
17. Kansas	18
18. Kentucky	18
19. Louisiana	18—under Louisiana Gift to Minors Act
20. Maine	18
21. Maryland	18—but donor may provide for continued custodianship until age 21

*The child has a right to the custodial property at this age regardless of whether it differs from the age of majority in that state.

State	Age of Majority
22. Massachusetts	18
23. Michigan	18
24. Minnesota	18
25. Mississippi	21
26. Missouri	21
27. Montana	18
28. Nebraska	19
29. Nevada	18
30. New Hampshire	21
31. New Jersey	18—but donor may provide for continued custodianship until age 21
32. New Mexico	18
33. New York	18—but donor may provide for continued custodianship until age 21
34. North Carolina	18
35. North Dakota	18
36. Ohio	18
38. Oregon	18—but donor may provide for continued custodianship until age 21
39. Pennsylvania	21
40. Rhode Island	21
41. South Carolina	18
42. South Dakota	18
43. Tennessee	18
44. Texas	18
45. Utah	21
46. Vermont	18
47. Virginia	18
48. Virgin Islands	21
49. Washington	18
50. West Virginia	18
51. Wisconsin	18
52. Wyoming	19

Appendix C

Summary of Allowable Investments under the Uniform Gifts to Minors Acts for the Various States

Alabama UGMA
Securities, life insurance policies, annuity contracts, money.
Alabama Code, Sections 35-5-1 to 35-5-10.

Alaska UGMA
Securities, life insurance policies, annuity contracts, money.
Alaska Stat., Sections 45.60.011 to 45.60.101.

Arizona UGMA
Securities, life insurance policies, annuity contracts, money.
Arizona Rev. Stat., Sections 44-2071 to 44-2080.

Arkansas UGMA
Securities, life insurance policies, annuity contracts, money.
Arkansas Stat. Ann., Sections 50-901 to 50-910.

California UGMA
Securities, money, life or endowment insurance policies, annuity contracts, real estate, tangible personal property, or any other types of property.
California Code, Sections 1154 to 1165 (West).

Colorado UGMA
Securities, life insurance policies, annuity contracts, interests as a limited partner in a partnership, interests in real property located in this state, tangible personal property, or money.
Colorado Rev. Stat., Sections 11-50-101 to 11-50-112.

Connecticut UGMA
Securities, interests in a general partnership, interests in a limited partnership, money, life insurance policies, endowment policies, annuity contracts, *proceeds* of life insurance or endowment policies and annuity contracts, interests in real property located in this state, tangible personal property.
Connecticut Gen. Stat. Ann., Sections 45-101 to 45-109 (West).

Delaware UGMA
Securities, life or endowment insurance policies, annuity contracts, money, tangible personal property, real estate.
Delaware Code Title 12, Sections 4501 to 4510.

District of Columbia UGMA
Securities, life insurance policies, annuity contracts, money.
District of Columbia Code Encyclopedia, Sections 21-301 to 21-311 (West).

Florida UGMA
Securities, life insurance policies, annuity contracts, money.
Florida Stat. Ann., Sections 710.01 to 710.10 (West).

Georgia UGMA
Securities, life insurance policies, annuity contracts, money.
Georgia Code, Sections 48-301 to 48-313.

Hawaii UGMA
Securities, life insurance policies, annuity contracts, money.
Hawaii Rev. Stat., Sections 553-1 to 553-9.

Idaho UGMA
Securities, life insurance policies, annuity contracts, money.
Idaho Code, Sections 68-801 to 68-810.

Illinois UGMA
Securities, money, life or endowment insurance policies, annuity contracts, personal property, real property located in this state including any interests therein, and any other types of property or interests therein (other than real property located outside this state).
Illinois Ann. Stat., Chapter 110 1/2, Paragraphs 201 to 211 (Smith-Hurd).

Indiana UGMA
Securities, money, life or endowment insurance policies or annuities.
Indiana Code, Sections 30-2-8-1 to 30-2-8-10.

Iowa UGMA
Securities, money, life or endowment insurance policies or annuity contracts.
Iowa Code Ann., Sections 565A.1 to 565A.11 (West).

Kansas UGMA
Securities, life insurance policies, annuity contracts, money.
Kansas Stat., Sections 38-901 to 38-912.

Kentucky UGMA
Securities, life insurance policies, annuity contracts, money.
Kentucky Rev. Stat., Sections 385.010 to 385.101.

Louisiana UGMA
Securities, life insurance policies, annuity contracts, money.
Louisiana Rev. Stat. Ann., Sections 9:735 to 9:742 (West).

Maine UGMA
Securities, life insurance policies, annuity contracts, money.
Maine Rev. Stat. Title 33, Sections 1001 to 1010.

Maryland UGMA
Securities, money, life or endowment insurance policies, annuity contracts, real estate, tangible personal property, or any other types of property.
Maryland (Estates and Trusts) Code Ann., Sections 13-301 to 13-310.

Massachusetts UGMA
Securities, money, life or endowment insurance policies or annuities.
Massachusetts Gen. Laws Ann., Chapter 201A, Sections 1 to 11 (West).

Michigan UGMA
Securities, life insurance policies, annuity contracts, money.
Michigan Comp. Laws Ann., Sections 554.451 to 554.461.

Minnesota UGMA
Securities, life insurance policies, annuity contracts, money.
Minnesota Stat. Ann., Sections 527.01 to 527.11 (West).

Mississippi UGMA
Securities, life insurance policies, annuity contracts, money.
Mississippi Code Ann., Sections 91-19-1 to 91-19-19.

Missouri UGMA
Securities, life insurance policies, annuity contracts, money.
Missouri Ann. Stat., Sections 404.010 to 404.100 (Vernon).

Montana UGMA
Securities, life insurance policies, annuity contracts, money.
Montana Rev. Code Ann., Sections 72-26-101 to 72-26-404.

Nebraska UGMA
Securities, life insurance policies, annuity contracts, money.
Nebraska Rev. Stat., Sections 38-1001 to 38-1010.

Nevada UGMA
Securities, life insurance policies, annuity contracts, money.
Nevada Rev. Stat., Sections 167.010 to 167.110.

New Hampshire UGMA
Securities, money, life or endowment insurance policies, or annuity contracts.
New Hampshire Rev. Stat. Ann., Sections 463-A:1 to 463-A:10.

New Jersey UGMA
Securities, life insurance or endowment policies, annuity contracts, tangible personal property, interests in a partnership or limited partnerships, money.
New Jersey Stat. Ann., Sections 46:38-13 to 46:38-41 (West).

New Mexico UGMA
Securities, life insurance policies, annuity contracts, money.
New Mexico Stat. Ann., Sections 46-7-1 to 46-7-10.

New York UGMA
Securities, life insurance policies or annuity contracts, interests in limited partnerships, interests in real property, tangible personal property, money.
New York EPTL, Sections 7-4.1 to 7-4.12 (McKinney).

North Carolina UGMA
Securities, money, life insurance policies.
North Carolina Gen. Stat., Sections 33-68 to 33-77.

North Dakota UGMA
Securities, life insurance policies, annuity contracts, money.
North Dakota Cent. Code, Sections 47-24-01 to 47-24-10.

Ohio UGMA
Securities, money, life or endowment insurance policies, annuity contracts, real estate, tangible personal property, or any other types of property.
Ohio Rev. Code Ann., Sections 1339.31 to 1339.39 (Page).

Oklahoma UGMA
Securities, life insurance policies, annuity contracts, money.
Oklahoma Stat. Ann. Title 60, Sections 401 to 410 (West).

Oregon UGMA
Real or personal property.
Oregon Rev. Stat., Sections 126.805 to 126.880.

Pennsylvania UGMA
Securities, interests in limited partnerships, money, endowment policies, life insurance policies, annuity contracts, real property.
Pennsylvania Cons. Stat. Ann. Title 20, Sections 5301 to 5310 (Purdon).

Rhode Island UGMA
Securities, money, life or endowment insurance policies or annuity contracts.
Rhode Island Gen. Laws, Sections 18-7-1 to 18-7-11.

South Carolina UGMA
Securities, life insurance policies, annuity contracts, money.
South Carolina Code, Section 35-3-10 to 35-3-120.

South Dakota UGMA
Securities, life insurance policies, annuity contracts, money.
South Dakota Compiled Laws Ann., Sections 55-10-1 to 55-10-39.

Tennessee UGMA
Securities, life insurance policies, annuity contracts, money.
Tennessee Code Ann., Sections 35-7-101 to 35-7-110.

Texas UGMA
Securities, life or endowment insurance policies, annuity contracts, money, tangible personal property, real estate.
Texas Code Ann., Property Code, Sections 141.001 to 141.014.

Utah UGMA
Securities, life insurance policies, annuity contracts, money, interests in real property located in Utah, tangible personal property.
Utah Code Ann., Sections 75-5-601 to 75-5-609.

Vermont UGMA
Securities, life insurance policies, annuity contracts, money.
Vermont Stat. Ann. Title 14, Sections 3201 to 3209.

Virgin Islands UGMA
Securities and money.
Virgin Islands Code Ann. Title 15, Sections 1241 to 1250.

Virginia UGMA
Securities, life insurance policies, annuity contracts, money.
Virginia Code, Sections 31-26 to 31-36.

Washington UGMA
Securities, life insurance policies, annuity contracts, money.
Washington Rev. Code Ann., Sections 21.24.010 to 21.24.900.

West Virginia UGMA
Securities, life insurance policies, annuity contracts, money.
West Virginia Code, Sections 36-7-1 to 36-7-11.

Wisconsin UGMA
Securities, life insurance policies, annuity contracts, money.
Wisconsin Stat. Ann., Sections 880.61 to 880.71 (West).

Wyoming UGMA
Securities, life insurance policies, annuuity contracts, money.
Wyoming Stat., Sections 34-13-101 to 34-13-110.

Appendix D

**Summary of Gift Taxes of the Various States
(as of September 1, 1984)**

State	Gift Tax
Alabama	None
Alaska	None
Arizona	None
Arkansas	None
California	None
Colorado	None
Connecticut	None
Delaware	See A
District of Columbia	None
Florida	None
Georgia	None
Hawaii	None
Idaho	None
Illinois	None
Indiana	None
Iowa	None
Kansas	None
Kentucky	None
Louisiana	See B
Maine	None
Maryland	None
Massachusetts	None
Michigan	None
Minnesota	None
Mississippi	None
Missouri	None
Montana	None

State	Gift Tax
Nebraska	None
Nevada	None
New Hampshire	None
New Jersey	None
New Mexico	None
New York	See C
North Carolina	See D
North Dakota	None
Ohio	None
Oklahoma	None
Oregon	See E
Pennsylvania	None
Rhode Island	See F
South Carolina	See G
South Dakota	None
Tennessee	See H
Texas	None
Utah	None
Vermont	None
Virginia	None
Washington	None
West Virginia	None
Wisconsin	See I
Wyoming	None

(A)

Delaware: Taxable gift is the amount subject to federal gift tax and computed the same as federal except that federal exclusion not allowed.

RATES:
Exclusion: $3,000
first $25,000 over exclusion, 1%
$25,001–$50,000 over exclusion, 2%
$50,001–$75,000 over exclusion, 3%
$75,001–$100,000 over exclusion, 4%
$100,001–$200,000 over exclusion, 5%
over $200,000 over exclusion, 6%

(B)

Louisiana: Donor has $30,000 specific lifetime exemption plus $3,000 annual exclusion per donee.

Rates: first $15,000 over annual exclusion plus lifetime exemption, 2%; over $15,000, 3%.

(C)

New York: Gift tax is from 1.5% to 15.75% of taxable gifts. Gift tax is cumulative: tax for calendar quarter is based on gifts for that quarter and previous quarters less tax for previous calendar quarters. Gifts to a spouse are tax-free.

There is a unified credit allowable as follows: (1) if the tentative tax is $2,750 or less, the credit is the full amount of the tax; (2) if the tentative tax is greater than $2,750 but less than $5,000, the credit is an amount by which $5,500 exceeds the tax; and (3) if the tentative tax is $5,000 or more, the credit is $500, provided, however, the amount of the credit cannot exceed the aplicable amount of the tentative tax before the application of the tax.

RATES:
first $50,000 of taxable gift, 2%
$50,001–$150,000, $1,000 + 3% over $50,000
$150,001–$300,000, $4,000 + 4% over $150,000
$300,001–$500,000, $10,000 + 5% over $300,000
$500,001–$700,000, $20,000 + 6% over $500,000
$700,001–$900,000, $32,000 + 7% over $700,000
$900,001–$1,100,000, $46,000 + 8% over $900,000
$1,100,000–$1,600,000, $62,000 + 9% over $1,100,000
$1,600,001–$2,100,000, $107,000 + 10% over $1,600,000
$2,100,001–$2,600,000, $157,000 + 11% over $2,100,000
$2,600,001–$3,100,000, $212,000 + 12% over $2,600,000
$3,100,001–$3,600,000, $272,000 + 13% over $3,100,000
$3,600,001–$4,100,000, $337,000 + 14% over $3,600,000
$4,100,001–$5,100,000, $407,000 + 15% over $4,100,000
$5,100,001–$6,100,000, $557,000 + 16% over $5,100,000
$6,100,001–$7,100,000, $717,000 + 17% over $6,100,000
$7,100,001–$8,100,000, $887,000 + 18% over $7,100,000
$8,100,001–$9,100,000, $1,067,000 + 19% over $8,100,000
$9,100,001–$10,100,000, $1,257,000 + 20% over $9,100,000
over $10,100,000, $1,457,000 + 21%

(D)

North Carolina: Class A donees: lineal issue, lineal ancestor, husband, wife, stepchild, legally adopted child. $30,000 of gifts to Class A donees is exempt. Class B donees: brother, sister, descendant of either, or aunt or uncle (by blood). Class C: all others except gifts for charitable purposes.

RATES:

Class A: first $10,000 after exemption, 1%
             $10,000–$25,000, 2%
             $25,000–$50,000, 3%
             $50,000–$100,000, 4%
             $100,000–$200,000, 5%
             $200,000–$500,000, 6%
             $500,000–$1,000,000, 7%
             $1,000,000–$1,500,000, 8%
             $1,500,000–$2,000,000, 9%
             $2,000,000–$2,500,000, 10%
             $2,500,000–$3,000,000, 11%
         over $3,000,000, 12%

Class B: first $5,000, 4%
             $5,000–$10,000, 5%
             $10,000–$25,000, 6%
             $25,000–$50,000, 7%
             $50,000–$100,000, 8%
             $100,000–$250,000, 10%
             $250,000–$500,000, 11%
             $500,000–$1,000,000, 12%
             $1,000,000–$1,500,000, 13%
             $1,500,000–$2,000,000, 14%
             $2,000,000–$3,000,000, 15%
         over $3,000,000, 16%

Class C: first $10,000, 8%
             $10,000–$25,000, 9%
             $25,000–$50,000, 10%
             $50,000–$100,000, 11%
             $100,000–$250,000, 12%
             $250,000–$500,000, 13%
             $500,000–$1,000,000, 14%
             $1,000,000–$1,500,000, 15%
             $1,500,000–$2,500,000, 16%
             $2,500,000 and over, 17%

If gifts exceed $3,000 in one year, only the excess is taxable. Donor gets total
exemption of $30,000 deducted from gifts made to donees in Class A, less al-
lowed exemptions in prior years. Exemption may be taken in one year or spread
over a period of years. Exemption is apportioned when applied to gifts to more
than one donee in any year. Gift to a spouse is tax-free.

(E)

Oregon: 12% of the total net gifts. Lifetime specific exemption $200,000 for gifts in 1983–1984; $500,000 1985–1986. Annual exclusion $3,000. No tax after 1986.

(F)

Rhode Island: 2% to 9% of full and fair cash value at time of transfer. $25,000 exempt; first $3,000 of gifts to any donee in any year are not considered as gifts.

RATES:

Net Gift (after deducting exclusions and exemption)		Tax on Col. 1	Rate on Excess
(1)	(2)	(3)	(4)
$ 0	$ 25,000	$ 0	2%
25,000	50,000	500	3%
50,000	100,000	1,250	4%
100,000	250,000	3,250	5%
250,000	500,000	10,750	6%
500,000	750,000	25,750	7%
750,000	1,000,000	43,250	8%
1,000,000	. . . .	63,250	9%

(G)

South Carolina: Gift tax: Rates: $40,000 of taxable gift, 6%; $40,000–$100,000, $2,400 plus 7% over $40,000; over $100,000, $6,600 plus 8% over $100,000. Exclusions and deductions follow Fed. Gift Tax Code (Section 2503; 2522–2517; 2523–2524) as of 12/31/75; $10,000 exclusion per donee is allowed. Lifetime $60,000 exemption is allowed, exemption is reduced by amount of exemption allowed for gifts after 1969 (effective for gifts made after 12/31/78). Unlimited marital deduction for gifts to spouse.

(H)

Tennessee: Class A: husband, wife, son, daughter, lineal ancestor, or descendant brother, sister, stepchild, son-in-law and daughter-in-law, legally adopted child. Class B: all others except charities, nonprofit institutions, etc. Marital deduction: one-half of the gift to the spouse. Annual exclusion for Class A gifts: $3,000 for gifts made before 1984; $5,000 for 1984 gifts; $7,500 for 1985 gifts; and $10,000 for gifts made in 1986 and thereafter.

EXEMPTIONS:

Class A: $10,000
Class B: $5,000

RATES:

Value of Gift Passing to Class		Class A		Class B	
		Tax on Col. 1	Rate on Excess	Tax on Col. 1	Rate on Excess
(1)	(2)	(3)	(4)	(5)	(6)
$ 0	$ 40,000	$ 0	5.5%	$ 0	6.5%
$ 40,000	50,000	1,650	6.5%	2,275	6.5%
50,000	100,000	2,300	6.5%	2,925	9.5%
100,000	150,000	5,550	6.5%	7,675	12 %
150,000	200,000	8,800	6.5%	13,675	13.5%
200,000	240,000	12,050	6.5%	20,425	16 %
240,000	440,000	14,650	7.5%	26,825	16 %
440,000	. . . . . .	29,650	9.5%	58,825	16 %

(I)

Wisconsin: Donees are classed as follows for gift tax purposes: Class A: lineal issue, lineal ancestor, son- or daughter-in-law, mutually acknowledged or legally adopted child, his spouse and issue. Class B: brother, sister, descendant of either. Class C: uncle, aunt or descendant of either. Class D: all others unless exempt.

Exemption (to each donee): Class A: lineal issue and others, $10,000. Class B, C and D: none. Gifts to a spouse are entirely exempt.

RATES:

Class A: lineal issue and others
    first $25,000 less exemption, 2.5%
        $25,000–$50,000, 5%
        $50,000–$100,000, 7.5%
        $100,000–$500,000, 10%
    over $500,000, 12.5%

Class B: first $25,000, 5%
        $25,000–$50,000, 10%
        $50,000–$100,000, 15%
        $100,000–$500,000, 20%
    over $500,000, 25%

Class C: first $25,000, 7.5%
$25,000–$50,000, 15%
$50,000–$100,000, 22.5%
over $100,000, 30%

Class D: first $25,000, 10%
$25,000–$50,000, 20%
over $50,000, 30%

Tax is annual tax on gifts made during calendar year without regard to gifts made during prior calendar years except so far as personal exemptions are concerned. Property value $3,000 (in addition to Class A exemption) transferred in any calendar year by any donor to any donee is exempt.

TAX PLANNING FOR TUITION

A newsletter devoted to reducing tuition costs through intelligent tax planning

Tax Planning for Tuition is a new and unique newsletter designed to give you continuing and accurate information on the latest ideas, tax cases, and rulings dealing with successful (as well as unsuccessful) plans to pay for college and private school tuition and related costs with *before-tax* dollars. Each issue of the newsletter contains:

   * Case studies and the latest IRS rulings on tuition planning in real family situations.

   * Questions from subscribers on tax planning for tuition and answers from the experts.

   * A special "how to do it" section containing instructions on implementing various tax-saving ideas which will reduce your tuition costs through tax savings.

   Whether your children are infants or already in college, you can benefit from the ideas offered by the newsletter: it is for early planners, late planners, and nonplanners. Edited by Alexander A. Bove, Jr., it offers all the necessary data to carry out the plan through your professional advisors.

   A one-year subscription (four issues) is offered at the introductory price of $27.50 (tax-deductible). For information or subscriptions, send your name and address to Sacker Financial Publications, 11 Beacon Street, Suite 1010, Boston, Massachusetts.

Index